Lives, Great and Simple

Sarah A. Tooley

Copyright © BiblioLife, LLC

BiblioLife Reproduction Series: Our goal at BiblioLife is to help readers, educators and researchers by bringing back in print hard-to-find original publications at a reasonable price and, at the same time, preserve the legacy of literary history. The following book represents an authentic reproduction of the text as printed by the original publisher and may contain prior copyright references. While we have attempted to accurately maintain the integrity of the original work(s), from time to time there are problems with the original book scan that may result in minor errors in the reproduction, including imperfections such as missing and blurred pages, poor pictures, markings and other reproduction issues beyond our control. Because this work is culturally important, we have made it available as a part of our commitment to protecting, preserving and promoting the world's literature.

All of our books are in the "public domain" and some are derived from Open Source projects dedicated to digitizing historic literature. We believe that when we undertake the difficult task of re-creating them as attractive, readable and affordable books, we further the mutual goal of sharing these works with a larger audience. A portion of BiblioLife profits go back to Open Source projects in the form of a donation to the groups that do this important work around the world. If you would like to make a donation to these worthy Open Source projects, or would just like to get more information about these important initiatives, please visit www.bibliolife.com/opensource.

GENERAL GORDON. ALEX MACDONALD, M.P.

PRINCESS ALICE.

LIVES, GREAT AND SIMPLE.

BY

MRS. G. W. TOOLEY.

LONDON:
KENT & CO., 23, PATERNOSTER ROW, E.C.

1884.

CONTENTS.

	PAGE
GENERAL GORDON	5
PRINCESS ALICE	20
ALEXANDER MACDONALD	38
HENRY IRVING	48
LORD WOLSELEY	68
DR. WILLIAM CHAMBERS	86
LORD LAWRENCE	96
ROBERT DICK	116
ANTHONY TROLLOPE	130
SIR WILLIAM FAIRBAIRN	140
ROBERT TANNAHILL	151
JAMES GARFIELD	161
JANET HAMILTON	174
CHARLES DICKENS	183
THOMAS EDWARD	198
THOMAS CARLYLE	213
HENRY SCOTT RIDDELL	229
WILLIAM LEIGHTON LEITCH	237
HENRY M. STANLEY	248
EDWARD IRVING	268

LIVES, GREAT AND SIMPLE.

GENERAL GORDON.

GENERAL GORDON, popularly known as "Chinese" Gordon—a title given him from the renown he gained during the Tai-ping rebellion in China—is descended from a race of soldiers. For a century and a half his ancestors have been connected with the military profession. His father, Lieutenant-General Henry William Gordon, was a cultivated soldier, kind-hearted and genial, but well fitted to take command. He could on occasion show great sternness of character. He married Elizabeth Enderby, daughter of Samuel Enderby, of Blackheath. Their family consisted of five sons and six daughters. Three sons entered the army. The youngest of these was Charles Gordon, who was destined to be the most illustrious of the race of Gordon soldiers.

General Gordon's mother was a singularly placid and sweet-tempered woman, full of noble fortitude. While the Crimean War was raging her remarkable self-possession showed itself. She moved about amongst the wounded and dying, with her kindly helping hand, although her three sons and several near kinsmen were to the front of the army. She was a descendant of a family of merchants and explorers. Her father had opened up the Southern Hemisphere for trade by means of his whaling vessels, which took out settlers to New Zealand and Australia. Two of his vessels were employed to carry out the first batch of convicts to Botany Bay. The cargo of tea sent by the British Government to Boston, which occasioned the first outbreak of the American Revolution, was carried by his vessels. They were boarded by the rebels, who broke open the chests, and emptied the tea into the water, thus showing their contempt for the tax imposed upon tea, and striking the first blow for American Independence.

The early years of Charles Gordon were not marked in any special manner. His health was delicate, and prevented him from especially distinguishing himself in his studies. He was educated at Taunton, and at the Royal Military Academy, Woolwich. While there the fire and energy which was in him began to show itself. On being rebuked for incompetency, and told by his commander that he would never make an officer, he tore the epaulettes from his shoulders, and flung them at his superior's feet. The utter distaste he had for anything like adulation also showed itself at this period. He chanced to enter the room one day where his mother was proudly displaying to some admiring friends one of his beautifully executed maps. He took it from her hands, tore it in two, and threw it upon the fire. This relic, which the fond mother rescued from the flames, was preserved by her, and shown to still more admiring friends when her son had gained world-wide fame in China.

Leaving the Royal Academy of Woolwich, Gordon entered the service as an Officer of Engineers, and was ordered to Pembroke, August, 1854. In December of the same year, much to his satisfaction, he was sent to the Crimea. On January 1st, 1855, he reached Balaclava, and reported himself at head-quarters. For a month no duty was assigned him, so he occupied himself in surveying the miserable position of the allied armies. The cold was intense, and the supply of food very poor. Officers and men were occupied more with thinking how they were to live than with the progress of the siege.

At the end of a month Gordon was ordered to serve in the trenches before Sebastopol, a rough beginning for so young a soldier. It was a terrible time for the army through that severe Russian winter. Month after month of weary waiting, with no active engagement to rouse the men to enthusiasm, made it a peculiarly trying time for the officers. Sebastopol surrendered September, 1855, after eleven months' siege. For four months afterwards Gordon was employed in destroying the forts, dockyards, quays, barracks, and store-houses. This work ended his service in the Crimea.

He had shown himself strong of purpose and strong of nerve. During one engagement a bullet fired at him whizzed past within an inch of his head. In writing home he made but slight reference to his narrow escape, merely remarking that the Russians "are very good marksmen; their bullet is large and pointed." Colonel Chesney, in writing of this time, says: "Gordon had first seen war in the hard school of the 'black winter' of the Crimea. In his humble position as an Engineer subaltern he attracted the notice of his superiors, not merely by his energy and activity, but by a special aptitude for war, developing itself amid the trench work before Sebastopol in a personal knowledge of the enemy's movements *such as no other officer attained*. We used to send him to find out what new move the Russians were making." Gordon was decorated with the Legion of Honour at the end of the campaign, which was a special mark of distinction for so young an officer.

After working, as Assistant Commissioner, in helping to lay down the new frontiers for Russia, Turkey, and Roumania, and afterwards in the same kind of work in determining the Russian boundaries in Asia, Gordon left home in July, 1860, for China, where he was destined to so brilliantly distinguish himself.

China was at this time convulsed by the great civil war known as the Tai-ping Rebellion. A village schoolmaster, named Hung-tsne-schnen, laid claim to Divine power. He gave out that he was inspired, and by the accounts of his strange visions and miraculous powers, drew to his side a vast army from among the discontented masses of China. He professed to have seen God, and said that the Almighty regarded him as the second Celestial Brother. The person whom he had seen, and whom he professed to his followers was God, was nothing more nor less than a Christian missionary, dressed in flowing robes, distributing tracts. The rebellion steadily gained ground. Hung traversed the provinces, breaking the idols, and effacing the Confucian texts from the walls of schools and temples. In 1851 the rebel leader had so strong a following that he assumed the title of the Heavenly King, the Emperor of the Great Peace. He chose five warrior Kings or Wangs from among his kinsmen as his subordinates, and with these, marched through China, gaining converts and devastating the country as he went. After a march of 700 miles, this huge army of fanatics secured Nanking, which became the capital of the Heavenly King. Here he established himself in royal state, surrounded by his Wangs or Kings, which number increased from five to several hundreds. The greatest cruelties were practised upon the peaceful inhabitants of the country. There was nothing in the teaching of the Heavenly King to inspire men to a moral life. Quite the reverse; yet so superstitious were the Chinese that, deluded by his miraculous pretensions, he was able to draw millions to his standard.

The Imperial Government waged war with the rebels, and were for driving them to the sea-ports. In consequence, the safety of the foreign traders at Shanghai, an important consular port, was menaced. The merchants became alarmed, and commissioned two American filibusters, Ward and Burgevine, to raise a force to capture Sung-Kiang from the rebels. They failed in the attempt, and the Faithful King marched upon Shanghai, where he was repulsed by the allied forces of French and English, who had joined the Imperial army, and Ward, the commander of the Ever Victorious Army, in putting down the rebels.

Charles Gordon, after his landing in China in 1860, had taken part in the capture of the Summer Palace from the rebels, and had been successful in driving them from several of their strongholds. For several months he was engaged in surveying the district around Shanghai—a perilous task in those troublous times. But it gave him an opportunity for studying the Chinese and their country. He was not favourably impressed by it. In writing of it he said: "There is nothing of any interest in China; if you have seen one village you have seen the whole country." In the same letter he gives a description of the fishing with cormorants: "It is extraordinary to see the quantities of fishing cormorants there are in the creeks. These cormorants are in flocks of forty and fifty, and the owner, in a small canoe, travels about with them. They fish three or four times a day, and are encouraged by the shouts of their owners to dive. I have scarcely ever seen them come up without a fish in their beaks, which they swallow, but not for any distance, for there is a ring to prevent it going down altogether. They get such dreadful attacks of mumps, their throats being distended by the fish, which are alive; when the birds seem as if they were pouter pigeons. They are hoisted into the boats, and there are very sea-sick. Would you consider the fish a dainty?"

He had an experience on April 5th, 1862, of one of the terrific dust storms common in China. A canal fifty miles long and eighteen feet wide and seven feet deep was completely filled up by the falling dust. The storm lasted sixteen hours. Gordon, who was on a travelling expedition, was caught in it, and obliged to take refuge in a village.

The most romantic part of Gordon's career began in March, 1863, when he was appointed to the command of the Ever Victorious Army, in place of Burgevine, who had been dismissed for corrupt practices. He was, at the same time, made a Chinese Mandarin. The appointment did not give satisfaction to Gordon's father, who would have preferred to see him serving as a British officer rather than as a Chinese commander. But he undertook the post out of pity for the suffering inhabitants, who were being pillaged and slaughtered by the followers of the Faithful King. He determined to put forth every effort to rid China of this devastating force. His first success was achieved at Fushan, which he captured from the rebels. This was followed by the taking of Chansu, for which he was promoted to the grade of Hung-Ping, or Brigadier-General.

His little army was in a wretched condition when he first took the command. It was badly drilled, badly paid, and badly disciplined. Before long it was the best drilled force in the country, and by getting good pay for the men, he endeavoured to stop their system of looting the towns which they captured. He introduced the use of an uniform which made the rebels think that they were foreign soldiers coming to fight them, and inspired them with awe. The men soon learnt to love him, while at the same time they felt that his word was law. By strict measures he quelled mutiny in the bud, and by kindly treatment of the prisoners captured, turned them into faithful soldiers in his own army. On one occasion his men showed signs of rebellion, and refused to embark on an expedition. Colonel Gordon appeared in the midst on hearing of the insurrection, and ordered every man who refused to embark to step forward. One man only ventured to do so. The Colonel presented his revolver at the man's head, and reiterated his command, which, it is needless to add, was speedily obeyed. Many an officer would have had his whole force in mutiny by taking such action, but Colonel Gordon had wonderful control over his men, through the fearlessness of character which he always displayed. They regarded him with awe and wonder, and seemed too paralized by his presence to offer resistance.

With his force of three thousand men he captured successively Taitsan and Quinsan, important strongholds of the rebels, and pushed forward to join the Imperial forces surrounding Soochou. An arrangement was made with the Wangs or Kings heading the rebels in the city by which, in consideration of their lives being spared, they were to secretly facilitate the entrance of the troops into Soochou. The place surrendered, and the Imperial troops took possession, Colonel Gordon retreating with his men a few miles distant to prevent their looting. Meantime, without his knowledge, the five Wangs were murdered by the Imperialist leaders, contrary to the compact entered into. Now that they were independent of Gordon's help they would not act in accordance with his clemency. Knowing nothing of what had occurred, he entered Soochou, and went innocently to the house of an uncle of one of the murdered Kings. It was immediately surrounded by Tai-pings, who were in great excitement as to what had become of the five Wangs, not knowing that they had been slain. They determined to keep Gordon as a hostage for the good treatment of their leaders. He was in a perilous position, but contrived to escape, and soon learnt of the murder of the Wangs. He burst into tears when he heard of their fate, so grieved was he that the men to whom he had pledged his word of honour that their lives should be spared if they surrendered, should be thus murdered in cold blood. He determined to give up his command, and would have done so, but Burgevine, the former commander, had joined the rebels, and Gordon felt that now every effort would be needed to free the distressed people from the misery into which they were plunged. The country was in a state of horrible desolation and famine. The rebels swept all means of sustenance away from the places through which they passed, and the starving creatures were even eating the flesh from the dead bodies. Gordon determined to free, if possible, the peaceful inhabitants from the outrages of the Tai-pings.

His name had now become a terror to the rebels. They believed that he led a charmed life, for he moved fearlessly amid showers of bullets without injury. Only once was he wounded, and then he remained calmly at his post, with the blood streaming from his leg, still giving his orders, until the doctor dragged him forcibly away. He wore none of the accoutrements of war, but carried, as his only weapon, a short cane, which the rebels thought must be a magic wand. "Gordon's magic wand of victory" they called it. Mere life he never valued, nor sought to avoid danger. On one occasion he had a marvellous escape. He was sitting on a bridge, leisurely smoking his cigar, when a bullet struck the stone beneath his seat. It did not disturb his serenity; he sat calmly on until a second struck, when he thought it time to retire to his boat below. Hardly had he done so, when the bridge fell a heap of ruins, nearly crushing his boat as he hastened away.

After the taking of Soochou, Gordon entered the field again on the 19th of February, 1864. He recaptured town after town from the rebels until only two remained in their hands. At that juncture he received orders to return home. Before leaving he had the satisfaction of seeing the Tai-ping rebellion thoroughly crushed. The Heavenly King, after causing all his wives to be put to death, committed suicide. The Emperor of China showed his deep gratitude to Colonel Gordon for his services by conferring upon him the highest Chinese honour—that of the Yellow Jacket and the Peacock's Feather, which are equivalent to the Orders of the Garter and the Bath in this country. A large sum of money was offered him, but that he refused. He had never worked from mercenary motives. After the taking of Soochou, an Imperial gift of 10,000 taels had been sent to him, but he flogged the treasure-bearers from his presence with his "magic wand," and wrote to the Emperor, indignantly declining his gift. The whole of his pay as a Commander, and part of his private income, he had expended in procuring comforts for his men. He would never accept pay for his services beyond the regular income of a commanding officer. Had he been disposed, he might have returned to his native country laden with wealth. But his only aim in this campaign had been to benefit the Chinese, and to rid them of their cruel oppressors.

Before leaving China the merchants of Shanghai presented him with an address, expressive of their gratitude for the good he had achieved by the crushing of the rebellion. When he left the Chinese felt that they were losing their best friend; even the rebels loved and admired him. "I know," he said, "I shall leave China as poor as I entered it, but with the knowledge that, through my weak instrumentality, upwards of 80,000 to 100,000 lives have been spared. I want no further satisfaction than this."

The Government at home rewarded him with only one step in the army. Later on he was made a Companion of the Bath. He had no wish to be made a hero, and had a great horror of any of his deeds being published. In the privacy of his home at Southampton he would entertain his friends with accounts of his numerous adventures, which sounded like a romance, so full of incident had his life in China been. But he never cared to be publicly lionized.

From 1865 to 1871 Colonel Gordon acted as Commanding Engineer at Gravesend. This period was about the happiest of his life. He lived in freedom from weighty cares, rarely entered society—to which he had a great dislike—and devoted his leisure time to philanthropic work. He took great delight in rescuing poor boys from the gutter, taking them from their old surroundings, clothing, feeding, educating, and then procuring them a start in life. His "Kings," he called them. On a map, which hung over his mantelpiece, he marked with pins the journeyings of those who had gone to sea. The pins were moved from place to place as he got tidings of the boys' whereabouts. He held them fervently at heart, and made each one of them a subject of daily prayer. Of the esteem in which these boys held their benefactor the inscriptions on the walls, in defiance of orthography, "God bless the Kernel," will testify. His house became so full of waifs and strays that he could not accommodate them, so was forced to give up this scheme. He transferred his attention to ragged schools, infirmaries, and workhouses, where he was a constant visitor, ever ready with a cheerful word and a helping hand.

In his habits he was most abstemious. A friend writes: 'Coming home with us one afternoon late, we found his tea waiting for him—a most unappetizing stale loaf and a tea-pot of tea. I remarked upon the dryness of the bread, when he took the whole loaf (a small one), crammed it into the slop-basin, and poured all the tea upon it, saying it would soon be ready for him to eat, and in half-an-hour it would not matter what he had eaten. He always had dry, humorous little speeches at command that flavoured all his talk, and I remember the merry twinkle with which he told us that many of the boys, thinking that being invited to live with the Colonel meant delicate fare and luxury, were unpleasantly enlightened upon the point when they found he sat down with them to salt beef, and just the necessary food." Presents of fruit and flowers were often sent to him by admiring friends, but he immediately despatched them to the sick in the hospitals and workhouses. His large garden he let out in plots to the poor for the cultivation of vegetables.

Of himself and his doings he rarely talked, nor did he care to be held up to public notice. When the first biography of him was being written, the author presented it for his approval. Colonel Gordon tore out every leaf which referred to his personal acts of bravery. In vain the dismayed author protested that his book would be spoilt; Gordon would have his way. Had he been less reticent, his deeds would have received more public recognition; but he ever suppressed himself.

After serving for two years at Galatz as British Commissioner on the Danube, Colonel Gordon entered the service of the Egyptian Khedive, and became Governor of the tribes in Upper Egypt, as successor to Sir Samuel Baker. He was offered a salary of £10,000 a year, but would only accept £2,000, which he considered sufficient to meet his expenses. His reason for refusing the larger sum was that he felt that the money would be wrung out of the suffering people.

The district over which Colonel Gordon had now to rule was the centre of the slave trade. This traffic was carried on to a fearful extent. Many of the slave dealers were like little kings in their territories, and the dread of the natives. At this time Lebehr Rahama—called the Black Pasha—was one of the most notorious, and his son Suleiman became more so. The Khedive had determined to suppress this traffic, but for no higher reason than that it threatened his Empire. Gordon was commissioned to carry this into effect. He set out for Gondokoro on the Nile, which was to be his headquarters. There he found himself in a strange region. River horses splashed and blew in the waters of the Nile, while great crocodiles basked in its mud. The laughing birds mocked him from the bushes when he took an evening stroll, and the inhabitants of the place stalked about with little or no clothing, considering a necklace sufficient full dress to appear in before the new Governor.

His first care was to gain the goodwill of the natives. He gave them presents, enlisted them in his service, and gradually gained their confidence. From Khartoum he had issued a decree which meant the suppression of slavery. The traders were already on the alert. But Colonel Gordon persevered in his work. He bought up the slaves as they were being taken through his territory, and gave them employment. The poor creatures almost worshipped him. Some of the slave dealers he took into his service, dealing with them as he had done with the Chinese rebels, whom he first captured and then enlisted in his army. He took long journeys across the country, listening to the grievances of the people, and trying to redress them. Nothing was neglected which he could do for the good of his subjects. He was kind and considerate even to the smallest things. Writing of an old woman whom he had supported, he says, " She had her tobacco up to the last."

Besides redressing the wrongs of the people, and hunting down the slave traders, he explored the country, often exposing himself to attacks from the hostile tribes, who were on the alert to spear his boats as they passed through the narrow channels of the river.

On October 6th, 1876, the "Little Khedive," as the natives had learnt to call Colonel Gordon, left for London, but by February, 1877, at the earnest request of the Khedive, he returned to Egypt as Governor-General of the Soudan, a much more important office than his previous one. It gave him what he most longed for—greater power to suppress the slave trade. On reaching Khartoum, the capital of his dominions, he went through a grand installation ceremony. An address was read, to which his subjects expected to hear a grand speech in reply. But all the new Governor said was: " With the help of God I will hold the balance level." This pleased the people more than any oration could have done. They felt that they had over them a man determined to dispense justice with an even hand, and to whom the welfare of his subjects would be the first consideration. During the three days of festivity he gave of his private means £1,000 to the poor. His residence was a palace as large as Marlborough House, and he had

200 servants in attendance. All this ceremony he thoroughly disliked. If he rose from his seat, everybody else did the same. He was guarded by six or eight sentinals, while eight or ten men were in readiness to assist him from his camel if he wished to alight during his journeys across the country. When he walked all his followers dismounted too, which rendered him so furious that he would in desperation resume his seat. He made a good deal of fun out of all this formality. Sometimes he would say in English to a chief who was paying a visit of state, "Now, old bird, it is time for you to go." This greatly pleased them; for they did not understand the language.

He was most energetic in dealing with the slave dealers, traversing the country at great personal peril, and was many times in imminent danger from the robber chieftains. The most daring of them was Suleiman, who after giving him a long chase finally surrendered, but only to break out again as soon as an opportunity came. Colonel Gordon rode over nearly 4,000 miles of desert during his first year of office. In consequence of not wearing bandages round his chest and waist he suffered greatly from the severe shaking on the camel's back.

The Khedive had neglected to provide Colonel Gordon with a sufficient escort when he sent him to visit King John of Abyssinia, in order to negotiate with that monarch in a dispute which had arisen with the Egyptian Government, the consequence was he was taken prisoner. An amusing account is given of the affair: "When Gordon Pasha was lately taken prisoner by the Abyssinians he completely checkmated King John. The King received his prisoner sitting on his throne, or whatever piece of furniture did duty for that exalted seat, a chair being placed for the prisoner considerably lower than the seat on which the king sat. The first thing the Pasha [Gordon] did was to seize this chair, place it alongside that of his Majesty, and sit down on it; the next to inform him that he met him as an equal, and would only treat him as such. This somewhat disconcerted his sable Majesty, but on recovering himself he said, 'Do you know, Gordon Pasha, that I could kill you on the spot if I liked?' 'I am perfectly well aware of it, your Majesty,' said the Pasha. 'Do so at once if it is your royal pleasure; I am ready.' This disconcerted the King still more, and he exclaimed, 'What! ready to be killed!' 'Certainly, replied the Pasha; I am always ready to die, and so far from fearing your putting me to death, you would confer a favour on me by doing so; for you would be doing for me that which I am precluded by my religious scruples from doing for myself— you would relieve me from all the troubles and misfortunes which the future may have in store for me.' This completely staggered King John, who gasped out in despair, 'Then my power has no terrors for you?' 'None, whatever,' was the Pasha's laconic reply? His Majesty, it is needless to add, instantly collapsed."

Shortly after this Colonel Gordon resigned the Governorship of the Soudan. He could not agree with the policy of the new Khedive's ministers; therefore preferred to resign his post. In reply to some remarks in praise of his Governorship he said, "I do not profess either to be a great ruler or a great financier; but I can say this—I have cut off the slave-dealers in their strongholds, and I have made the people love me." He had had three years of desperate labour, having ridden 8,500 miles, and been exposed to hardships and dangers innumerable. But he was satisfied to have ameliorated the condition of the wretched inhabitants of the Soudan.

On his return to London he was greeted as the "Uncrowned King." The press and the public at large were loud in his praises, but the Government seemed slow to recognize his services. After spending a few weeks at his home at Southampton, he started to India as Secretary to Lord Ripon, the Governor-General, but shortly resigned. The post was not at all suited to one who had lately reigned as a Sultan.

He next visited China, at the request of his old friend, Governor Li, with whom he had been associated during the Tai-ping rebellion. War seemed imminent between Russia and China. Colonel Gordon gave most valuable advice to the Chinese Government, and was instrumental in averting the war, but he would not act in an official capacity. He merely looked upon himself as a friendly visitor to the country. At his suggestion the Chinese Army was remodelled—the man who in former years had saved China, now taught her how to save herself.

After his return in 1881, he visited Ireland, and was

afterwards appointed Commanding Royal Engineer to the Mauritius, where he spent ten uneventful months. On March 6th he was made a Major-General, and shortly afterwards left the Mauritius for the Cape. He had consented to go there, at the request of the Government, to help in settling the disturbances with the Basutos. But it was a mistaken expedition; his advice was ignored and he could not act freely. He threw up the post after holding it for five months.

He now longed for rest, and set out on a pilgrimage to the Holy Land. Settling in a house outside Jerusalem, he lived on bread and fruits, and interested himself with marking out the Holy Sites ; many of which, according to his observations, were entirely wrongly placed. Bible in hand he devoted himself most assiduously to this interesting study. But General Gordon was not yet destined to retire from the field of public action. When at the close of last year (1883) news came of the terrible state into which the Soudan had fallen, through the ravages of the Mahdi or False Prophet, with his hordes of fanatical Arabs, and the incompetency of its rulers, there was an universal cry, " Where is Gordon ?" All eyes turned to him as the only one likely to restore peace to the Soudan. General satisfaction was felt when the Government commissioned him to proceed to Khartoum, and gave him full liberty to use such measures as his past experience of the country suggested to him for the relief of the Soudanese. With his usual promptitude he set out, arriving safely at Cairo. He left that place in high spirits, believing that his work of pacification would soon be accomplished. The whole country followed the stages of his dangerous journey across the desert, where he was liable at any moment to be massacred by the marauding Arabs. Again and again it was said that he had been captured. Prayers were offered in the churches for his welfare, and one long cry of satisfaction went up from the British nation when the telegraph flashed the news that the brave man had reached Berber in safety, February 11th. " Stewart and I are all right," he telegraphed. " Do not bother about us. Do not want Bedouins at Korosko; take them away ; do what you like with them. The people are coming in on all sides with enthusiasm. Hope soon the Soudan will be perfectly tranquil." On the 18th of February he reached Khartoum. The people crowded to kiss his hands and feet. It was their "Little Khedive" come back to them in their time of misfortune. They hailed him as their deliverer, and the "Sultan of the Soudan." He held semi-regal Durbars, and the people hung upon his words. "I come," he said to them, "without soldiers, but with God on my side, to redress the evils of the Soudan. I will not fight with any weapons but justice. There shall be no more Bashi-Bazouks." He and Colonel Stewart proceeded at once with the institution of reforms in the government of the country. Offices were opened in the palace, where complaints were heard and grievances redressed. The official records of unpaid taxes, which had doubtless been unjustly imposed upon the suffering people, were publicly burnt, together with the whips and instruments for administering the cruel bastinado. The prisons were thrown open, and their ghastly occupants, who had been left forgotten to rot in their chains, staggered out into freedom. He acknowledged the Mahdi as ruler of Kordofan. There was no other alternative. He had destroyed his status as a prophet, by taking eighteen wives contrary to the precepts of the Koran, and had therefore seized upon the office of a Sultan. General Gordon allowed him to retain it, hoping by such concession to keep him from pushing further towards Khartoum. The slave question he has not been able to satisfactorily settle, at least, at the present time. In fact some of his proclamations appear to countenance this traffic. This, however, is so at variance with General Gordon's past policy in the Soudan that it is hardly probable. It appears that the slave dealing in the Soudan is a part of Mohammedan law, which no one has authority to suppress. "Your grievance," said General Gordon to the chiefs, "has been that we interfered with what you call your property, your slaves. Very well, in future we shall not interfere either with your slaves or with any other of your institutions, bad or good." So far as news has reached this country the General's plan is to put certain restrictions upon the future possession and sale of slaves, which will make it less worth while for the Soudanese to keep up the traffic.

Through the energy of General Gordon the telegraphic communication between the Soudan capital and Cairo has been re-established, and the road between Berber and Suakim been opened up. It seemed as though he had achieved a bloodless victory. But the followers of the Mahdi, led by his General, Osman Digna, were more determined than had at first been supposed. They repulsed the Egyptian troops with great slaughter. British soldiers have been obliged to take the field against them, in order to restore peace to Egypt. General Graham, on the 4th of March, achieved a victory over the rebels at El Teb, and a week later, at Tamasi, the army of Osman Digna was routed after some of the most desperate fighting on record. Four thousand Arabs were slain and 6,000 wounded. Meantime the hostile tribes were rising near Khartoum, but General Gordon clung still to his peace policy. Writing on the 7th of March, he said "I am dead against the sending of any British expedition to reconquer the Soudan. It is unnecessary. I would not have a single life lost." With the retirement of the British forces, the hostile tribes became bolder. Khartoum was surrounded, all communication cut off, and again the nation was plunged in doubt and anxiety regarding the fate of the brave General. On the 16th of March, came the news that he had sallied forth at the head of his small force, but had been defeated by the Arabs, through the treachery of two of his Pashas, and the cowardice of his troops. He was able to retire again to Khartoum with the remnant of his followers. A more perilous position than his at the present time can hardly be imagined. It seems a matter of impossibility for a British force to be sent to his aid, so dangerous is the route. Khartoum is surrounded by a force of Arabs, numbering 4,000 foot and 100 cavalry. Bullets are falling within his palace, and many of his followers lying dead around him.

The eyes of all English people are now wistfully turned to this soldier-hero at Khartoum, blocked in on all sides, but still gallantly defending his position, and hoping on. He has proved himself a true soldier, a true statesman, and above all, a true Christian. He still lives in the hearts of the Soudanese, and is the only Christian for whom daily prayer is offered in the Temple at Mecca. A Mandarin of the highest order in China, a Pasha in Africa, a General in England, and the Governor of the Soudan, he is yet one of the humblest of men; has no personal ambition, and is scornful of all flattery and applause. In all parts of the globe his deeds are spoken of.

PRINCESS ALICE.

HER ROYAL HIGHNESS PRINCESS ALICE MAUD MARY was born at Buckingham Palace on the 25th of April, 1843. She was the third child and second daughter of Queen Victoria and the Prince Consort. She had the inestimable advantage of possessing parents whose gifts of mind and heart had drawn from their subjects the deepest admiration and love. Her father, Prince Albert, was the second son of the Duke of Coburg. He became the husband of the Queen when in his twenty-first year. At that time his handsome presence and manly chivalrous character won all hearts. No better husband could have been desired by the nation for their idolized young Queen. The Prince proved himself the people's truest friend. In all that related to the welfare of his adopted country; its social and agricultural conditions; its industries and commerce, he took the deepest interest. He held a high and exalted idea of the duties of royalty, and discharged those in connection with his own position with rare sincerity and power. No words can convey a better estimate of his worth than the beautiful lines of Tennyson :—

"And indeed He seems to me
Scarce other than my own ideal knight,
'Who reverenced his conscience as his king;
Whose glory was redressing human wrong;
Who spake no slander, no, nor listened to it;
Who loved one only and who clave to her—'
Her—over all whose realms to their last isle,
Commingled with the gloom of imminent war,
The shadow of His loss drew like eclipse,
Darkening the world. We have lost him: he is gone:
We know him now : all narrow jealousies
Are silent, and we see him as he moved;
How modest, kindly, all-accomplish'd, wise;
With what sublime repression of himself,
And in what limits and how tenderly;

> Not swaying to this faction or to that ;
> Not making his high place the lawless perch
> Of wing'd ambitions, nor a vantage ground
> For pleasure ; but thro' all this tract of years
> Wearing the white flower of a blameless life
> Before a thousand peering littlenesses,
> In that fierce light which beats upon a throne,
> And blackens every blot : for where is he
> Who dares foreshadow for an only son
> A lovelier life, a more sustain'd than his ?
> Or how should England, dreaming of *his* sons,
> Hope more for these than some inheritance
> Of such a life, a heart, a mind as thine,
> Thou noble father of her kings to be,
> Laborious for her people and her poor—
> Voice in the rich dawn of an ampler day—
> Far-sighted summoner of War and Waste
> To fruitful strifes and rivalries of peace—
> Sweet nature gilded by the gracious gleam
> Of letters, dear to Science, dear to Art,
> Dear to thy land and ours, a Prince indeed,
> Beyond all titles, and a household name,
> Hereafter, thro' all times, Albert the Good."

The beautiful simplicity of our good Queen's life, and the manner in which she has discharged her duties as Queen, wife, and mother are the pride of her subjects. As the years pass by, her pure life shines clearer and clearer. "From you," wrote the Princess Alice to her in later years, "I have inherited an ardent and sympathizing spirit, and feel the pain of those I love as though it were my own." With such parents the childhood of the Princess was singularly blessed. She was surrounded by a beautiful domestic simplicity. The Royal children were never allowed to come in contact with the actual Court life, but were entrusted to the care of persons of the highest character chosen by the Queen and Prince Consort. They themselves enquired into the minutest details of their education, heard them recite their poems, and inspected their drawings and work. Eagerly did the merry group of children vie with each other in winning an approving smile from their Royal parents. Sometimes they broke down in their recitations, when the Prince would bite his lips to keep from laughing at their woe-begone looks. The Swiss Cottage at Osborne had its museum, kitchen, storeroom and little gardens for their special use. They there learnt how to do household work, to cook, to garden and to direct in all particulars a small establishment. Their parents visited them as their guests, partaking of dishes prepared by the young Princesses. In deeds of charity they were taught to delight, and while enjoying the freedom of the Highlands, were allowed to visit the humblest cottages.

The Princess was a bright, merry, beautiful child. When she was a year old, her father spoke of her as "the beauty of the family," her mother adding that "she was a very vain little person." She soon became a great favourite with all around her. Lady Lyttleton, who up to 1851 had the supervision of the Royal children, wrote the following account of the Princess's fourth birthday:—"Dear Princess Alice is too pretty in her low frock and pearl necklace, tripping about and blushing and smiling at her honours. The whole family, indeed, appear to advantage on birthdays; no tradesman or country squire can keep one with such hearty simple affection and enjoyment. *One* present, I think, we shall all wish to live further off—a live lamb, all over pink ribbons and bells. He is already the greatest pet, as one may suppose.

"Princess Alice's pet lamb is the cause of many tears. He will not take to his mistress, but runs away lustily, and will soon butt at her, though she is most coaxy, and said to him in her sweetest tones, after kissing his nose often, ' Milly, *dear* Milly! *do* you like me?'" She became passionately fond of riding and of horses; delighted in gymnastics, skating, and all bodily exercises. She joined in her brothers' sports, and soon became bold and fearless as a boy. But with all this she displayed the most thoughtful consideration for the feelings of others. On one occasion a dresser of the Queen's passed by the Royal children as they were playing in the corridor. The Prince of Wales made a joke about her great height. The young Princess quickly tried to smooth over a remark which seemed a little unkind by saying, "It is very nice to be tall; Papa would like us all to be tall."

In her studies she was bright and clever. "Her copy-books were always neatness itself, and she wrote a very pretty hand." After reading history with Madame Roland, the French governess, it was the custom for the Royal children to make pen and ink sketches of scenes about which they had been reading. The Princess Alice was especially clever in the originality of her designs, and the spirited character of her drawing. For foreign languages and music she also showed very decided talent. In private theatricals, performed on birthdays and other festive occasions, she far outshone her brothers and sisters by her pleasing intonation of voice and the dignity and grace with which she acted her part. Still, as long as her very gifted and distinguished sister the Crown Princess remained unmarried, Princess Alice occupied a subordinate place. It was hardly thought at that period that she would develop into the clever woman she eventually became.

Her life was greatly changed after the marriage of her sister to Prince Frederick William of Prussia. She became the chief companion of her parents. The Duchess of Baden thus refers to this period :—

"Alice was now drawn more into the circle of the grown-up members of the family; but in spite of this she retained all the fascination of her charming graceful ways. A great vein of humour showed itself in her, as well as a certain sharpness in criticising people who were not congenial to her. Many a little conflict took place in the schoolroom ; but while the individualities of the sisters became more and more distinct, their happy relations to one another remained unchanged. She was a great favourite with her brothers and sisters, though they knew she was fond of mischief.

"To a naturally engaging manner quite exceptional, joyousness and power of showing affectionate emotion imparted an especial charm, which revealed itself in the fine lines of her face, in her graceful movements, and a certain inborn nobleness and dignity, Her attachment to my parents, 'Uncle Prussia' and 'Aunt Prussia,' was truly touching."

She was fifteen years of age at the time of her sister's marriage. But the constant intercourse with her noble father rapidly formed her into a thoughtful woman. She was led by him to take an interest in art, music, politics and religion far beyond what is usual. This higher state of culture she always maintained, Her father was her ideal of all that was noble and true. She strove to follow in his footsteps and to train her children, when she became a mother, after the methods which he advocated. The Queen, writing of her at this period, said : "She is very good, gentle, sensible and amiable, and a real comfort to me. I shall not let her marry as long as I can reasonably delay her doing so."

During the Ascot races in June, 1860, the two Princes, Louis and Henry of Hesse, sons of Prince Charles and nephews of the reigning Grand Duke, were among the visitors at Windsor Castle. It soon became evident that an attachment was springing up between Prince Louis and Princess Alice. After the return of the Princes, a letter arrived from the Crown Princess, in which she said that the Prince's mother had told her of his attachment. During a visit of the Queen and Prince Consort to the Continent, it was arranged for Prince Louis to pay a second visit to the English Court. The result of the visit is shown from the following interesting entry in the Queen's diary:—"While I was conversing with the gentlemen after dinner, I observed that Alice and Louis, standing before the fire, were conversing more earnestly than usual, and as I passed to go to the next room, both of them came towards me, and Alice said, with great agitation, that he had proposed to her, and he begged for my blessing. I could only squeeze his hand and say, 'Certainly,' and that we would see him in our room later. Got through the evening, working as well as we could. Alice came to our room. . . . . agitated, but quiet. . . . . Albert sent for Louis to his room; he went first to him and then called Alice and me in. . . . . Louis has a warm, noble heart. We embraced our dear Alice, and praised her much to him. After talking a little we parted; a most touching, and to me most sacred moment." The engagement of Prince Louis of Hesse to Princess Alice took place on the 30th of November, 1860, when she was seventeen years of age. It was entered into entirely from affection, and proved to be one of the happiest unions.

The Queen's Message to Parliament announcing the intended marriage of the Princess was received with general satisfaction. A dowry of £30,000 with an annuity of £6,000 was voted her in the House of Commons without a dissentient voice. "She will not," writes her father, "be able to do great things with it."

Prince Louis stayed over Christmas with his intended bride. He was much beloved by the Queen and Prince, who both felt that their precious daughter, though going into comparative poverty, would have as her husband a loving protector. He left on the 28th of December after a sorrowful parting, but with the hope of returning in the spring.

At the end of the year, when busy with preparations for Princess Alice's future household, the Prince Consort became ill. Soon the illness developed into typhoid fever. Great alarm was felt. All through that trying time the young Princess was her father's devoted nurse. When on the 14th of December he breathed his last, it was she, who, repressing her own grief with wonderful self-command, ministered to the comfort of her widowed mother. All communications from the Ministers and the Queen's household passed through her hand. Night and day she worked at State affairs to relieve her heart-broken mother. The whole nation noted with admiration the conduct of this young girl called, so suddenly, to face the death of an idolized parent, and to bear the weight of such great responsibilities. Her strength of mind and self-sacrifice have never been forgotten. The name of "Princess Alice" remains a household word in every British home.

At the last mournful hour her pent-up grief overcame her. As she placed the wreaths and flowers over the "dear, dead Prince," she cried in heart-rending voice to her dear friend, Princess Louise of Prussia, "Oh! dear Molly, let us pray to God to give us back dear Papa!"

In the June of the year following this great bereavement Prince Louis arrived at Osborne to claim his bride. The marriage took place on the 1st of July. It was celebrated in the quietest manner possible on account of the Queen's widowhood. The newly-wedded pair spent their honeymoon at St. Clare, near Ryde, Isle of Wight.

On the 9th of July Prince and Princess Louis of Hesse left England, in the Royal Yacht, for Darmstadt. The best wishes of a devoted people followed the Princess to her new home. The memory of her goodness was fresh in every heart. The following sonnet appeared in *Punch* at the time:—

"Dear to us by those calm earnest eyes,
  And early thought upon that fair young brow;
  Dearer for that where grief was heaviest, thou
Wert sunshine, till He passed where suns shall rise
And set no more: thou, in affection wise
  And strong, wert strength to Her who even but now
  In the soft accents of thy bridal vow
Heard music of her own heart's memories.

> "Too full of love to own a thought of pride
> Is now thy gentle bosom ; so 'tis best :
> Yet noble is thy choice, O English bride !
> And England hails the bridegroom and the guest
> A friend—a friend well loved by him who died.
> He blessed your troth : your wedlock shall be blessed."

Her reception at Darmstadt was most enthusiastic. She charmed all classes by her grace and amiability. Her home was a very unpretentious one. Vastly different from the royal palaces in which her life had hitherto been passed. But she was determined to make herself content in her adopted county. Writing to the Queen, she thus describes her home :—" Our rooms are very small, but so nicely furnished, and with such perfect taste, everything a present from my own dear Louis ; they look quite English." "You tell me," she writes on another occasion, " to speak to you of my happiness. You will understand the feeling which made me silent towards you, my own dear bereaved Mother, on that point; but you are unselfish and loving and can enter into my happiness, though I could never have been the first to tell you how intense it is, when it must draw the painful contrast between your past and present existence. If I say I love my dear husband, that is scarcely enough— it is a love and esteem which increases daily, hourly; which he also shows to me by such consideration, such tender loving ways. What was life before to what it has become now? There is such blessed peace being at his side, being his wife ; there is such a feeling of security ; and we two have a world of our own when we are together, which *nothing* can touch or intrude upon. My lot is indeed a blessed one ; and yet what have I done to deserve that warm, ardent love, which my darling Louis ever shows me ? I admire his good and noble heart more than I can say. How he loves you, you know, and he will be a good son to you. He reads to me every day out of *Westward Ho*, which I think very beautiful and interesting."

The first months of her married life were spent in visiting some of the chief German towns and, what to her was the most interesting, Coburg, the native place of her beloved father. These scenes of his early years were new to her. She surveyed them with that intensity of devotion which marked them as hallowed ground. There he had gambolled as a child, and there his budding youth had opened out into that noble manhood which made him a nation's pride. Tearfully and reverently she walked over the house and grounds of the Rosenau, every part of which was sacred to her father's memory. In the little garden that had been his she gathered two flowers to send to the sorrowing Queen.

The Princess's rooms at Darmstadt were too small to accommodate guests; for this reason she and her husband arranged to spend the winter and spring in England. Meantime preparations were made for building them a new palace at Darmstadt. Plans were sent in, "but," wrote the Princess to her mother, "even the simplest is far above what we poor mortals can build." However, she herself drew up a plan, and the new palace was begun on a site given them by the Grand Duke. The arrangements throughout were made under her direction and characterized by great artistic taste.

Prince and Princess Louis arrived in England, November, 1862, and remained until the following May. During this visit, their first child, Princess Victoria, lately married to Prince Louis of Battenberg, was born at Windsor Castle, April 5th, 1863.

After a short stay at Osborne and in London, they returned to Darmstadt with their infant daughter. The letters of the Princess at this period show her keen motherly solicitude for her little daughter, and give pretty glimpses of her in her new character. June the 8th she writes—"Baby sits up quite strong, and looks about and laughs. She has got on wonderfully, and she is so good. She was an hour with us yesterday evening, wide awake, and so good. She is as well and as strong as any child could be." Some months later she writes—". . . . My baby has this morning cut her first tooth, and makes such faces if one ventures to touch her little mouth. . . . ."

On her return to Darmstadt, Princess Alice began to take an active part in philanthropic work. She became the "Protectress" of the "Heidenreich Institution" for women From that time forward her efforts were unceasing in promoting the usefulness of that and kindred institutions. She took a really active interest in them, going into the minutest details, studying methods which had been adopted in her own and other countries, and furthering their introduction into Germany. During her father's illness she had given proof of her singular aptitude as a nurse. She continued to read and study books on the human body, the treatment of disease, and kindred subjects, feeling the necessity of every woman taking an intelligent interest in medical science. Emergencies arise when help is needed before a doctor can be found. The Princess advocated that it was the duty of women to fit themselves to act in these emergencies, and to be able to further a doctor's efforts by intelligent co-operation. Writing to the Queen, she gives the following account of a visit she paid to a poor sick woman. Describing the efforts of the "Heidenreich Institution" for the relief of poor women, she continues:—"All cases are reported to me. The other day I went to one *incog.* with Christa, in the old part of the town—and the trouble we had to find the house! At length, through a dirty courtyard, up a dark ladder into one little room, where lay in one bed the poor woman and her baby; in the room four other children, the husband, two other beds and a stove. But it did not smell bad, nor was it dirty. I sent Christa down with the children, then with the husband cooked something for the woman; arranged her bed a little, took her baby for her, bathed its eyes—for they were so bad, poor little thing!—and did odds and ends for her. I went twice. The people did not know me, and were so nice, so good and touchingly attached to each other; it did one's heart good to see such good feelings in such poverty. The husband was out of work, the children too young to go to school, and they had only four kreutzers in the house when she was confined. Think of that misery and discomfort!

"If one never sees any poverty, and always lives in that cold circle of Court people, one's good feelings dry up, and I felt the want of going about and doing the little good that is in my power. I am sure you will understand this."

A very pleasing tribute was paid the Princess in June, 1865. Two hundred and fifty of the women of Darmstadt subscribed to have a picture painted for her of Loch Katrine. They sent the painter, Mr. P. Weber, to Scotland to paint it, thinking that something from her own country would give her most pleasure.

In 1866 the new palace at Darmstadt was completed. The Princess herself directed the decorative part. She inherited her artistic taste from her father, and had been accustomed to watch his exquisite arrangement of pictures and other works of art. In her new home she gathered souvenirs of her parents and her brothers and sisters. Photographs, pictures, and presents to remind her of her dear native land. On the night on which the new palace was first occupied the Prince and Princess gathered their household together in the hall, while the chaplain prayed and pronounced a blessing.

At this time she became interested in another branch of philanthropic work—asylums for poor idiots. She attended some lectures on the subject given by a clergyman from the Odenwald, and took measures to found such an institution. But she was determined to separate the religious from the practical part of the work. Her idea was that people should feel bound to alleviate sickness and suffering out of love for their fellow-men irrespective of religious duty.

She held a bazaar in her new palace to raise the necessary funds for the enterprise. It was opened on the 6th of April 1866, and lasted four days. The sum of 16,000 florins was raised. This was the only occasion on which the Princess resorted to bazaars as a means for aiding her charities. She felt that on such occasions people came more for their own personal amusement than to aid the good work.

A terrible time of anxiety was now before her. War between Prussia and Austria was imminent. Hesse Darmstadt was on the side of Austria, so that in the event of war Prince Louis would be fighting against his brother-in-law the Crown Prince of Prussia. Earnestly did the Princess hope and pray that such a disastrous calamity might be avoided. She had, like her father, a detestation of war, looking upon the tendency to press every question to the point of the sword as a return to mediæval times. There seemed no possibility of an agreement in this dispute. Prince Louis had soon to assume command in the field.

The Princess now began to organize a staff of nurses for the wounded, and to collect necessary things for the hospitals. She sent to England to beg rags, linen, sheeting, &c., to have in readiness for the wounded soldiers. Her two little girls were left to the Queen's care until happier and more peaceful days came to Darmstadt.

In the midst of this excitement the Princess's third child was born, July 11th. Three days later her husband was forced to tear himself from her side and march to the front of the battle. Although in such a delicate condition, she had all the affairs of state to manage. Everything seemed dependent upon her. Her husband was cut off from communication with Darmstadt by the Prussians. No tidings could she get of his welfare. Long sleepless nights were followed by anxious days of waiting. The Prussians were pillaging the houses within sight of her palace. The terror-stricken people flocked around her for protection. Many of their goods she hid in her private rooms to be safe from the looting of the soldiers. Wives and mothers clung about her beseeching for tidings of their husbands and children, and she had none to give. All the time she dreaded lest her own darling husband was amongst the slain. Fearful as was this strain upon her strength, she was foremost in the hospital work, and was busy night and day in attending to the wants of those newly arrived from the battle-field. Money was scarce, and many deprivations did she undergo so that the poor people might have enough. Her parents-in-law, the Prince and Princess Charles, were the only ones left in Darmstadt to whom she could go for counsel, and they were bowed down with grief and needed her support. Added to all this there was the fear that the Duchy of Darmstadt might be claimed by the Prussians. In that case her husband's prospects of one day becoming Grand Duke would be lost.

There was a cessation of hostilities in August, but it was doubtful whether it would be a permanent peace. The Prussians still occupied Darmstadt. The Princess decided to join her husband in his quarters in the "Gelbe Haus" at Nierstein-Oppenheim, notwithstanding that cholera was raging there. She felt that she must be by his side come what might.

After a prolonged occupation by the Prussians, peace was concluded. The Prince and Princess entered Darmstadt amidst enthusiastic welcome. On the 12th of September, the infant princess, born in the midst of war and bloodshed, was christened at the palace, receiving the names Irène (Peace) Louise Marie Anna. The same day the peace for which the brave mother had so earnestly sought was ratified at Berlin. A few days later the Princess, and the Prince with his brave soldiers of the Hessian division, made their public entry into Darmstadt.

The experiences of the late war had impressed Princess

Alice more than ever with the need of organizations for the relief of the sick and wounded. In 1867 a committee was formed of six ladies and four doctors, having the Princess as president. This was the beginning of the "Ladies' Union." A central committee was to be held in Darmstadt under the Princess's direction. Other committees were spread over the country. The object of the "Union" was to assist "the nursing and supporting of the troops in times of war," and in times of peace to "train nurses, to assist other hospitals, or amongst the poor, or to nurse the rich"—to give, in reality, help wherever it was needed. By the year 1869 the members of the "Ladies' Union" had increased to 2,500. The Princess wished lay women and ladies of all classes to join. Hitherto nursing had been too much confined to religious orders.

Other schemes, for the good of women and girls, were started by her, with the help of her friend Fraülein Louise Büchner, the distinguished champion for the higher education of women. A committee was formed for the encouragement of "Female Industry." On the 25th of November, 1867, "The Alice Bazaar" was opened. It was for the purpose of receiving and disposing of ladies' needlework, and also for obtaining employment for women of all classes.

The Princess in company with her husband visited Coburg early in 1867 and there met, for the first time since the war, the Crown Prince and Princess of Germany. It had been a severe trial to the two sisters to feel that their husbands were fighting on opposite sides, but now war was over and they enjoyed the happiness of re-union. Prince and Princess Louis went to Berlin for a few weeks and afterwards to Paris, to be present at the Great International Exhibition, to which the Emperor Napoleon had invited all the Sovereigns and Princes of Europe.

Returning to Darmstadt, the Princess continued to take the greatest interest in the Institutions which she had been the means of founding. At Christmas she visited the hospitals, and took presents for the inmates. To this time belongs one of the most beautiful of the Princess's letters to her mother, written for the anniversary of her dear father's death:—

"Before going to rest, I take up my pen to write a few loving words, that they may reach you on the morning of the 14th [December]. The sound of that date brings with it that sad and dreary recollection which, for you, my poor dear Mamma, and for us, time cannot alter. As long as our lives last, this time of year must fill us with sad and earnest feelings, and revive the pain of that bitter parting.

"I ought not to dwell on those hours now, for it is wrong to open those wounds afresh, which God in His mercy finds little ways and means to heal and soothe the pain of.

"Dear darling Papa is, and ever will be, *immortal*. The good he has done; the great ideas he has promulgated in the world; the noble and unselfish example he has given, will live on, as I am sure he must ever do, as one of the best, purest, most God-like men that have come down into this world. His example will, and does, stimulate others to higher and purer aims ; and I am convinced that darling Papa did not live in vain. His great mission was done ; and what has remained undone he has placed in your dear hands, who will know best how to achieve his great works of love and justice. I shall think much, very much, of you on the 14th, and you will be more in my prayers than ever. Think also a little of your most devoted child."

On the 25th of November, 1868, the Princess gave birth to a son and heir. This was a great joy to the parents and to the country. It was christened on the 28th of December, receiving the names of Ernest Ludwig. His sponsors were the Queen of England and the King of Prussia.

In the year 1870 Prince Louis was seized with scarlet fever. Soon after Princess Victoria and the little Prince took the infection. Princess Alice undertook the nursing entirely herself. This involved her complete seclusion from the social world. It was during this time that her intimate friendship with David Friedrich Strauss began. She had become much interested in Voltaire, and arranged for Strauss to give her lectures upon that celebrated man during the weeks she was in enforced seclusion. They amounted to seven lectures in all, and were received by the Princess with the deepest interest. She acceded to the wish of Strauss that they should be published as a book and dedicated to her. It was a step which even the author feared might bring unpleasant criticism upon her. The rationalistic tendency of Strauss was well known, and the teaching of Voltaire greatly condemned. The Princess read the proof-sheets with her husband and returned them to Strauss with the following characteristic letter:—

"DEAR HERR PROFESSOR,—I return you your *Voltaire* with many thanks. My husband read through the fifth chapter of it yesterday; he does not think that its contents are such as to justify my refusing the dedication. The value which I place on the dedication of your book will always be far greater than any little unpleasantness which might possibly arise from my accepting it.—ALICE."

Princess Alice never allowed herself to be swayed by mere prejudice. She appreciated truth from any source. Although she did not hold many of the views of Strauss, she had at the same time sympathy with his efforts for putting the life and work of Voltaire before the people in a more charitable manner than had hitherto been done.

When her husband and two children had recovered from scarlet fever, she accompanied them to Mayence for change of air. The hospitals at Mayence, Offenbach and Giessen were visited by her for the purpose of consulting with their managers on the introduction of improvements.

This peaceful happy life was brought to a close by the declaration of war between France and Germany. The Princess had again to watch her soldier-husband march to the scene of war, and take her post at Darmstadt as general consoler, helper, and adviser. Now it was that her excellent nursing organizations proved their worth. The hospitals were soon filled with the wounded and dying. Among them the Princess moved like an angel of mercy. Soothing the agonies of the wounded men by her gentle touch and words of cheer. The soldiers in the Crimean War kissed the shadow of Florence Nightingale as she passed from bed to bed in the hospitals. A similar feeling must have filled the hearts of the poor men in the Darmstadt hospital as the Princess Alice tended to their wants. She visited the homes of the widows and orphans of those who had fallen in the war, providing for their wants out of her, now, much straitened means. The streets of the place were full of infection, but she heeded it not as long as there was one pain to lessen, one heart to cheer, or one dying one to comfort. Two of the most serious cases in the hospital she had removed to her palace to be under her special care. For six weeks one young man lay at death's door, but ultimately the

Princess had the joy of restoring him to his parents. The doctors said that his life had been saved chiefly through her efforts.

At the beginning of the war the "Alice Society for Aid to Sick and Wounded" had sixteen trained nurses ready to work. Their number was soon increased to 164. These were despatched to the ambulances near Metz, and to other hospitals. By her noble example the Princess inspired women and girls of all classes to give their aid. As well as caring for the sick and wounded, she rendered great assistance to the widows and orphans of the soldiers. "The Alice Society" did good service by finding them employment. Out of this sprang the "Alice Lyceum" for the intellectual culture of the higher classes. At the head of it was Fraülein Louise Büchner.

A second son had been born to the Prince and Princess in October, 1870, while the war was raging. Its christening took place on the 11th of February, 1871, when an armistice had been concluded, which it was hoped would result in peace. The young prince was named Frederick William after the victorious King of Prussia.

The following June Prince and Princess Louis went to Berlin to be present at the triumphal entry of the German troops on the conclusion of the peace. In the autumn they visited the Queen at Balmoral, and went from there to Sandringham. It was during this visit that the Prince of Wales was seized with typhoid fever. Princess Alice took her place at his bed-side, and nursed him with the same tender devotion which, ten years before, she had shown to her beloved father. On the 14th of December, 1871, the anniversary of the Prince Consort's death, a gloom overspread the country. It was feared that no hope of the Prince's recovery was left. A whole nation's heart went out in sympathy with those anxious watchers at his side. The presence of Princess Alice sustained the despairing wife and mother. When the joyous news was flashed through the country that the crisis was safely over, it was to her the nation turned with grateful feelings. Through her efforts and God's blessing the heir to the British Empire was restored.

The first breach in the Princess's own family occurred in June, 1873. She had been for some time in delicate health, and had visited Italy for change. Exhausted after this journey she was in bed in her room when the two young princes came in to wish her good morning. At her desire they were left by the nurse to play. In their fun and merriment they ran from room to room looking out of the windows. The Princess followed Prince Ernest who had run off. She was only absent from her room a few seconds, but in that time Prince Fritz had climbed to the window and fallen on to the terrace below. He was picked up insensible, and died shortly afterwards in the arms of his agonized mother. The loss of this beautiful and gifted boy was a blow from which she never recovered.

For some years the Princess, though living one of the most useful and beautiful lives, had been beset by religious doubts. After the death of her little son all these were removed. From that time forward she became an earnest believer in God and immortality. She wrote to a friend at this period, "The whole construction of philosophical conclusions which I had formerly built up I now find to be based on nothing; nothing has remained; and what should we be in life if we had no faith and no conviction that there is a God who governs the world and each single one of us? I feel the necessity of prayer; I like to sing hymns with my children, and we have each our favourite hymn."

A complete change came over her after this sad bereavment. "Some time afterwards," writes the same friend, "she told me herself, in the most touching manner, how this change had come about. I could not listen to her story without tears. The Princess told me she owed it all to her child's death, and to the influence of a Scotch gentleman [Mr. Leitch] a friend of the Grand Duke's and the Grand Duchess's, who was residing with his family at Darmstadt."

In the year 1877 Prince Louis of Hesse, on the death of his father and uncle, ascended the throne of the principality of Hesse-Darmstadt as Grand Duke Louis Fourth. This entailed upon the Princess many heavy responsibilities. She had a high feeling of the requirements of her position, and strove to act up to her high ideal of what a sovereign should be. Her new duties did not prevent her from taking the same interest as ever in her various institutions. While in England she had met Miss Octavia Hill, "the warm-hearted friend of the poor," and had felt the greatest admiration for the work that lady was doing in London.

The Princess translated into German some of Miss Octavia Hill's essays *On the Homes of the London Poor*, and published them with a preface by herself. She hoped that some of these methods which had been so successful in England would be adopted in Germany. The Princess herself, in strictest incognito, visited some of the worst houses, in a sanitary respect, in Mayence. It was her intention to make plans for improved dwellings for the poor.

The Grand Duchess's health was a cause of some anxiety. In 1878 she came to Eastbourne with her family for the summer months, spending some time with the Queen at Osborne. During this visit she was busy among the poor, and in visiting the Sunday-schools of the district. In the cottages of the fishermen she was a welcome guest. Few visitors to Eastbourne during the summer of 1878 will forget the universal kindness and sympathy of the Princess. She consented to become the patroness of Mrs. Vicars' Albion Hill Home for Fallen Women, at Brighton, at that lady's urgent request. She visited the " Home," and when asked by Mrs. Vicars for permission to tell the inmates who their visitor was, replied, " I only come as one woman to visit another."

" Shortly after the Princess's return to Darmstadt her eldest daughter Princess Victoria was suddenly attacked with diphtheria. The infection spread until the Grand Duke and five of the children—only one escaping—were prostrate with it. Great sympathy was felt with the Grand Duchess in this new trial. Prayers were offered in the churches for the recovery of this beloved family. All were spared save the sweet little Princess May—" Sunshine," as her fond mother used to call her. She died on the 16th of November. In breaking the news of the loss of their little one to the Grand Duke, the Duchess, overcome at the sight of his grief and forgetful of the doctor's injunctions, threw her arms about his neck and kissed him. On the 7th of December she was seized with the malady. The anxious days of nursing had told upon her already weakened constitution, and could ill resist the disease. The worst was feared. On the 13th the doctors prepared her husband for the loss which was awaiting him. To the last she seemed to take an interest in everyone, enquiring after the poor and sick, and conversing with her ladies-in-waiting. In the afternoon she read a letter from her mother, took a little nourishment, and composed herself to sleep. From that sleep she never awoke. Her happy spirit passed away at 1 a.m. on the 14th of December, the anniversary of her beloved father's death. She died murmuring to herself, "From Friday to Saturday—four weeks—May—dear Papa——!"

On the 17th of December her remains were removed from her own palace to the chapel in the Grand Ducal Castle. Many were the visitors who came to pay their tribute to the "idolized young mother" of her people. Her deeds of mercy, her work in the hospitals, and her tender solicitude for her husband and five children through the past weeks were spoken of in hushed voices. Among the mourners came an old peasant woman from the Odenwald. She advanced timidly to where the velvet pall covered the remains of the beloved Princess. Murmuring a little prayer, she laid upon it a wreath of rosemary and two white flowers, tokens of her grateful affection. Then, unnoticed as she thought, she plucked a rosebud from one of the splendid wreaths upon the coffin, and hiding it beneath the folds of her old woollen dress, moved sorrowfully away. It was to her a precious memorial of the lady who had ever been the friend of the poorest. High court dignitaries could not restrain their emotion as they gazed upon the scene of mourning. It affected great and poor alike.

The beloved Princess was buried in the Mausoleum at the Rosenhöhe. The British flag, by her own request, was placed upon her coffin. Dear as was the land of her adoption, she could never forget the land of her birth. Over the spot where she rests a beautiful monument by Boehm has been placed. It represents the Princess in a recumbent position holding Princess May in her arms.

The loss which her husband and family sustained in her death can hardly be estimated. She was all in all to them. To a character singularly amiable and sweet were added the highest intellectual gifts. Broad and open in her sympathies, she always endeavoured to judge people according to their worth, and was singularly free from prejudice. She was taken at the time when her influence was being most felt. But—

"She being dead yet speaketh—all may hear
The message left us by her lovely life
In deeds that live, in actions that endear,
As Princess, sister, daughter, mother, wife!"

ALEXANDER MACDONALD, M.P.

ALEXANDER MACDONALD, the first "Working Men's Member of Parliament," rose from being a poor pit lad to take an honourable position among the legislators of Great Britain. Impressed at an early period of his life by the misery and the great disadvantages under which the poor miners and their families laboured, he determined to consecrate his whole life and energy to improving their condition. He devoted himself to the good of humanity, regardless of the sneers and harsh criticism which beset him on all sides, and had the gratification of knowing that thousands of men, women, and children were raised from bondage and degradation to comparative comfort through his instrumentality.

He was born at Newmonkland, in the county of Lanarkshire, in the year 1821. His father and grandfather were both miners. Their position was little better than that of slaves. The pit owners tyrannized over their workmen in a manner which can hardly be credited at the present time. It was not until the year 1775, that any attempt was made to release the miners from their state of bondage. Even then it was but a nominal freedom, as they had not the right of free contract and hire. They laboured under this injustice until the year 1799, when the privilege of fixing the rate of value for their own labour was conceded to them. This was but a small advance. For many years they continued in great wretchedness until Alexander Macdonald came boldly forward as the champion of their rights, and brought before the eyes of the nation the grievances under which they suffered.

Mr. Macdonald was descended from the famous Scottish clan of the MacDonalds, the great Lords of the Isles. His grandfather fought under the banner of Charles Edward Stuart in the rebellion of 1745. He followed the fortunes

of his prince until utter ruin came upon him. The bold
Highlander descended to the Lowlands, and sank lower and
lower until he became an ordinary pitman. He was forced
to leave his heather hills and pure mountain air for the soot
and grime of the coal mine. The claymore was exchanged
for the pick and shovel. In place of the stirring notes of
the pibroch sounding through his native glens, he heard
only the coarse talk of the pitmen, and the monotonous
sound of their picks as they worked in the bowels of the
earth. What a change for the man who had stood proudly
amongst his clan at the battle of Preston Pans when the
MacDonalds had claimed, and obtained the post of honour,
to the right of the whole Highland army, on that memorable
battle-field.

Not the least illustrious of the clan was the brave Highland girl, Flora MacDonald. When the fortunes of "Bonnie Prince Charlie" were at their worst, and he was chased through his native land as a fugitive, she dressed him in the clothes of a waiting maid—a coarse calico gown, a light-coloured quilted petticoat, and a mantle and hood, calling him Betty Burke. She obtained a pass from her stepfather, Sir Alexander MacDonald, who had joined the English, to take him through the country without fear of detention. Travelling with her man-servant and the disguised prince she reached, after many narrow escapes from detection, Kilbride, in the Isle of Skye. But here they were in the country of Sir Alexander MacDonald, who was in the service of the government, and consequently in danger. Flora MacDonald took into her confidence the Lady Margaret, Sir Alexander's wife. This lady was secretly a Jacobite, and risked even her lord's displeasure to aid the fugitive. Her house was filled with soldiers, so that to hide him there was impossible, but she committed him to the care of her husband's factor, MacDonald of Kingsburgh. The faithful Flora escorted him thither. But his extraordinary appearance drew people's attention. One woman exclaimed that she "had never seen such a tall impudent jaud in her life. What lang strides she taks, and how her coats wamble about her ! I daur say she's an Irishwoman, or else a man in women's clothes?" she said to Flora. When crossing a stream Charles either held his petticoats indelicately high, or else permitted them to float on the water. "Your enemies," remarked a friend to him, "call you a pretender ; but if you be, I can tell you you are the worst at your trade I ever saw." After many narrow escapes the celebrated wanderer escaped to France. His faithful followers were divested of their lands, reduced to beggary, and many had, like the grandfather of Alexander Macdonald, to work for their living in the most menial way.

After receiving a very little education at the parish school of Newmonkland, Alexander Macdonald entered the coal pit early in his eighth year. There were no regulations at that time with regard to the labour of children, and no Compulsory Act of Education. The miners were so poor that they were anxious to put their children to work at the earliest age, and even the women had to share in the labours of the pit, "Before I reached my tenth year," writes Mr. Macdonald, "being able to read the newspapers, I read with great avidity the reports of meetings addressed by Richard Oastler, the factory king, and others, in their advocacy on behalf of the children and females employed in mines. The fearfully degraded condition of the miner and his offspring made a very strong impression on me, and this was increased by my own bitter experience. Thus early I made a resolve to endeavour, or at least to contribute, as far as I could, my share to the elevation of those employed in mines."

He worked from two o'clock in the morning until five at night ; but so great was his thirst for knowledge that after those long hours of toil he attended a night school for two hours. The intense application to which he subjected himself greatly injured his eyesight. But his heart was set on emancipating his fellow-toilers. To be able successfully to do this he must gain knowledge to fit him for public life. Although a mere youth he took part in the great Lanarkshire strike in 1842. This brought him in contact with the leading men among the miners, and enabled him to greatly extend his observations. At the close of the strike he suffered severely from the tyranny of his employers, and had great difficulty in obtaining work. When he did again get employment he was more than ever determined to pursue his education. He sat up the greater part of the night studying Latin, Greek, Grammar and Mathematics. By the most careful living, and at the cost of much personal deprivation he had, by the year 1846, saved £250 out of his scanty wages. This he determined to spend on getting an University education.

He entered the Glasgow University at the age of twenty-one. The care with which he had for several years studied the different branches of education enabled him to take a creditable place among his fellow-students. His savings, however, were not sufficient to pay the expenses of a college course for three years. To enable him to do this he was forced to resume the pick and the shovel, and toil in the mine during the spring and autumn vacations. He thus earned money to support himself during the winter session. A young man of less dignity of character would have felt ashamed to thus descend from University life to work in a coal mine. He would have feared the taunts of his companions. But Alexander Macdonald felt that all honest labour was creditable, and having his eye fixed upon the future when, his college course done, he should enter the world's arena to fight on behalf of the oppressed class to which he had belonged, he toiled cheerfully.

His periodical return to pit life kept up his interest in the miners, and gave him opportunities for further investigation into their condition. From time to time he contributed letters to any newspapers that would receive them, with regard to the miserable state of the mining population; calling attention to any special grievance which came under his notice. He thus began quietly, but surely his work of reform.

Leaving the University in 1851, he became a teacher, in which capacity he continued until 1854. But throughout that period he was at work for the miners as vigorously as before. They soon began to learn who was their advocate and friend, and came to him imploring his further exertions when the troubles of 1854 came upon them. With a willing heart Alexander Macdonald threw up his post of teacher, and devoted himself entirely to promoting their good. He became a Miners' Secretary and Agent, and from that time forward until the day of his death toiled unweariedly in the cause of these suffering people. It was to be his life's work. The memory of his own unhappy childhood, when, instead of a joyous schoolboy life, he had to spend the long, weary hours in the gloomy mine, growing prematurely old through his laborious and depressing work, was vividly before him. It spurred him on to bring about the emancipation of the miners' children.

An Act had been passed, through the efforts of Lord

Ashley, afterwards the Earl of Shaftesbury, for the expulsion of females from the mines, and imposing restrictions with regard to age. The objects for which Mr. Macdonald determined to work were the better education of the miners' children, the reduction in the hours of labour, the ventilation of the mines, the appointment of better mine managers (at that time they were a low, brutal class of men), and the introduction of measures for the protection of life and limb. He had the satisfaction of seeing all these attained. But it was a gradual work, and met with opposition at every step. In 1855 the Mines' Act was passed, for the extension of protection to the miners.

Mr. Macdonald found it necessary to extend the area of his operations to make his labour successful. For this purpose he travelled into England, visited the principal mining districts, talked with the men, stirred them up to an intelligent interest in the methods for bettering their condition, and brought their grievances before the public. Calumny was heaped upon him from all sides, " demagogue," "agitator," "fire-brand," "communist," "sower of mischief," "the destroyer of trade," and various other epithets were pelted at him. He worked on unheedful of all abuse until the country recognized that he was not a mere fanatical agitator, but an honest and true man. He never advocated "strikes," preferring always the settlement of all disputes between masters and men by arbitration. He was wont to refer with great pride to the loyalty with which the miners invariably accepted the decisions of an umpire.

During his travels in England he worked so hard in travelling from place to place, that almost the only sleep he obtained was taken in the railway carriage. He was rewarded by success. Sir George Lewis, then the Secretary of State, was induced through Mr. Macdonald's representation to introduce in 1860 a Bill on the subject of mining. This Bill provided that every pitman's child should have some amount of education. Almost alone he urged on the government the necessity for legislation for the protection of the miners. This resulted in the Act of 1862. In 1865 he was the means of getting a Select Committee to enquire into the condition and complaints of the miners. He attended all the sittings of this committee, in order to give information and start such questions as he thought would benefit the class he represented. The agitation was continued until 1872. In that year most of the changes for which he contended became law. The age at which children could enter the mines was raised to twelve years, except under unusual circumstances, their amount of labour reduced, their working hours shortened, and the managers of the mines were required to be men of greater education.

Another branch of the subject now occupied Mr. Macdonald's attention, This was the Labour Laws. The system of contract for hiring pressed most unfairly upon the men. They were often sent to prison for three months with hard labour for some trifling breach of contract. On the other hand the masters were under no such penalty, and could break their contracts at will. A modification of these rules was brought about by the labours of a Royal Commission.

In the year 1874 the working men of Stafford interviewed Mr. Macdonald for the purpose of testing whether he was a "fit and proper person" to represent them in Parliament. He stated his political views, which were deemed so acceptable that he was chosen, from among several others for the office. He would not consent to bind himself to any particular set of views. When asked if he would vote for the Permissive Bill, for Female Suffrage, for Anti-Vaccination, and for the Abolition of the Contageous Diseases Act, he replied that he should not vote for one of those measures. In the face of this the Stafford electors supported him, and he was returned as their Liberal Member. Confidence was placed in him because of his devotion to the working men's cause. Each year he arranged to give his constituents an abstract of his work. If they approved, a vote of confidence in him was to be passed; and if they were dissatisfied, a vote of censure, upon which he would immediately resign his seat by accepting the Chiltern Hundreds. This arrangement was duly carried out. But never had the Stafford electors to repent their choice. Mr. Macdonald remained their representative until the day of his death.

The return of a working man to Parliament was looked upon as rather a dangerous innovation. He was received with looks of distrust or hostility. Many people thought that this was too rapid a stride in the advance of democracy, and prophesied that it would end disastrously. Mr. Macdonald waited until the first burst of opposition had subsided, and his detractors began to see that he was not an uneducated pushing agitator, but a man to be respected. He took an entirely independent position in the House. From the general run of politics he held aloof, and devoted himself almost entirely to the legislature affecting the working classes. His speeches received respectful attention. He had a dignified bearing; did not speak often, but when he did, it was to the point. He chose those subjects with which he was thoroughly acquainted Such conduct gradually disarmed all prejudice. It was admitted that Alexander Macdonald, though a "Working Men's Candidate," was an honour to St. Stephens. His position was not gained by money, but by intrinsic merit. When he was returned for Stafford he told the electors that he had no money to give to their charities or public institutions. His work for the miners had been purely disinterested. He never at any time received a salary from them, although in the year 1860 and in 1872, they expressed their gratitude by giving him handsome testimonials. He was a poor man, and many times in the early part of his career, had walked the London streets without the money to buy even a bite of bread, while at the same time his whole energies were being spent for the amelioration of his fellow-men. He never thought of his own deprivation, or of his unceasing toil if the object he sought could be gained. In 1866 he had a severe illness, which was brought on by overwork. This attack left behind it a partial deafness, from which Mr. Macdonald suffered through the latter portion of his life.

In the same year in which he was returned to Parliament a Second Commission was appointed to enquire into the miners' grievances. Mr. Macdonald was placed upon it in company with eight other gentlemen. The Lord Chief Justice was the chairman. All of them dissented from Mr. Macdonald's views, and he found himself in a minority of one. But when the question was carried into the House of Commons the decision of the Committee was reversed. The House sided with him. In 1875 the Act was passed. It provided for a better regulation of the Labour Laws, by which the men were protected from injustice in the matter of contract and hire.

The scandalous Truck system was the next abuse to which Mr. Macdonald turned his attention. It was the custom for the coal masters to have provision shops near to the mines. At these the men received payment in goods instead of money. No choice was left them. Out of a week's earnings the poor miner received only a trifling sum in cash, the remainder was given in groceries, &c. The majority of the proprietors of these "tommy shops," as they were called in some districts, were unprincipled men. The goods sold were very inferior, and the charge made for them far above the regular market price. Yet the men dared not rebel. If they refused to buy from their master's shop, dismissal from their work was the result. When Mr. Macdonald brought the matter before Parliament the disclosures made were of such an infamous nature, that sharp and effectual legislature followed. Now there is not a Truck-shop of any note in the country.

In 1876, the Compensation Bill was brought before Parliament by Mr. Macdonald. For several years he fought out its battle. In time other politicians took it up. Finally it resulted, in the year 1880, in the passing of the Employers' Liability Act. By it masters are made answerable for injuries received by their workmen, if it can be proved that they occur through any neglect in providing preventative measures against accident. Plain language was one of Mr. Macdonald's characteristics. He never minced matters. When disasters occurred in mines where the owners, to avoid expense, had failed to take precautionary measures he did not call it an *accident*, but *murder*. " He had," said one of his friends, "a bull-dog tenacity of purpose, nothing swerved him from the main object of his life—the interest of the miners of this country." He was made Secretary of the Miners' Association of Scotland, and President of the Miners' National Union. Besides his efforts on behalf of the pitmen, he took great interest in the measures affecting seamen.

His observations were not confined to Great Britain alone. He was almost as much at home in the mining districts of the United States as in his own country. The measures which he introduced into Parliament also became law in the States. Three times he visited California. He was four times in Utah, besides sundry journeys to Wyoming, Nebraska, and Kansas. He had a personal knowledge of almost every place in America where coal mines were situated. Many adventures befel him in his journeyings to these outlandish places. While travelling by rail to California for the first time—he had usually gone by stage-coach—the conductor entered the cars, as the train was passing over the the Sierra Nevada, and advised the passengers to get ready their fire-arms, as a band of robbers were preparing to " put up" the train. All were ready for the encounter, but the train passed by without any interference. On reaching Sacramento Mr. Macdonald went to the house of the manager of the line. He was greeted by the words " Is the shooting done ?" " What shooting" he enquired ? He was then told that the band of desperadoes who threatened the train had quarrelled, and were too busily engaged in shooting each other to interfere with the travellers. A telegram was sent to the nearest military post for assistance in case the robbers should come upon the inhabitants of the mountain station. The cool answer returned was that they were "to keep themselves safe, and by all means encourage the shooting." In those times it was a common thing for the trains to be stopped in the mountain regions by a band of armed robbers, who plundered the passengers of all they possessed. When visiting Hays City, Kansas, Mr. Macdonald was shown the graveyard, and told that of the thirty-nine men buried there, thirty-seven had " died in their boots." At Sheridan it was worse still ; for there every man interred had met with a violent death.

The last piece of national work which Mr. Macdonald did was to attend a Central Board Meeting at the Queen's Hotel, Leeds, October, 22nd, 1881. He was in failing health, and thus addressed his fellow-members: "The work has been begun by others ; I am getting old. I shall soon leave you younger men to take up the work ; go into your districts and carry it to a successful issue." Up to the last day of his life his mind was engaged upon miners' legislation. The last words that he wrote were addressed to a friend on the 30th of October, the day before his death. He thus concluded the letter, " I am worried to death on this powder question. It will be sad beyond measure if the work of half a century be reversed." In a postscript he added, " Every man should be at work ; I cannot." The next day his busy life came to a close. He died on the 31st of October, 1881, at Wellhall, Hamilton, Scotland. He was buried in the cemetery of his native place, Newmonkland, on the 7th of November. As the mournful cortege passed along thousands of people stood bareheaded. A true friend of the people was gone from their midst. Resolute and determined when fighting as the champion of the working classes, he was, in his home, gentle and playful as a child ; full of hospitality and kindliness. Few men worked harder. "My every spare moment," he once said, "is devoted to manual labour ; the axe, the knife, the spade, are all handled freely by me. When at home I only feel pleasure at the close of the day in knowing that I have performed as much work as keeps me from the category of an eater and not a worker."

At a meeting of the Yorkshire Miners' Association held shortly after Mr. Macdonald's death, the following resolution was passed :—" This Council is of opinion that the death of Mr. Alexander Macdonald, M.P., is a great loss to the mining community and working men generally, seeing that he has been the unflinching advocate of all desirable objects, both for miners and others, for the last thirty years, as much in their moral, social, and intellectual interest, as for protection to the lives and limbs of our mining population above and below ground.

"We also desire to express our sincere and heartfelt sorrow with the bereaved family in this their hour of trouble, and trust they will be consoled in their loss at the remembrance of the great and good work he has done for his fellow-workmen during his long, useful, and honoured life.

"Further, we are of opinion that a memorial should be raised by voluntary subscription to the memory of the great man and his work, who is now numbered with the great majority."

The latter part of the resolution was carried into effect. On Saturday, November 17th, 1883, a marble statue of the late Mr. Macdonald, M.P., erected to his memory by the Miners of England and Scotland, was unveiled at Durham, by his friend and fellow-worker, Mr. Thomas Burt, M.P. It holds a unique place in the history of Great Briton, being the first statue erected to a working man by working men. But far greater than any monument of bronze or marble, is the monument Alexander Macdonald has himself erected in the hearts of tens of thousands of working men throughout the civilized world.

HENRY IRVING.

JOHN HENRY BRODRIB IRVING stands foremost among actors. Entering upon his profession purely from love, he devoted his energies to it in a marvellous manner. When only a boy of thirteen he deprived himself of food in order to buy books, and devoted every spare hour, before and after his office work, in studying. Although possessing great natural gifts, his success was long in coming. For fifteen years he toiled without attracting special notice. During that time he acted an astonishing number of characters, giving to each representation a large amount of study. He was fastidious in the correctness of the smallest detail. It is this persistent determination to work up to a high ideal that has made him the most cultured and polished actor of his time.

He was born at Keinton, near Glastonbury, Somersetshire, on the 6th of February, 1838. His early years were passed with a maternal aunt, Mrs. Penberthy, at Halseton, a little town among the Cornish mines. It was a desolate spot, but full of romance and weird legends; ghost stories were particularly relished, and " guise dancing " a favourite sport. This pastime consisted in the villagers dressing up in grotesque costumes in which they entered each other's houses, causing terror among the children. An ancient dame, nearly a century old, terrified young Irving with her stories of hobgoblins and such like: he determined to take his revenge. Appearing suddenly in her room, with his two cousins, after she had gone to bed, he conducted a sort of prayer for impenitent story-tellers, while the infuriated old dame vainly sought to belabour the culprits with her stick.

Young Irving had such schooling as the place afforded; the principal books to which he had access were the Bible, a volume of old English ballads, and " Don Quixote." These stirred his youthful fancy. The romantic scenery of

Cornwall also played its part in awakening his poetic instincts, but this life was soon to be changed for the bustle and stir of London. In 1849, when eleven years old, he joined his parents in London, and was placed at a school in George Yard, Lombard Street, kept by Dr. Pinches.

During these early years, Henry Irving displayed his aptitude for acting. In the school theatricals he played a distinguished part. Dr. Pinches took alarm at his pupil's love for these performances, and for recitations. He strove to restrain him, and forbade his recitation of Bell's poem of "The Uncle," which young Irving was very anxious to give at one of the school entertainments. The remembrance of this must have been vividly before him when, in the height of his fame, he recited this same poem to an enraptured audience.

He had very little opportunity during his youth for seeing plays. Edmund Kean was brought up to the stage from his very babyhood, but Mr. Irving served no such apprenticeship. His first visit to a theatre was made while at Dr. Pinches' school, to see Mr. Phelps play *Hamlet*, at Sadler's Wells. This performance greatly impressed him. The character of *Hamlet* was rivetted on his mind. He dwelt upon it until in 1874 his own marvellous conception startled London into frantic applause. On another occasion he paid a furtive visit to the *Adelphi* and saw a dramatic version of Charles Dickens' Christmas story "The Haunted Man," together with "The Enchanted Isle," and the farce of "Slasher v. Crasher," but the theatre where he had received his first impressions remained his favourite place of resort.

When fourteen years of age young Irving became a clerk in the office of an East India Merchant. It was not a very congenial start in life but he varied the monotony of office work by attending the "City Elocution Class." Its meetings were held in Sussex Street, Leadenhall Street, and here dramatic performances were given periodically by the class. Irving soon became a great favourite. In the pieces which were played he took a prominent place. One of the rules of the class was that each member should know the words of his part; in this the new member never failed. One of his most successful efforts was the part of *Wilford* in selected scenes from "The Iron Chest." The following description is given of Irving at the time of his joining the "Elocution Class":—" One evening a youth of some fifteen years old presented himself as a new member; his appearance was such as would make ladies say, 'what a nice boy!' He was rather tall for his age, dressed in a black cloth suit, with what was called a round jacket, and deep white linen collar turned over it; his face was very handsome, with a mass of black hair and eyes bright and flashing with intelligence. He was called upon for his first recitation and fairly electrified the class with an unusual display of elocutionary skill and dramatic intensity. The new member was the now world-famous Henry Irving. Poor Henry Thomas (teacher of the elocution class) has long since gone over to the majority, but had he lived he would have delighted in the thought that he had some share in fostering and developing the genius of one so deservedly esteemed as the foremost actor of his age."

In the year 1854 Irving was fortunate in securing a very sympathetic friend—Mr. William Hoskins, a leading actor at Sadler's Wells. This gentleman was so struck by the young clerk's eagerness to study for the stage that he arranged to give him early morning lessons before office hours. Mr. Creswick may, however, be said to be Irving's first tutor. He taught the future *Hamlet* to grasp a dagger tragically. Before his departure for Australia, Mr. Hoskins introduced his pupil to Mr. Phelps, the manager of Sadler's Wells, who offered Irving an engagement; this he refused, preferring to study and practise in private for some time longer. Mr. Hoskins gave him a letter, saying "You will go upon the stage; when you want an engagement present that letter and you will find one."

For two years longer the youth remained in London, studying hard to fit himself for the profession he had already determined to adopt. He took lessons in fencing at a school of arms in Chancery Lane, and soon learnt to use the sword with ease and grace.

His first appearance in public was far from being a success. David Garrick achieved immediate success. No sooner did he step upon the boards of the little theatre in Goodman's Fields than his fame as an actor was made. With Mr. Irving his early attempt looked like failure. It was in the year 1856 that, nervous and anxious, the young actor first faced a public audience in the New Lyceum Theatre, Sunderland. The play was that of "Richelieu;"

he took the part of *Orleans*. Appropriately enough it fell to him to recite the first words of the play :—" Here's to our enterprise." All confidence forsook him. Never before had the poor Duke of Orleans so stuttered and stammered. Few would have prophesied the future greatness which was before him.

His second attempt was even worse than the first. He played the part of *Cleomenes* in "A Winter's Tale." In the fifth act his nervousness quite overcame him when for a moment he found himself the centre of attention. Forgetting the words of his part he wildly gasped :—" Come on to the market place and I'll tell you further," a line from another play, and rushed from the stage. This unlooked-for invitation to the market place upset the other actors who could barely restrain their laughter. Full of grief and shame poor Irving passed a troubled night expecting that the morrow would bring dismissal from the calling he so loved ; but the manager was considerate and encouraged him until, in time, he overcame his nervousness. His second failure was due to his having only a very limited time in which to learn his part; he refused to study it on Sunday, consequently had only a very short time left on Monday morning.

After his first appearance in Sunderland, Mr. Irving accepted an engagement at the Theatre Royal, Edinburgh, for two and a half years. He now made great progress, having some of the leading actors of the day as fellow-players. At this period of his career the number of characters he assumed is noteworthy ; nothing seemed to come amiss to him. During the first three years of his provincial tour he appeared in four hundred and twenty-eight different characters. He played in them all with such wonderful ease and adaptation that it was difficult to decide what was his special vocation ; but the critics said Comedy.

On one occasion, in 1859, he had the coveted honour of playing *Claude Melnotte* in the " Lady of Lyons " to the *Pauline* of Miss Julia St. George. It is recorded that the young actor was "called before the curtain several times."

The rising actor made his first appearance in London in 1859 at the Princess's Theatre. Through an introduction by his friend, Mr. Toole, he had entered upon a three years' engagement ; but finding that he had only six lines to speak in the opening part of a four act play he threw up the engagement in disgust and resumed his provincial career. He was resolved not to return to the Metropolis until his success as an actor was established.

It was in Manchester that he first played the coveted part of *Hamlet*. The announcement that he intended to take it for his benefit night created some amusement among the members of the company. It seemed rather a daring experiment for the young actor. He acquitted himself, however, in a manner which clearly showed that he had grasped the character of the *Dane*. Those who had made merry at his ambition now began to predict a great career for him.

During his stay in Manchester he exposed the trickery of the famous Davenport Brothers. In the winter of 1864-5 these impostors were creating a great sensation by their "dark séances." They professed to be under the influence of departed spirits, and to be thus enabled to perform miraculous feats. The Rev. Doctor Ferguson acted as their showman. In company with two friends Mr. Irving imitated their performances in private, and with such success that it was arranged to give a public exposé. This took place in the Library Hall of the Manchester Athenæum, on Saturday afternoon, February 25th, 1865. Mr. Irving played the part of Dr. Ferguson. He was got up as an exact representation of him, and in his opening speech imitated his manner, voice, and gesture with inimitable mimicry. His two friends acted the part of the Davenport Brothers, and were successful in performing all the tricks done by them. The "manifestations" were received with loud applause, and many witty remarks passed freely between the "Doctor" and the audience. Irving, in his assumed character, insisted upon an unbroken chain of contact, "else," said he, " you may be touched in places you least expect." " In the pocket," wittily retorted one gentleman. " Yes," was Irving's quick repartee, "in the pocket, or the head, or in any other empty receptacle." The performance was a great success. Mr. Irving's clever mimicry of the "Doctor" drew forth bursts of applause. The various phenomena of the "dark séance"—the floating of musical instruments in the air, the tying of the two men in the cabinet, followed by the sight of hands and faces at the window, and the sound of musical instruments inside, although, when the doors were opened, the men were found fast bound to their chairs—were rendered with exactitude. Everything that the "Davenport Brothers" professed to do through spirit influence was successfully imitated by Mr. Irving and his two friends. The exhibition was entirely free, the tickets being given away. By public desire a second performance was given in the Manchester Free Trade Hall, the proceeds of which were devoted to charities. Testimonials were offered to Irving and his assistants, but steadily refused. They had no wish to make a profit out of the exposé. So successful had the venture been that the manager of the theatre tried to induce Mr. Irving to repeat it on the stage. This he declined to do, and in consequence lost his engagement. During this period in Manchester he had been very successful as a comedian, and was received as a recognized actor upon his return to London in 1865. Time had yet to show what greater power lay in him. He accepted an engagement at St. James's Theatre, and there appeared on the 6th of October, 1866, as *Doricourt* in "The Belle's Stratagem." He subsequently played a variety of parts in the Queen's Theatre, and the Gaiety, making a steady rise in public favour.

About this time he became identified with the portraiture of villany in its various forms. It soon became apparent that *his* villains were not exaggerated "horrors," but were real pictures of man in his worst aspects. He played *Count Falcon* in Ouida's "Idalia," *Bob Gassett* in "Dearer than Life," *Redburn* in "The Lancashire Lass," and many other characters of this type, including *Bill Sykes* in "Oliver Twist."

The public were first aroused to the fact that there was among them an actor of great original powers by Mr. Irving's impersonation of *Digby Grant* in the "Two Roses," at the Vaudeville, in June, 1870. His powers were so versatile that the critics were puzzled, but at length fixed on Comedy as his *forte*. He was pronounced the first comedian of the day. Mrs. Sartoris (Adelaide Kemble) wrote to him at this time, that he reminded her of her own family more than any actor she had seen, and urged him to devote himself to the higher drama.

Mr. Irving's ambition had risen far above being a mere

comedian. He was looking forward to more serious work. In order to test public opinion, he recited Hood's poem, "The Dream of Eugene Aram," on his benefit night at the Vaudeville. The enthusiasm which greeted this effort was tremendous. The audience listened spell bound. This was the beginning of his fame as a tragedian.

In 1871, resolving to devote himself to tragedy, Mr. Irving entered upon an engagement at the Lyceum, then under Mr. Bateman's management. He drew that gentleman's attention to "The Bells,"—an adaptation of "Le Juif Polonais," of Erckmann-Chatrian. The leading character, *Mathias* was considered an impossible impersonation. On the 25th of November, 1871, "The Bells" was first brought out at the Lyceum ; Mr. Irving's warmest admirers were astonished by his wonderful realization of the character of *Mathias*. The critics were dumbfounded ; they had pronounced him wholly a comedian, and yet his power to delineate one of the most difficult characters in tragedy had now set London in a perfect uproar of enthusiasm. The play ran for 150 nights, and then had an equal success in the provinces.

On the 28th of September, 1872, Mr. Irving took the part of *Charles I.* The following extract from the *Daily News* will show the impression caused by it :—" Through "Charles I." runs a melancholy beauty, which finds expression in many musical passages, and which intensifies, as the play proceeds, into absolute pain. During the last act there was scarcely a dry eye in the house ; women sobbed openly, and even men showed an emotion which comported ill with the habitual serenity of the stalls. Much of this uncomfortable gratification was due to the acting of Mr. Irving, who has once more created a great rôle. In intensity of suggestiveness his *Charles I.* will compare with his *Mathias* ; while in breadth, dignity, and harmonious colour, it surpasses it. . . . Nothing more regal can be desired than his bearing, nothing more harmonious than the effect of every look and gesture, nothing more touching than his delivery of the poetic beauties that abound. From the outward appearance of the king (he might be an incarnate portrait of Vandyke) down to each little detail of posture, everything is elaborated with conscientious care, and the result is a vivid creation of art."

"Charles I." was followed by "Eugene Aram." Every one was prepared to admire, but Mr. Irving's impersonation far exceeded the greatest expectations. Determining to still further establish his fame, he appeared as *Richelieu*, on the 27th of September, 1873, adding still fresh claims to be considered the first actor of his day.

Public excitement became intense when it was announced, in the autumn of 1874, that the great actor would play *Hamlet*. At three o'clock in the afternoon the crowd began to gather round the pit door of the Lyceum, extending down the covered way far into the Strand; impatience and expectancy were written on every face, for Irving was that night to decide whether the times were too degenerate for the revival of Shakespeare. A burst of applause greeted the actor as he stepped upon the boards. His thoughts must have travelled back to the time when as schoolboy he had been enraptured by seeing Mr. Phelps play *Hamlet*. The impressions received then had strengthened with years. His longing to impersonate Shakespeare's great creation had received but one fulfilment—on the occasion of his benefit night at Manchester, when, amidst the half concealed merriment of his fellow-actors, he took the rôle of the Dane. Their ridicule had been stopped and turned into wonder when their aspiring comrade showed them *his* conception of *Hamlet*. He was now to imprint that character anew with his genius. Representatives of art and letters flocked to the Lyceum to witness the trial. The *Hamlet* that stood before this vast expectant audience was entirely different to the one of tradition. After the first outburst of applause two acts went by in silence, and Irving left the stage depressed, feeling that he had not reached his ideal. As the play progressed the audience, at first slow to understand this new conception, began to appreciate it; the interest quickened with each succeeding act. The *Hamlet* before them was a human one. His nervous uneasy manner bespoke the disturbed mind. His melancholy escaped in low murmurings, with half-drawn sighs and wearied action. There was a total absence of the loud frantic declamation which other actors had used in this great character. Mr. Irving's *Hamlet* was always the chivalrous gentleman, though stung to the quick by the foul murder of his father. His conduct was forced, by a sense of justice to his murdered parent, but was foreign to his gentle heart. The famous soliloquy "To be, or not to be," escaped his lips in the natural manner of a deep nature communing with itself ; it was not thundered forth at the audience, but came sentence by sentence as the humour stirred the dreamy, melancholy man. His conflicting emotions in the scenes with *Ophelia* and in his interview with his mother were finely marked. As the play advanced the immense gathering drank in the spirit of his *creation.* True, he spake the words of Shakespeare, but he invested them with a meaning never before applied. As the curtain fell upon the last scene in the tragedy the actor received his reward in the almost wild delight with which that vast assembly thundered forth its applause until nearly one o'clock in the morning. The following day the leading journals of the metropolis were loud in praise of this great achievement. Never before had the play awakened such interest; nearly everybody was quoting "Hamlet." The success, too, had been attained without those scenic aids with which Mr. Irving now surrounds his representations.

"Hamlet" was played for two hundred consecutive nights, ending June 29th, 1875. It was followed by "Macbeth" and "Othello," in which characters Mr. Irving appeared with great originality. The success which he had achieved brought much harsh criticism, but the majority esteemed him as the first actor of the day. Mr. Gladstone tapped him familiarly on the shoulder one day as he walked down Bond Street, and gave him his warm congratulations. Charles Dickens had some years before remarked on the "singular power" of Mr. Irving. When at the end of the season he took the part of *Philip* in the poet laureate's drama of "Queen Mary," a warm friendship was established between himself and Mr. Tennyson.

In the autumn of 1876 Mr. Irving made a tour through the provinces, everywhere meeting with the most enthusiastic reception. At Dublin he received academic honours and an address from the students of Trinity College.

Address to HENRY IRVING, Esq., *presented by the Graduates and Undergraduates of Trinity College, Dublin.*

"Sir, the engagement which you bring to a conclusion to-night at the Theatre Royal, has given the liveliest pleasure to the graduates and undergraduates of Trinity College, Dublin.

"To the most careful students of Shakespeare you have, by your scholarly and original interpretation, revealed new depths of meaning in 'Hamlet,' and aroused in the minds of all a fresh interest in our highest poetry. . . . Acting such as yours ennobles and elevates the stage, and serves to restore it to its true function as a potent instrument for intellectual and moral culture.

"Throughout your too brief engagement our stage has been a school of true art, a purifier of the passions, and a nurse of heroic sentiments ; you have even succeeded in commending it to the favour of a portion of society, large and justly influential, who usually hold aloof from the theatre."

By command of Trinity College " Hamlet " was played. The vast audience included the Lord-Lieutenant of Ireland and His Grace the Duke of Connaught. Five hundred of the students occupied the pit. All the leading men of Dublin were present to do honour to Mr. Irving. As he entered, the pit rose to receive him. Never before had there been such an enthusiastic reception. At the conclusion of the play the students escorted him to his hotel in triumphal procession.

The Lyceum Theatre was re-opened with "Macbeth." "Richard III." followed in January, 1877. On the first night of the performance Mr. Irving was presented by Mr. Chippendale with the sword of Edmund Kean. The Baroness Burdett Coutts gave him the ring of David Garrick engraved with the following description :—" This ring, once Mr. Garrick's, is presented by the Baroness Burdett Coutts to Mr. Henry Irving in recognition of the gratification derived from his Shakespearean representations ; uniting to many characteristics of his great predecessors in histrionic art (whom he is too young to remember) the charm of original thought, giving delineations of new forms of dramatic interest, power, and beauty." The play, as represented at the Lyceum, strictly followed the text. For two centuries Shakespeare's words had been mutilated and interpolated by Colly Cibber's version. Mr. Irving now acted the play as written by Shakespeare, giving to the character of *Richard* a reality never before attained.

After another tour in the provinces Mr. Irving appeared as *Louis XI.*—one of his most marvellous representations. The appearance of the cynical, mean, hypocritical old king is perfect. From the time he crosses the stage until the play closes infirm old age is before the spectator. The one hand keeps up a perpetual tremor, lines of advancing decay are upon the face, and the various moods of the old tyrant are expressed to a nicety. Mr. Irving studies minutely every detail of dress and has an extraordinary talent for suggestiveness; one look, one movement of the head or hand conveys a meaning which words would fail to express. "This *Louis XI.*," says an able critic, "is as individual to every spectator who saw him as ever was any human being who was known to his fellow-creatures by his ways and his talk."

On the 12th of August, 1878, Mr. Irving laid the foundation stone of the Harborne and Edgbaston Institute, Birmingham. His services were in constant demand for such occasions, showing how highly he was esteemed by men of culture. A short time before he had been elected President of the Perry Bar Institute. He gave a characteristic address upon the occasion in defence of the stage. "If there be any," he said, "who are for veiling from human sight all developments of evil, they, indeed, must turn from the theatre door, and must desire to see the footlights put out. But they must also close Shakespeare, avoid Fielding, Dickens, Thackeray, George Eliot; pronounce Kingsley immoral, and, as far as I can understand, read only parts of their Bible. It is not by hiding evil, but by showing it to us alongside of good that human character is trained and perfected." He has lost no opportunity for upholding the moral dignity and intellectal character of his profession. On one occasion he read a paper before the Church of England Temperance Society. He then occupied the unique position of an actor among bishops. He did not fail to speak his mind to his clerical audience. " Make the theatre," he said, " respected by openly recognizing its services ; make it more respectable by teaching the working and lower middle classes to watch for good or even creditable plays, and to patronize them when presented. Let members of religious congregations know that there is no harm, but rather good, in entering into ordinary amusements, so far as they are decorous. Use the pulpit, the press, and the platform to denounce, not the stage, but certain evils that find allowance on it. . . . Gentlemen, change your attitude towards the stage, and, believe me, the stage will co-operate with you in your work of faith and labour of love."

No actor has been so supported by the clergy as Mr. Irving. There is a good joke told of the manager of a Scotch theatre. Peeping into the house before the curtain rose on the night of Mr. Irving's first appearance, he was so astounded at the sight of so many parsons in the stalls that he thought the actor must surely be going to hold a prayer meeting before the performance.

A new epoch in Mr. Irving's career began in 1878. Upon the retirement of Mrs. Bateman from the Lyceum he became its manager. His first act was to engage the services of Miss Ellen Terry who has contributed so much, during the later years of Mr. Irving's career, to his success. "Hamlet" was chosen for the opening piece. Miss Terry played *Ophelia*, Mr. Chippendale *Polonius*, Mr. Mead the *Ghost*, Mr. Forrester *Claudius*, Mr. F. Cooper *Laertes*, Miss Pauncefort *Gertrude*, and Mr. Irving his celebrated part of *Hamlet*. The play ran for 108 nights. It was followed by several of Mr. Irving's well known representations. At the end of the first seven months of his management the total receipts amounted to £36,000.

The actor spent his summer holiday in a Mediterranean cruise in the Baroness Burdett Coutts's yacht. Perhaps the fair land of Italy inspired him with its poetry, for the great event of his next theatrical season was the production of "The Merchant of Venice," November 1st, 1879, The scenic arrangements were perfect. Venice in its charming beauty, with its graceful gondolas and busy Rialto fascinated the audience. True to his artistic taste Mr. Irving left out no detail which would correctly represent the "Bride of the Sea." In his character of *Shylock* he looked the Jew to perfection. But he invested the character with a new dignity. There is a grandeur about his *Shylock* which no actor has before given. By adroit touches he enlists sympathy with the old man in spite of his monstrous demand for his "pound of flesh." Instead of one continued feeling of hate for the unrelenting Jew, the audience are moved at times to pity and sympathize with him. Christians have made him what he is. All trades have been closed against him save that of usury; what wonder then that his faculties in that direction are sharpened.

It is a Christian who robs the old man of his child. With masterly art the curtain is unexpectedly raised after Jessica's elopement, to disclose the Jew, unconscious of his loss, returning to his deserted house. Even in the trial scene when the malice of *Shylock* is most strongly depicted, Mr. Irving makes him the hero of the scene by the look of noble scorn he casts upon his tormentors. The thoughts of the audience are carried back to an earlier portion of the play, when in answer to Antonio's demand for a loan of money the Jew replies :—

> " Signor Antonio, many a time and oft
> In the Rialto you have rated me
> About my moneys, and my usances :
> Still I have borne it with a patient shrug ;
> For sufferance is the badge of all our tribe ;
> You call me misbeliever, cut-throat dog
> And spat upon my Jewish gaberdine,
> And all for use of that which is mine own.
> Well then, it now appears you need my help :
> Go to then ; you come to me, and you say,
> ' Shylock, we would have moneys ;' you say so ;
> You that did void your rheum upon my beard,
> And foot me as you spurn a stranger cur
> Over your threshold ; moneys is your suit.
> What should I say to you ? should I not say,
> ' Hath a dog money ? is it possible
> A cur can lend three thousand ducats ?' or
> Shall I bend low, and in a bondman's key,
> With bated breath, and whispering humbleness,
> Say this :—
> ' Fair sir, you spat on me on Wednesday last ;
> You spurned me such a day ; another time
> You call'd me dog ; and for these courtesies
> I'll lend you thus much moneys ? ' "

The Jews were in ecstacies over this representation. They felt that Mr. Irving's vindication of *Shylock* was a vindication of their race. The popularity of the play was greatly enhanced by the grace and charm of Miss Terry's *Portia*. It was played for two hundred and fifty consecutive nights—the longest run on record in the history of the Shakespearean drama.

This marvellous success was followed, in September, 1880, with a revival of " The Corsican Brothers." In this weird play of the twin brothers Mr. Irving found scope for his peculiar power of delineating the mysterious with picturesque effect. He has always had a bias for the supernatural, doubtless instilled into his youthful fancy by the ghostly legends to which he listened when a boy among the Cornish mines.

During the five years of Mr. Irving's management he has only introduced one new play. This was Mr. Tennyson's drama of "The Cup," which was first acted at the Lyceum January 3rd, 1881. Further on in the season some excitement was felt amongst theatre goers by the announcement that Mr. Irving and the American actor, Mr. Edwin Booth, were to play alternately the parts of *Othello* and *Iago*. It was the first time that Mr. Irving had taken the part of *Iago*, and he did not fail to invest it with new touches. The conjunction of two such celebrated actors made this revival of "Othello" one of the most celebrated in dramatic history.

Returning to Shakespearean dramas on March 11th, 1882, Mr. Irving appeared, for the first time, as *Romeo*, and Miss Terry as *Juliet*. Many portions of the play were restored, and the pictorial effect was strikingly beautiful. A banquet was held to celebrate the one hundredth performance, the Earl of Lytton presiding. He bore the very highest testimony to the character of Mr. Irving's acting. "Romeo and Juliet" was followed by the last of Mr. Irving's Shakespearean revivals—"Much Ado about Nothing." The character of *Benedick* suited the actor to perfection, and was distinguished by rare humour. Miss Terry's *Beatrice* was charming and captivating. This successful comedy was withdrawn, after a run of two hundred and twelve nights, to make way for Mr. Irving's farewell performances before leaving for a tour in America.

Mr. Irving's farewell benefit took place on Saturday, July 28th, 1883. Never before did an actor receive such an ovation. At noon the crowds began to gather round the theatre doors. Hundreds were turned away unable to get within the walls. The actor appeared in several of his well-known characters, and the entertainment was varied by a laughable sketch by Mr. J. L. Toole, and with songs by Mr. Sims Reeves. As the curtain fell upon the last act there were loud cries for "Irving." Wreaths and bouquets fell fast upon the stage as the curtains parted and he appeared before them, very pale, and evidently much moved. In a short speech he bade farewell to his audience. Then the band played "Auld Lang Syne," and the entire

Lyceum Company appeared upon the stage. Handkerchiefs were enthusiastically waved from floor to roof, while sobs mingled with the deafening cheers. The actor's success was complete. No further proof was needed to show how high a place Mr. Irving held in the hearts of Englishmen.

A further demonstration of Mr. Irving's popularity was given on the 4th of July, 1883, at a banquet in his honour at St. James's Hall. The Lord Chief Justice Coleridge presided. There were present ambassadors of State, English nobles, judges, admirals, generals, and clergymen; literature, science and art sent distinguished representatives. Never before did such a brilliant company assemble to do honour to an actor. Dr. Lightfoot, the Bishop of Durham, regretting his enforced absence, wrote in the very highest terms of praise of the guest of the evening. "All who desire the elevation of public morals," he wrote, "must sympathize with this desire to do honour to one who has exerted himself so nobly to raise the tone of English dramatic art." The Lord Chief Justice, in his speech, remarked: "The general tone and atmosphere of a theatre, wherever Mr. Irving's influence is predominant, has been uniformly higher and purer. The pieces which he has acted, and the way he has acted them, have been always such that no husband need hesitate to take his wife, no mother to take her daughter, where Mr. Irving is the ruling spirit."

Among his fellow-actors Mr. Irving is deservedly popular, for throughout his career he has taken the deepest interest in all societies and organizations for the help of actors and actresses. Mindful of his own early struggles, he is ever ready to help forward those who are painfully climbing the ladder of fame. On Monday, July 9th, 1883, a supper in his honour was given by Mr. Bancroft at the Garrick Club. It was attended by British, American, and French actors, and was a characteristic gathering, being an assemblage of actors to honour one who was admittedly their king.

After some farewell performances in Glasgow, Edinburgh, and Liverpool, Mr. Irving and Miss Terry, with the Lyceum Company, sailed for America, October 11th, 1883. An enthusiastic crowd watched the good ship *Britannic* as it sailed from Liverpool. Mr. Irving, deeply moved, stood bare-headed on the deck, returning the salutations of those assembled to bid him good-bye. By his side stood Miss Terry, who kissed hands until the crowd faded from their view, and they were fairly "Westward Ho!"

Mr. Irving's tour in America has been a great success. Crowded houses welcomed him at the leading American cities. The sale of tickets has been immense, and general delight expressed at his Shakespearean representations. Men of all ranks and professions have been eager to do him homage, not excepting America's great preacher, Henry Ward Beecher. Referring to his visit to Mr. and Mrs. Beecher at Brooklyn, Mr. Irving says: "One would have had to lay in a stock of vanity to even dream of such a reception as we have had. Mr. Beecher has evidently been a hard worker all his life; a persistent man, and nothing is done without it. Miss Terry and I were invited to visit Mr. Henry Ward Beecher. We went on Sunday to his church. He preached a good stirring sermon, full of strong common-sense. It was what might, in some respects, be called an old-fashioned sermon, though it was also exceedingly liberal. The spirit of its teaching was the doctrine of brotherly love. The preacher told his congregation that a man was not simply a follower of Christ because he went to church on Sundays. A man could, he said, be a follower of the Saviour without going to church at all. He could also be a follower of Christ if he wished, and belong to any church he liked—Baptist, Wesleyan, Lutheran. A pagan could be a follower of Christ if he lived up to his doctrine of charity. To do good is the chief end and aim of a good life. It was an extemporaneous sermon so far as the absence of manuscript or notes went, and was delivered with masterful point and vigour, and with some touches of pure comedy—Mr. Beecher is a great comedian. After the service he came to us and offered his arm to Miss Terry. She took one arm, his wife the other. I followed with his son and several other relations. A few members of the congregation joined the little procession. Following Mr. Beecher and the ladies, we walked down the aisle and into the street to his house. There was something very simple and dignified about the whole business, something that to me smacked of the primitive churches without their austerity. Mrs. Beecher is seventy-one years of age; a perfect gentlewoman, Quaker-like in her dress and manners, gentle of speech, but with a certain suggestion of firmness of purpose. Beecher struck me as a strong, robust, genial, human man —a broad, big fellow. We had dinner—the early dinner that was in vogue when I was a boy." Continuing the account of his visit, Mr. Irving says: "It used to be said of Lord Beaconsfield that his oriental blood and his race instincts gave his fondness for jewels; but Beecher seems to have the same kind of taste. He brought out from a cabinet a handful of rings, and asked me which I thought Miss Terry would like best. Then he took them to her, and she selected an *aqua marina*, which he placed upon her finger and begged her to accept as a souvenir of her visit to Brooklyn. 'May I?' said Miss Terry to Mrs. Beecher. 'Yes, my dear, take it,' said Mrs. Beecher, and she did. It was quite touching to see the two women together—so different in their stations, their years, their occupations. Miss Terry was the first actress Mrs. Beecher had ever known. To begin with, she was very courteous; her greeting was hospitable, but not cordial. The suggestion of coldness in her demeanour gradually thawed, and at the close of the visit she took Miss Terry into her arms, and the two women cried. 'One touch of nature makes the whole world kin.'"

After his American tour Mr. Irving appeared at the Lyceum, May 31st, 1884, in the comedy "Much Ado About Nothing." The enthusiastic reception given him and Miss Terry is beyond description. Flowers and wreaths were showered upon the stage. The theatre rang with frantic shouts of welcome. Miss Terry was moved to tears by the demonstration. Mr. Irving replied in a suitable speech expressive of his pleasure at returning again to the Lyceum, and referring to the great kindness which had been shown him in America.

Great as is Mr. Irving's popularity as an actor, he excels equally as a manager. Nothing is neglected which will give effect to his pieces, and everything passes his scrutiny. His brother actor, Mr. Booth, referring to the thoroughness of Mr. Irving's inspection, says: "He sits on the stage during rehearsals, watching every movement and listening to every word. If he sees anything to correct or alter, he rises and points out the fault, giving the proper form, when the scene is repeated. He commands all points with the understanding that his will is absolute law, that it is not to be disputed, whether it concerns the entry of a mere messenger who bears a letter, or whether it is the reading of an important line by Miss Terry. From first to last he rules his stage with an iron will, but as an offset to this he displays a patience that is marvellous." In the choice of scenery and stage furniture Mr. Irving is most fastidious. Everything at the Lyceum bears the impress of his artistic taste. During his late American tour he carried his stage furnishings with him, from that imposing structure, the high altar used in "Much Ado About Nothing," down to the commonest deal table.

The high position which Mr. Irving holds among the cultured classes has already been referred to. In private life he is equally esteemed. He has in him a fund of humour which makes him an irresistible companion. In his house in Bond Street he surrounds himself with books, pictures, statues, nic-nacks, all in confusion, yet a pleasing whole—an artistic disarray. At Hammersmith he has a fine old house as a rural retreat, where he passes a holiday sauntering about the grounds attended by his three large dogs. He delights in a good joke. During a visit to Shakespeare's birthplace at Stratford-on-Avon he entered into a conversation with a rustic native. "Can you tell me whose place that is over there?" he said to the man, pointing to Shakespeare's house. "Dunno," was the short answer. "Come, come, you must know who lives there. Is his name Shakespeare?" "Dunno." "But can't you tell us whether he's alive now?" "Dunno." "But surely you must know whether he was famous—whether he ever did anything?" "Yes, he—he—." "Well, what did he do?" "He writ summit." "That's it; we were sure you knew all about him. What did he write?" "He writ a boible." The amusement which the greatest of Shakespearean actors derived from this dialogue can be readily imagined.

A very touching and pathetic story is told of the hardships which Mr. Irving underwent as a young and rising actor with small pay. There was in connection with the Theatre Royal, Manchester, at the time when Mr. Irving was engaged there, an actor named Joseph Robins. He had formerly been in business as a gentleman's hosier and had kept enough of his old stock to last him for several years. "When I first met him," says Mr. Irving, "he was engaged in a very small way on a very small salary at a Manchester theatre. Christmas came in very bitter weather. Joe had a part in the Christmas pantomine. He dressed with other poor actors, and he saw how thinly some of them were clad when they stripped before him to put on their stage costumes. For one poor fellow in especial his heart ached. In the depth of a very cold winter he was shivering in a suit of very light summer underclothing, and whenever Joe looked at him the warm flannel undergarments, snugly packed away, weighed heavily upon his mind. Joe thought the matter over, and determined to give the actors who dressed with him a Christmas dinner. The dinner was to be served at Joe's lodgings, and before it was placed on the table Joe beckoned his friend with the gauze underclothing into a bedroom, and pointing to a chair silently withdrew. On that chair hung a suit of underwear which had been Joe's pride. It was of a comfortable scarlet colour; it was thick, warm, and heavy; it fitted the poor actor as if it had been manufactured especially to his measure. . . . . That actor never knew—or if he knew, he never could remember—what he had for dinner on that Christmas afternoon. He revelled in the luxury of warm garments. . . . . Proud, happy, and comfortable, he felt little inclination to eat, but sat quietly and thanked Providence and Joe Robins with all his heart." "You seem to enter into that poor actor's feelings very sympathetically," observed the friend to whom Mr. Irving related this incident. "I have good reason to do so," replied Mr. Irving, "for I was that poor actor."

The following testimony to the charm of Mr. Irving's private character, will form a fitting conclusion:—"It is not the least pleasant of Mr. Irving's characteristics, that in private intercourse he never seems possessed by a conciousness of his public position. . . . He is never anxious to make his own achievements the topic of conversation. A man of refined sensibilities often surrounds himself with a reserve which many mistake for pride. Mr. Irving's 'aloofness,' as George Eliot would call it, is thus misconstrued, and strangers sometimes suppose that he is by nature cold and unsociable. Those who have a better knowledge of him can speak of his genial companionship, and even of the heartiness with which, in moments of enjoyment, he can enter into a frolic. The quiet humour which illustrates the keen observation of the man of the world is sometimes succeeded by a gaiety which is irresistible. When he abandons himself to the fun of a good story, and gives the rein to mimicry, it is hard to realize that this is only one side of his nature. At all times he inspires admiration and esteem, and amidst the homage to the actor and the student, they feel themselves privileged whose good fortune it is to know him as the kind friend and the polished gentleman."

LORD WOLSELEY.

LORD WOLSELEY, one of the most distinguished of British military commanders, was born at Golden Bridge House, County Dublin, on the 4th of June, 1833, and is the eldest son of the late Major G. J. Wolseley, of the 25th King's Own Borderers.

He is descended from one of the most ancient families in Staffordshire, their possession of the Manor of Wolseley dating before the conquest. Many scions of the house of Wolseley have distinguished themselves as soldiers, notably, Colonel William Wolseley, who defeated the Irish army on the 29th of July, 1689, having first relieved the garrison of Enniskillen. In the following year he led the Enniskilleners to victory at the ever memorable battle of the Boyne, when King William finally defeated his rival, James II. The grandfather of Lord Wolseley began life as a soldier, but subsequently settled down into the more peaceful calling of the Church. He became the Rector of Tullycorbet, County Monaghan.

As a boy Lord Wolseley showed a remarkable aptitude for the military profession. He was of very studious habits, and read all the chief works on military history, taking also a great interest in surveying and the practical work of a military engineer. Four or five times a week he took expeditions to perfect himself in these studies. It seems to have been his aim to gain a most thorough and precise knowledge of the profession to which his parents and his own inclinations had destined him. Glorious as is the thought of stirring warfare to the young military aspirant, young Wolseley was not led away by it to neglect the thorough training in mathematics, engineering, fortification, and land surveying, so necessary for the skilled soldier.

He received his education at a day school near Dublin, and from private tutors, working all the time most assiduously at his military studies.

Lord Wolseley began his career as a soldier in March, 1852, when he was appointed Ensign in the 80th Regiment. He was not destined to fret long in inactivity; for a few months later he left England for foreign service. It was the time of the second Burmese War. A series of unbroken successes were dimmed by a humiliating disaster which occurred just at the time when Ensign Wolseley arrived in Burmah. The Burmese leader, Myat-toon, had established himself near Donabew. On the 3rd of February, 1853, a column under Captain Loch was despatched against him, but was compelled to retreat. General Godwin, anxious to retrieve the prestige of his army, summoned every soldier to the front. Wolseley's regiment among others was hurried to the scene of action.

On the 19th of March, Myat-toon's stronghold was successfully stormed. Ensign Wolseley threw himself into this his first experience of actual warfare with characteristic vigour. He was well in front of his men, and within twenty yards of the breastwork, when suddenly the earth gave way under his feet, and he fell into a covered pit having pointed stakes at the bottom. These treacherous pits had been made by the Burmese all around the ground near their stronghold. Wolseley was much shaken by his fall, but escaped unwounded.

The first attempt on the enemy's position being unsuccessful, a second attack was decided on. Lieutenant Taylor led the 51st Light Infantry, and when Major Holdrich called for volunteers from his own regiment, Ensign Wolseley at once stepped to the front. Quickly collecting his men he was ready for the attack. He and Taylor, well in advance of their men, made a rush for the honour of first gaining the enemy's breastworks. As the two young officers ran up the narrow path leading to the breastwork they both received a wound in the thigh. In a few seconds Taylor bled to death, but Wolseley, with great presence of mind, pressed his fingers upon the veins of his thigh, and so stopped the flow of blood; happily in his case the artery had not been severed. Lying helpless upon his back, his one hand pressing his wound, with the other he bravely waved his sword, and

F

cheered his men on to victory. He would not suffer himself to be carried to the rear until the position was gained,

After this severe encounter Ensign Wolseley was in a very critical state. For six months he had a soldier in constant attendance upon him, and was in great danger of bleeding to death. Ultimately he recovered, although the weakness in the left leg has occasioned him inconvenience throughout his life.

This was indeed a baptism of fire. Those who saw the gallant Taylor and Ensign Wolseley start on their perilous enterprise, gave them up for lost men. An officer, who had lent Wolseley his only shirt, besides the one on his back, ruefully ejaculated, "There goes my change of linen!" as he saw the gallant young officer rush to the breastworks; for he never again expected to see either his friend or his shirt. The latter was a weightier consideration than might be supposed ; for in these long marches through forest and jungle, an officer's kit was reduced to the smallest quantity. Changes of linen were barely included.

Ensign Wolseley spent the autumn of 1853 with his family in Dublin, and when his health was sufficiently restored, visited Paris. He did not rejoin his own regiment, but was promoted, as a reward for his bravery, to a lieutenancy in the 90th Light Infantry.

He was not allowed to remain idle long. Already the distant murmurings of war were heard along the Turkish frontier, and soon was to be enacted that ever memorable contest, the Crimean War. The combined expedition of British and French troops sailed from Varna on the 3rd of September, 1854. The English were under the command of Lord Raglan, and our Allies, the French, were commanded by Marshal St. Arnaud. They were accompanied by a vast armada of warships and transports. This mighty expedition landed at Old Fort, near Eupatoria, on the 14th of September. A few days later was fought the first of the Crimean struggles—the battle of the Alma. After the victory of the Alma, the siege of Sebastopol was undertaken, which for tediousness and the hardships endured by the soldiers through a Russian winter spent in the trenches, is unparalleled in the history of British warfare.

Alma was followed by the victories of Balaklava, and of Inkerman. Sebastopol showed not the slightest sign of surrender, and preparations had to be made for passing the dreaded winter. Lord Raglan sent home asking for every soldier that could be spared, to be despatched to meet the demands of the siege. The 90th, in which Wolseley was Lieutenant, was still at the Horse Guards fretting for action. The Chief had determined that they should go nowhere until they had first served in India. Wolseley and a brother officer were so irritated at being thus prohibited from service in the Crimea, that they were about to exchange into a corps before Sebastopol, when Lord Raglan's imperative demand for more men came, and the 90th was ordered to embark.

The regiment reached Balaklava on the 4th of December, 1854, and two days later was in the trenches before Sebastopol. Soon after his arrival Wolseley was appointed to the post of Acting-Engineer. The work he had to do was most severe. He had to be on duty always twelve hours at a time, and oftener twenty-four. There was the rocky nature of the soil to contend with, and the fearful cold of an Arctic winter. The snow sometimes lay on the plain twelve to eighteen inches deep. The construction of siege works under these conditions was no light task. The men were starving, as the food supply was wretchedly scarce owing to the bad transit arrangements. While the troops were perishing for lack of food, and the officers glad to snatch a mouldy biscuit, ship loads of food and clothing were rotting on the quays of Balaklava. There was scarcely any fuel. Roots and anything that could be gathered in that desolate region were utilized for making fires. It would be difficult to imagine anything more utterly wretched than the condition of the Allied Armies during this winter in the Crimea.

Lieutenant Wolseley was commissioned by General Harry Jones, of the Engineering Department, to make a plan in water colours of the position of Inkerman and the trenches. But the cold was so intense that the water froze on his brush, and he was obliged to use charcoal to melt the ice, and keep the water from freezing. Under these trying circumstances he finished the survey to the complete satisfaction of the General.

Cold and want were not all that these brave men in the trenches had to endure. They were never safe day or night.

The enemy was continually opening fire upon them. On one occasion as Wolseley was giving orders to two sappers, a round shot took one man's head off, and drove his jaw-bone into the other man's face. Incidents of this kind were so common during this prolonged siege that they were scarcely noticed. It was said of Wolseley by a brother officer who served with him in the trenches that he was "the bravest man he ever knew." He never turned his back on an approaching shell, but fronted it, determining that if he was killed it should never be said that he fell while running away from a shell, or while turning his back on the enemy.

With the return of spring, after these months of hardships in the trenches, the whole of the Allied Artillery opened fire upon the Russian stronghold, April 9th, 1855. Several bombardments were made, the third taking place on the 6th of June, when the Russian works began to show signs of the heavy fire to which they had been subjected. On the 7th was made the memorable assault on the Quarries, in which Wolseley, now made Captain, played a conspicuous part. All the officers and men intended to take part in this arduous task were kept off duty for twenty-four hours in order to be fresh for the attack. But Wolseley was called upon to fill the place of a Captain who had fallen early in the day, so that when the time came for the assault upon the Quarries he had undergone a day's hard work. This did not deter him from joining in the attack. The fighting was of a most desperate nature. Three times the enemy expelled our soldiers from the Quarries, and three times Wolseley returned with the victorious column, until finally the enemy was driven back. But at daybreak the enemy issued out again in strong numbers to try and recapture the Quarries. Our men were so overcome by the night's work that it was in vain the officers tried to rouse them from their sleep. Finding their efforts vain, the officers, only numbering twenty, determined, with just the handful of men they could rally to their side, to open fire upon the enemy. The bugler sounded, and never before did such a lusty cheer rise from so small a band. So well did they use their lungs that the Russians, mindful of the repulses they had met, refused to advance thinking that a large force awaited them. They retreated, leaving the Quarries in possession of the heroic little band.

Captain Wolseley had been on duty for twenty-four hours, and after his indefatigable exertions completely lost his voice. Exhausted from a wound he had received upon the thigh he fell down from fatigue, and was found by an officer lying on a heap of slain. So concluded, what Wolseley himself declares was "the hardest day's work I ever did in my life."

After a period of rest he was again in the field, and on the 30th of August received wounds which incapacitated him from further service during the campaign. He was engaged with some sappers in reconstructing some gabions which the Russians had pulled up, when a round shot struck a gabion, scattering the stones with resistless force. "Look out!" cried Wolseley, but both sappers fell to the ground. The one had his head taken off, and the other was disembowelled. Wolseley himself fell at their side senseless, and apparently dead. A sergeant of sappers finding that he still breathed, conveyed him, with the help of Prince Victor of Hohenlohe, to the doctor's hut. Wolseley sank on the ground exhausted, and the doctor, after a hasty glance at him, said curtly, "He's a dead un." This roused the gallant captain, who, though almost smothered with blood, managed to articulate, "I am worth a good many dead men yet." This remark brought the doctor to his side. Capt. Wolseley's condition was most shocking. The following detailed description will give some idea of the extent of his injuries:—
"His features were not distinguishable as those of a human being, while blood flowed from innumerable wounds caused by the stones with which he had been struck. Sharp fragments were embedded all over his face, and his left cheek had been almost completely cut away. . . . . Both his eyes were completely closed, and the injury to one of them was so serious that the sight has been permanently lost. Not a square inch of his face but what was battered and cut about, while his body was wounded all over, just as if he had been peppered with small shot. He had received also a severe wound on his right leg, so that both limbs had now been injured; the wound in the left thigh, received in Burmah, rendering him slightly lame."

After his wounds were dressed Captain Wolseley was conveyed on a stretcher, carried by four soldiers, to St. George's Monastery on the sea coast near Balaklava. For several weeks he was pent up in a gloomy cell. His eyes were too much injured to bear the light. In fact, at that time it was hardly probable that he would ever regain his sight Gloomy must the future have appeared to the active young soldier thus prostrated at the beginning of his career. As he passed those dreary days in the cave, shut out from the excitement of the war, and far removed from friends and kindred, his mind must have been sorely tried as he thought of his helpless blindness, and the small chance there was of his ever again wielding the sword, and cheering his men on to victory. As he lay in this wretched condition the news reached him of the fall of Sebastopol, which for seven long weary months had withstood the utmost efforts of the Allied Armies.

Captain Wolseley left the Crimea shortly after the conclusion of the peace with Russia. He was one of the last men to quit the country. Before he left he was sufficiently recovered from his injuries to be able to assist in surveying the Crimea. He was appointed Deputy-Assistant-Quartermaster-General, and had many narrow escapes from being captured by the Russians, who, smarting under their defeat, were annoyed to see the British officers reconnoitring and sketching close to their advanced posts.

After a brief rest at Aldershot and Portsmouth Captain Wolseley embarked with his regiment for China. The voyage was a most disastrous one. The *Transit* was in an unsound condition, and finally got wrecked by crashing on to a coral reef. The crew were obliged to pass a kind of Robinson Crusoe life for eight days on the Island of Banca. Captain Wolseley lost everything he possessed in the world, as nothing could be carried away from the shipwrecked vessel.

Startling intelligence reached the shipwrecked crew on the Island of Banca. The news was brought by Her Majesty's Gunboat *Dove*, arrived from Singapore, that the Bengal Native Army was in full mutiny. This changed Capt. Wolseley's destination. The 90th Regiment was embarked for India instead of proceeding to China. On the 27th of September, 1857, Captain Wolseley reached Cawnpore, which then presented a most desolate appearance. The cantonments and bungalows had been burnt down on every side. As he passed along its streets the horrors which had lately been enacted there caused his blood to fire. The monster Nana Sahib had butchered hundreds of women and children, and their bodies, while still palpitating, had been thrown into the neighbouring well.

Captain Wolseley's first fight during the Indian Mutiny was at Bhitoor, the residence of Nana Sahib. It was destroyed October 19th, and the troops bivouacked close by for the night. The cook of Wolseley's mess prepared his master's dinner by means of the legs of the monster's billiard-table. They were used for fuel.

Delhi had fallen by this time, and the mutiny was practically quelled. But Lucknow was still in a critical condition. It had been relieved on the 25th of September, by General Havelock and Sir James Outram. But the entire British force occupying it only amounted to 3,000 fighting men, while the rebel hordes surrounding it numbered 70,000. On the 14th of November Sir Colin Campbell, with the British army, started to its final relief. Captain Wolseley was hotly engaged throughout the operations, particularly distinguishing himself at the storming of the Mess-house. Sir Colin had heard of his bravery in the Crimea, and singled him out to lead the assault. With his usual bravery Captain Wolseley rushed ahead of his men in the face of a heavy fire, and succeeded in planting the British flag on the roof of the Mess-house. Twice it was struck down by the enemy, and twice it was replaced by Wolseley. At length the fire became so severe that he and his men were forced to seek cover.

Having accomplished the storming of the Mess-house, Captain Wolseley, though without orders, proceeded to take the Mootee Mahul fortress, and brilliantly succeeded. What was his astonishment shortly after to hear that Sir Colin Campbell was furious at him for exceeding orders. He was told to take the Mess-house, and he had in addition driven the enemy out of the Mootee Mahul! The next morning the enraged old soldier espied Captain Wolseley, and after an explosion of wrath at his daring to exceed instructions, ended by congratulating him upon his bravery, and promised to recommend him for immediate promotion.

After this Captain Wolseley took part in the capture of Lucknow, and at the close of the Mutiny was gazetted as

Lieutenant-Colonel. He was only twenty-six years of age at this time.

For the next five months Wolseley was established in comfortable quarters in the fine old palace near Lucknow, and was engaged in laying out the new cantonments, the old ones having been destroyed by the rebels. At the end of that time he was offered a position on the staff of Sir Hope Grant, who was about to proceed to China to bring the Imperial Government to terms,

Colonel Wolseley embarked on this expedition on the 26th of February, 1860, and reached Hong Kong on the 13th of March. On the 16th of June he accompanied the Commander-in-Chief to Shanghai. It was the duty of the troops to protect the peaceful inhabitants from the ravages of the rebels known as the Taipings, who for eight years had been desolating the country. The traders at Shanghai were in especial fear, as the Imperial Government seemed bent on driving the rebel hordes towards the sea, in which event the sea-coast towns, like Shanghai, would have been at their mercy. It was the work of the British troops to keep these rebels in check. Throughout the campaign Colonel Wolseley showed his usual heroism. Whenever the General, Sir Hope Grant, wanted an officer to undertake an important charge, he would enquire, "Where's Wolseley? Send him,"

Colonel Wolseley was in charge of the Topographical Department of Sir Hope Grant's army. His duties were very severe. He had to survey a country totally unknown, but the skill which he had acquired as a youth in surveying and engineering work served him now, and enabled him to render most valuable assistance to his general. He took part in the capture of the Taku Forts, and was present at the looting of the Summer Palace, one of the most glorious of Imperial residences. It was entered by the troops just after the flight of the Emperor. Its appearance of magnificent grandeur was a sight never to be forgotton. For two hundred years this had been the Imperial residence. During, that time gems and treasures of the most superb kind had been accumulated. Its walls were rich in gold, and its floors of polished marble. Through this magnificent palace the troops rushed pell-mell, destroying and pillaging on all sides. The booty was afterwards sold for £24,000.

The British troops after humiliating the Imperial Government, embarked for England. It remained to Col. Gordon and his "Ever Victorious Army," composed principally of native troops, to finally crush out the Taiping rebellion.

Colonel Wolseley arrived in England May 1st, 1861, after an absence of four years. Up to this period he had had an eventful career. He had distinguished himself in Burmah, had faced death during that terrible winter before Sebastopol, and again when bravely struggling his way through the streets of Lucknow, while matchlock-men aimed at him from " tower, turret, and bartizan." He had marched weary miles through swamp and jungle, and faced pestilence and famine. Three times he had lost his belongings; once at the shipwreck of the crazy old *Transit*, again during the Indian Mutiny, and lastly in China, where he returned one evening to find his tent completely flooded.

Our hero was next to distinguish himself in another quarter of the globe. In December, 1861, he was despatched to Canada as Assistant-Quartermaster-General. At this time the struggle was going on between the Northern and Southern States, and it seemed likely that England would become embroiled in the warfare; but this was happily averted. It was at the time when war seemed eminent that Colonel Wolseley was despatched to Canada. He reached Halifax after a miserable voyage in the *Melbourne*, which showed her unseaworthy qualities early in the voyage. It seemed to be Colonel Wolseley's fate to sail in unseaworthy vessels. His experiences on the *Melbourne* were only paralleled by those on the *Transit*.

From Halifax he proceeded to Montreal, which was the head-quarters for the army in the Dominion. He was soon engaged at Rivière du Loup in making arrangements for the troops. It fell to his lot to lodge, feed, and clothe them, and see them started on their journey to their various destinations at the leading towns. The administrative skill which has since so greatly distinguished Lord Wolseley was fully shown upon this occasion. This large force passed through his hands without any hitch or accident, save the desertion of one man.

As the dispute between England and America, concerning the seizure of the vessel *Trent* by the Americans, had been settled, the troops were not needed for warfare. Colonel

Wolseley took a leave of absence for six weeks, during which time he paid a hazardous visit to the seat of war, where the Federate and Confederate forces were in deadliest strife. He had many narrow escapes of being captured as a spy by the Northerners, who had blockaded the ports of the South, and were suspicious of every stranger journeying that way. On one occasion Wolseley and a friend had taken refuge in a hut, when they were horrified by the sight of a Federal officer followed by a band of soldiers. He entered the hut, but Wolseley contrived to enter into easy and friendly conversation with him, and by judiciously proffering him a cigar disarmed his suspicions.

After a series of adventures Wolseley crossed safely over into the Confederate States, and paid a visit to General Lee's head-quarters. He gives the following interesting description of the famous General : " He is a strongly-built man, about five feet eleven in height, and apparently not more than fifty years of age. His hair and beard are nearly white ; but his dark brown eyes still shine with all the brightness of youth, and beam with a most pleasing expression. Indeed, his whole face is kindly and benevolent in the highest degree. In manner, though sufficiently conversible, he is slightly reserved ; but he is a person that, whenever seen, whether in a castle or a hovel, alone or in a crowd, must at once attract attention as being a splendid specimen of an English gentleman, with one of the most rarely handsome faces I ever saw. . . . . You have only to be in his society for a very brief period to be convinced that whatever he says may be implicitly relied upon, and that he is quite incapable of departing from the truth under any circumstances."

After his visit to General Lee, Wolseley paid one of equal interest to Bunker's Hill, to see General Stonewall Jackson, whom he thus describes : " Dressed in his grey uniform, he looks the hero that he is ; and his thin compressed lips and calm glance, which meets yours unflinchingly, gave evidence of that firmness and decision of character for which he is so famous. He has a broad open forehead, from which the hair is well brushed back ; a shapely nose, straight and long ; thin colourless cheeks, with only a very small allowance of whisker ; a cleanly shaven upper lip and chin ; and a pair of fine greyish-blue eyes rather sunken, with overhanging brows, which intensify the keeness of his gaze without imparting any fierceness to it. . . . . The religious element seems strongly developed in him; and though his conversation is perfectly free from all puritanical cant, it is evident that he is a man who never loses sight of the fact that there is an Omnipresent Deity ever presiding over the minutest occurrences of life as well as over the most important. Altogether, as one of his soldiers said to me when speaking of him, ' he is a glorious fellow.' And, after I left him, I felt that I had at last solved a mystery, and discovered why it was that he had accomplished such almost miraculous feats. With such a leader men would go anywhere, and face any amount of difficulties." For myself, adds Wolseley, " I believe that, inspired by the presence of such a man, I should be perfectly insensible to fatigue, and reckon on success as a moral certainty."

Colonel Wolseley continued his duties in Canada as Assistant-Quartermaster-General, under Colonel Lysons, until 1867. Colonel Lysons' term of office expired in the autumn of that year, and Colonel Wolseley was nominated as his successor. The following year he left for England on two month's private leave. Once during his residence in America he had been obliged to return home for medical advice concerning the wound in his thigh received in Burmah. His present leave of absence was for a happy purpose. He was married, during his stay, to Miss Erskine, who returned with him to Canada.

In 1870 the disturbances which arose in the Red River Settlements gave Colonel Wolseley the opportunity for displaying his powers as a Commander. After eighteen years of service in some of the most memorable of British battle-fields he was well fitted to lead the expedition which the Government had determined to send to the Red River, to quell Louis Riel's revolt. This audacious usurper had defied the Canadian Government, establishing himself at Fort Garry as " President" of the so-called " Republic of the North-West." He had illegally confined sixty British subjects at Fort Garry, and had put to death one Thomas Scott who attempted their rescue.

On the 21st of May Colonel Wolseley assumed command of the forces and proceeded on his perilous journey to Fort Garry. There were rivers, cataracts, and falls to pass, besides long weary marches over strange country. The difficulties which beset the gallant commander in conveying a large armed force and war materials through such a route, can be easily imagined. On re-embarking the military stores at Lake Superior it was found that all the tent poles had been left behind. This was told to the commander in fear and trembling, but Colonel Wolseley met the report of this negligence with a merry laugh, and the query, "you have not forgotton the axes too?" Receiving an answer in the negative, he pointed to the primeval forests around, saying : "Then you can help yourself to as many tent-poles as you require." This was his happy way of meeting a difficulty.

Colonel Wolseley reached Fort Garry within twenty-four hours of the time he had stated before setting out on the expedition. That he could calculate so closely as to the length of time so hazardous a journey would take, is a proof of his remarkable foresight and correct calculation. Louis Riel fled from his stronghold when he heard of the advance of the army. Colonel Wolseley led his men triumphantly to Fort Garry and hoisted the British flag. He had gained a bloodless victory.

He returned to Canada with all his men save one, who was taken ill at Fort Garry. There had been no casualty throughout that perilous enterprise. The entire force reached Toronto and Montreal in good health.

On his return to England Colonel Wolseley received the honour of knighthood for his services in Canada. He became Sir Garnet Joseph Wolseley, K.C.M.G. After six months on the half-pay list, he was appointed Assistant-Adjutant-General, Discipline Branch, at the Horse Guards. This was an important post, as he had to deal with the movement and supply of troops.

Sir Garnet Wolseley next distinguished himself in the Ashantee War. He was sent by the Government to the Gold Coast as Civil and Military Commander. King Koffee with his savage hordes had practically blockaded the British ports, and the lives of the settlers were in danger. Sir Garnet started on his enterprise assuring his friends that if he came back at all he should land in England by the 1st of April. But he was more than punctual, for he landed at Portsmouth on the 21st of March.

Arriving at Cape Coast he found the inhabitants in a terror-stricken state. The Government had not supplied him with troops, and to raise a force from the natives seemed impossible. He sent home urgent requests for troops, as he felt that if tranquillity was to be restored to the Gold Coast, King Koffee must be thoroughly subdued. The Government failed to see the position in its true light, and were backward in complying with his demands. At last, after months of weary waiting, during which time Sir Garnet was prostrated by fever, a European army was sent out to him. With this, thoroughly organized, he began the invasion of Ashantee. Before starting he fixed the date on which he should lead his troops into Coomassie, King Koffee's capital. As on other memorable occasions he was true to time. When within fifteen miles of the capital some severe fighting ensued. The Ashantees fought desperately at Amoaful, and at the village of Ordahsu, where Sir Garnet had a narrow escape from death. After these two victories the Commander prepared for his final march to Coomassie. Sir Archibald Alison thus describes the advance of the Highlanders : " Then followed one of the finest spectacles ever seen in war. Without stop or stay the 42nd rushed on cheering, their pipes playing, their officers to the front ; ambuscade after ambuscade was successfully carried, village after village won in succession, till the whole Ashantees broke, and fled in the wildest disorder down the pathway on their front to Coomassie. The ground was covered with traces of their flight, umbrellas, and war-chairs of their chiefs, drums, muskets, killed and wounded, covered the whole way, and the bush on each side was trampled as if a torrent had flowed through it. No pause took place until a village about four miles from Coomassie was reached, when the absolute exhaustion of the men rendered a short halt necessary. So swift and unbroken was the advance of the 42nd, that neither Rait's guns, nor the Rifle Brigade in support, were ever brought into action."

Shortly after this brilliant feat, Sir Garnet with his entire force, marched triumphantly into Coomassie. Arriving in the market place he called for " three cheers for the Queen," which British throats gave so lustily that the natives fled panic stricken. He succeeded in bringing King Koffee to terms of peace, and returned home to be honoured on all sides. The gallant troops were reviewed by the Queen at Windsor amid general èclat. Sir Garnet was promoted to the rank of Major-General in the Army, and received from Parliament a vote of thanks for his services and a grant of £25,000.

In February, 1875, Sir Garnet was sent out to Natal to put down the outbreak of Langalibalele's tribe. Having succeeded in this he was in the following year appointed to the Governorship of Cyprus, then newly annexed. In this capacity he exhibited the greatest skill as a civil commander. The population was labouring under heavy abuses. Sir Garnet laboured during his short term of office to redress their wrongs by abolishing iniquitous taxes, reforming the land system, and keeping all officials in wholesome check by doing away with bribery.

Useful as was his work in the establishment of law and order in Cyprus, the gallant soldier longed for the battle-field. War was then raging on the Afghan frontier. Referring to it he wrote at this time: "All our thoughts here are now turned to the Afghan frontier, and I long to be in the saddle leading our men through these passes which former wars have made so familiar to us in history. I like being Governor of a new place like Cyprus during peace, but when 'the blast of war blows in our ears,' I long to run to the sound, and take my fair share of its dangers and excitements."

The life of Sir Garnet Wolseley is a history of successful battle-fields. He was recalled from Cyprus to be "Commander-in-Chief of the forces in South Africa, and High Commissioner for Natal, the Transvaal, and the neighbouring countries." The war with the Zulu King Cetewayo was raging. Our soldiers had received severe defeat by him at Isandlwhana. A general relief was felt by the country when Sir Garnet was despatched to try his skill against this redoubtable warrior king. *Punch*, referring to the appointment, wrote:—

> "When Wolseley's mentioned, Wellesley's brought to mind;
> Two men, two names of answerable kind.
> Called to the front, like Wellesley, good at need,
> Go, Wolseley, and like Wellesley, greatly speed."

Arrived in Zululand, Sir Garnet gave chase to King

Cetewayo, who had fled after Lord Chelmsford's victory at Ulundi. The war was practically over when Sir Garnet arrived, but the King was at large. The Commander-in-Chief soon captured him, and sending him a prisoner to Cape Town proceeded with the pacification of Zululand. The Basutos, encouraged by their chieftain Secocoeni, refused to come to terms. Accordingly Sir Garnet made preparations to attack his mountain fastness and capture him. Before starting from Pretoria the Commander assured his friends that he would take his afternoon tea in Secocoeni's house on the 28th of November, and fixed the date when his troops would be at certain places. *All these arrangements were literally fulfilled.* He took his tea in Secocoeni's mansion as he had predicted. There was some desperate fighting before the chieftain was captured. He had taken refuge in a cave with 600 of his followers. This was blockaded until Secocoeni, ill and starving, surrendered on the 2nd of December. On the 9th Sir Garnet Wolseley reached Pretoria with his captive, "who was the second great African potentate that he had captured within six months." Sir Garnet returned to England, having accomplished his mission—the pacification of Zululand.

On the outbreak of the war in Egypt in 1882 Sir Garnet Wolseley was again called upon to take command. He was sent with a force of 17,000 men to the help of the Khedive, whose Government was threatened by Arabi Pasha, his Minister at War. Arabi had a vast following, and the Egyptian Khedive was powerless to withstand him.

Before leaving England Sir Garnet, with his usual precision, prepared his plan of campaign ; every part of which was carried out to the letter. Every detail for the provision, embarkation, and disposition of this large army was arranged by the Commander himself. Arriving in Egypt he issued a proclamation to the people that it was the mission of the British army to re-establish the authority of the Khedive. Cautiously, step by step, he advanced through the country to Arabi's head-quarters. By a masterly stroke the Suez Canal was seized. This important operation was completed by the British Navy between 3 and 8 a.m. of Sunday, the 20th of August, and Sir Garnet arrived at Port Said with the 1st Division the same day. On the following he pushed on to Ismalia. Some time elapsed before Sir Garnet finally quitted that place. Meanwhile, the press at home were grumbling at what they called "unnecessary delay," But the sagacious Commander was bent on securing his way as he went, and dealing one decisive blow at Arabi.

An encounter, which almost amounted to a general action, took place with Arabi's troops at Kassassin, on the 9th of September. The enemy retreated towards Tel-el-Kebir. General Graham followed, and drew up within three-quarters of a mile of the place. The men were anxious to advance and make a dash upon Arabi, but the prudent Commander-in-Chief decided to withdraw his troops into camp. Much disappointment was felt by eager young officers, but future events showed the wisdom of it.

Sir Garnet now moved his troops to the front, and had all in readiness for the decisive blow. His plan was "to make a night march, and carry the enemy's position at dawn at the point of the bayonet." The distance to be traversed from the camp to Tel-el-Kebir was seven and a half miles. This had to be accomplished at midnight by an army whose front covered nearly four miles of ground. At 6.15 on the evening of the 12th of September this vast array moved silently out of camp. Not a bugle or trumpet sounded, lest the enemy should catch the alarm. On they moved across the star-lit desert, until within a few miles of the enemy. Then they halted until the first streaks of dawn appeared in the east. At five o'clock the enemy's works were lit up with a rosy light, and after a careful survey the General gave the order for attack. Just at that time the enemy became aware of the advance of the foe, and Arabi's men poured forth all along the line of the entrenchments a stream of rifle-fire. The Highland Brigade instantly advanced to the charge; but so fierce was the fire that 200 men were shot down, though they had only a distance of 150 yards to cross before gaining the ditch. A terrible hand-to-hand struggle ensued. The Egyptians were shot down in hundreds as they fled. Arabi's camp was captured, and by 6.30 "the last shot was fired by the Highlanders—one hour and twenty minutes after the first." So ended the battle of Tel-el-Kebir, the most brilliant of Sir Garnet Wolseley's victories, and one of the greatest achievements in modern warfare.

In the hour of his triumph the General did not forget a

faithful follower who lay dying. Lieutenant Wyatt Rawson, who had pioneered the Highland Brigade through the night march, was mortally wounded. Sir Garnet rode back some miles to see him. Entering the tent, he knelt by the bed-side of the wounded officer, and taking his hand strove to cheer him. The dying man asked, with proud satisfaction: "General, did I not lead them straight?" "Yes," was the reply, "I knew you were well to the front all the time, old fellow."

Such scenes as these show the esteem and devotion with which Sir Garnet Wolseley is ever held in by his followers. He has the gift of inspiring confidence, and can instil into the men whom he leads something of his own valour. These, with his wonderful adminstrative powers, have made him England's first soldier.

On his return from Egypt, Sir Garnet received numerous honours, among them being a peerage.

On the 20th of November Sir Garnet Wolseley was created a peer of the United Kingdom, by the title of "Lord Wolseley of Cairo, and of Wolseley in the county of Stafford."

Dr. WILLIAM CHAMBERS.

THE name of *Chambers*, connected as it is with so much of the instructive and popular literature of the day, has become a household word. William Chambers, the originator of *Chambers' Journal*, was moved to his literary enterprise by the remembrance of the need for cheap and good literature, which he had experienced when a friendless boy in Edinburgh. He, with his brother, after encountering and overcoming great difficulties, succeeded in working a revolution in the book trade. They were the means of putting instructive reading into the hands of the people at a price which even the poorest could afford, and had the satisfaction of seeing their efforts rewarded by an unprecedented success.

Born in the ancient royal burgh of Peebles, on the banks of the Tweed, William Chambers passed his early years amidst the beautiful mountain scenery of that district. His father had, in 1799, married Jean Gibson, one of the belles of the neighbourhood, who possessed a small fortune. With her he settled in a neat little house near the Eddleston Water, a tributary of the Tweed. In that unpretentious home their son William Chambers was born on the 16th of April, 1800. Shortly after his birth they removed to a house in the main street of Peebles, in order to start a drapery business.

William Chambers received a very ordinary education. He passed through the school of Peebles, where he had instruction in the three R's, and finished with a dose of Latin; the mark of which he bore to his dying day, in the shape of a small protuberance on the top of his head, occasioned by a blow from the schoolmaster's ruler, given as a punishment for his hesitancy in answering a question in Latin grammar.

He had a great love for books, and in company with his brother Robert—two years his junior—devoted every spare hour of the day to reading. The two boys read through the circulating library, besides devouring every other book within their reach; they were bent on gaining knowledge. Between the ages of 10 and 12 years they had, to a large extent, digested the *Encyclopædia Britannica*, and thus acquired a knowledge of the physical sciences, which they could not have learnt at school; for there was not a map, nor any book on history, geography, or science ever used in the schools which they attended.

In addition to the information they gained from books, their imaginations were stirred by the weird stories of an aged relative. She would tell them of fairies and hobgoblins, and the wonderful legends of the district, until their youthful minds were full of vague mysteries. A book—*Satan's Invisible World Discovered*—which came into their possession at this time, tended to intensify the stories of Aunty Peg. Fortunately for the boys they received a healthier bias in listening to the talk of the neighbours who dropped in for a chat with their parents. Articles in the *Edinburgh Review* came up for discussion, together with the telescope just then formed by Sir William Herschel, which was the great event of the day. So their youth was passed until their father's misfortunes began.

In 1813 Mr. Chambers lost all his money through an unfortunate business transaction. His home was broken up in the December of that year, and he removed with his family to Edinburgh. There, after a time, he obtained employment as manager of some salt works at Joppa, four miles from Edinburgh.

Through these family reverses William Chambers was obliged to seek employment. In May, 1814, he was apprenticed for five years to a bookseller in Edinburgh, and left to struggle in that city alone. Out of his scanty wages of four shillings per week he had to pay for lodgings, and meet all his requirements. By living on threepence-halfpenny a day he contrived to make both ends meet, and also saved money enough to buy an apparatus to make experiments in electricity. He had a book in which his modest expenditure wa duly entered, and was thus able to check his outlay if he found it exceeding his means. He could not afford to have many companions; his only one at this time was James King, an apprentice to a seedsman, and a boy who like himself was working his way up in the world.

Young Chambers did not neglect self-improvement because he had to work hard for a living. His spare time was spent in scientific experiments with his friend James King, and in studying French. In the summer he rose at five o'clock to have a spell at reading, but when winter came he could not afford a light, and so was obliged to give that practice up. Amongst other books he read Smith's *Wealth of Nations*, Locke's *Human Understanding*, Paley's *Moral Philosophy*, and Blair's *Belles Lettres*. It was his custom to make a memorandum of the leading books he read, and to record the principal facts contained in them. By this means he became thoroughly impressed with what he read, and had always his notes for reference.

The time when he began life in Edinburgh was a particularly eventful one in the history of literature. Sir Walter Scott was writing, in secret, at his house in the Canongate, the first of those wonderful romances which were shortly to take the public by storm. *Waverley* was published in 1814, the same year that William Chambers became a printer's apprentice. He was in the very midst of the excitement, and was kept busy running backwards and forwards, carrying relays of copies to supply the eager customers as they thronged the shop door, and speculated as to who the author of *Waverley* was. Doubtless he joined in the general anxiety to find out the unknown author, and when the secret popped out, took his gaze of wonder and admiration as the familiar figure of Sir Walter Scott passed along the Edinburgh streets.

Scarcely had the excitement of the Waverley Novels subsided when the *Scotsman* newspaper made its first appearance. Young Chambers determined to purchase the first copy that was issued. He took his stand amongst the crowd who gathered round the office, and eagerly waited to dart forward and secure the prize when the papers should be handed out. A stronger arm was before him, however, and he had to be content with the second copy. Tenpence was the price of it, owing to the costly Government stamp which had then to be affixed to newspapers. It was a large sum to spare out of his scanty wages, but delighted with his possession, he troubled not that he had to live on short allowance in order to secure it; such was his great thirst for knowledge.

In 1817, following directly upon the publication of the *Scotsman*, the first number of *Blackwood's Magazine* was published. This was another event of interest to the eager boy so full of literary tastes and sympathies.

In the winter of 1815-16 he was fortunate enough to get the offer of some very congenial employment. A baker, who was passionately fond of reading, but had not leisure for it, engaged young Chambers to come to his bake-house and read aloud to him and his sons as they prepared the bread, promising a hot roll each morning as payment. This offer was gladly accepted, not so much for the sake of the roll, as that it gave him an opportunity to carry on his early morning reading, which the expense of a light had hitherto prevented him from doing through the winter. Punctually at five o'clock each morning William Chambers made his appearance at the little underground cellar, occupied by the baker, and which was situated in the block of buildings since pulled down to make way for the North British Railway Terminus. Seated in the corner of the window on an old sack, and with a tallow candle stuck in a bottle by way of light, he entertained the bakers for two hours and a half. *Roderick Random* was the first book he read. It gave great satisfaction; the bakers had to cease again and again from their labours to hold their sides, which were aching with laughter. The reading was continued from other works of Smollett, and the novels of Fielding; at the end of it the hot roll was always forthcoming, and young Chambers, after brushing off the flour, started off for his master's shop in Calton Street, ready for the day's duties.

His Sundays were passed with his parents at Joppa. He looked forward to this as a great treat; for he was able to get a talk with his mother, to whom he was most tenderly attached. She was a noble woman, who had to battle with much trouble and privation. She felt anxious for her boy struggling alone in the city, and each week when he parted from her, gave him earnest admonitions to "avoid low company, to mind whom he was come of, and aye to haud forrit." Right well did William Chambers carry out his mother's injunctions. He ever held "forrit," and never made a backward step throughout his career.

His father's affairs did not prosper at Joppa; he was dismissed from his employment, and fell into ill-health. When the news of these fresh misfortunes reached young Chambers he hastened home to comfort his mother. It was a bitter cold night, and the rain pouring down when, after his day's work, he set out on his long walk to Joppa. He reached home at midnight, all was quiet in the house, and stealing up to his mother's bedside, he talked with her of the future, and laid his insignificant savings at her disposal. He was unusually rich in possessing half-a-sovereign, which had been given him by a gentleman to whom he had been sent by his master with the agreeable intelligence that he had gained a lottery prize. This precious little piece of gold he placed in his mother's hand as she pressed his at parting, and started out in the dim morning light for Edinburgh to earn more.

In May, 1819, his apprenticeship came to an end. His master was anxious to retain him in his service, but he preferred to start on his own account. It was rather a rash determination for a young man, whose entire capital consisted of five shillings, but William Chambers meant to "haud forrit," and having overcome many obstacles he was ready to battle with this one. A London bookseller, who was conducting a trade-sale in Edinburgh, hearing that young Chambers wished to start in business, offered to supply him, on credit, with a selection of books to the value of ten pounds. He gladly accepted this offer, and with his five shillings bought wood to manufacture a stall. This he erected in Leith Walk, and proudly arranging his stock of books, William Chambers began business. Who out of the crowds which passed by him thought that the poorly clad youth, whom they saw offering his few books for sale, was destined to attain such world-wide fame? His modest stock was soon disposed of, and he had, after paying all obligations, a few pounds in hand. Such was the first start in life of a man who died crowned with honours, and with the reward of a baronetcy within his grasp.

His out-door sale was all very well for fine days, but there were the wet ones to find employment for. Having three pounds in hand he purchased a small hand-press and some type, and started printing. His machinery was very much worn, and would only print half a sheet at a time. in spite of these difficulties he executed a small edition of the songs of Robert Burns, and bound them in boards with a coloured wrapper. They were soon all sold, giving him a profit of eight pounds. His next endeavour was to start and print a periodical. It was issued fortnightly under the title of the *Kaleidoscope*, and was edited by his brother Robert. But this strain of hard work was telling upon the strength of William Chambers; he was obliged to abandon the *Kaleidoscope* after a few issues.

After a period employed in bookselling and job printing, he conceived the idea of starting a journal. He had had good opportunity, during his Edinburgh life, for observing the growing demand for cheap literature. His idea was to start a paper which would elevate and instruct as well as amuse, and which would by its cheapness compete with the trash so eagerly sought after. On the 4th of February, 1832, the first number of *Chambers' Journal* was issued. With a beating heart the young editor watched the reception of his work. His efforts were rewarded by the unprecedented sale of 30,000 copies in a few days. That was confined to Scotland; but at the issue of the third number copies were sent to a London agent for diffusion throughout England, and the sale rose to 50,000. Robert Chambers, who at first refused to join his brother in his new enterprise, now became the editor of the *Journal*. William managed the printing and business department, writing occasional articles. From this time was dated the firm of W. and R. Chambers.

The immense benefit derived by young people from the publication of the *Journal* is best illustrated by a letter which Mr. W. Chambers received from the head-master of an important London school:—" You sowed the seeds of my advancement forty years ago. In a village in Cambridgeshire there were five poor boys whose united weekly wages amounted to seven and sixpence; one of them had given him, by a gentleman off the stage coach, a *Chambers' Journal*. The boy read it; and got four more to hear it read. I was one of them; and we agreed to take it weekly. But the difficulty was, how was it to be paid for? One shilling and sixpence a week would not afford literature. I was always presented with a halfpenny a week for the missionaries, and so were two others. The other two could not contribute; but as their share, they would walk seven miles to fetch it. For ten years we stuck together, and were able to do a great deal to educate ourselves. Now mark the result: I am the head-master of a large and important free school; another was, till lately, the head-master of Queen Elizabeth's Grammar School at Bristol; another became a clergyman; the fourth is now a retired builder; and the fifth is one of the largest sheep-farmers in New Zealand." This letter is by no means a solitary instance; Mr. Chambers was constantly being cheered by receiving testimony from one and another of the good gained from reading the *Journal*. In the country towns the young men were so eager to get it that they would walk several miles to intercept the carrier, and mechanics were seen busily reading it as they walked home from their employment on Saturday afternoons.

Encouraged by their success, the firm of W. and R. Chambers issued on the 4th of February, six weeks after the publication of the *Journal*, the *Penny Magazine*. This was followed, in 1834, by *Information for the People*, a series of popular, scientific, and historic treatises. At different periods they brought out the *Cyclopædia of English Literature, The People's Editions of Standard English Works, The Educational Course*, and *Papers for the People*. William Chambers, who managed all business connected with the firm, was most careful to husband all resources, to avoid debt, and never to speculate, and to these measures he attributed their marvellous success.

Mrs. Chambers was not forgotten by her sons in their prosperity. It was their first care to provide for her maintenance in comfort. Their father had died before their success came.

William Chambers married in 1833 the daughter of Mr. John Clark, of Westminster, and settled in Edinburgh as one of the most respected of its citizens. The toils of business were relieved by congenial intercourse. Among his friends he numbered the late Lord Cockburn, Sir Adam Fergusson, James Hogg the Ettrick Shepherd, Dr. Andrew Combe, and Mr. James Simpson.

At the celebrated dinner parties of Lord Murray, which were at that time unrivalled for the rareness and delicacy of the dishes, William Chambers was a frequent guest. Another friend of his was Mr. Henry Siddons, son of Sarah Siddons the actress. This gentleman had very fine legs, and consequently a weakness for showing them. He persisted in adhering to "shorts and tights," with Hessian boots, when that style of dress was fast giving place to trousers. So attached was he to it, that he left orders that he was to be buried in that dress, which he accordingly was, bottle-green dress coat, shorts and tights, and Hessian boots all complete. Mr. Chambers could well remember how he had gazed with admiration on this ancient beau when, as a boy, he met him walking one Sunday afternoon on the Calton Hill, and on another occasion saw him disporting his fine legs while skating on Duddingstone Loch.

Business transactions frequently called Mr. Chambers to London. There he enjoyed the friendship of Richard Cobden, John Bright, Sir James Kaye Shuttleworth, Sir James Clark, Dr. Neil Arnott, Douglas Jerrold, Mark Lemon, Charles Knight, and the Rev. Sydney Smith. With the latter gentleman his acquaintance began in rather an amusing manner. It was in the year 1844; Mr. Chambers was sitting quietly in his room at Greek Street, Soho Square, when he saw a carriage drive up to the door. From it alighted an aged gentleman in shovel hat and gaiters, whom he heard enquiring for "Mr. William Chambers." He was quite at a loss to know who this ecclesiastical dignitary could be. His doubts were at an end when the attendant ushered in the "Rev. Sydney Smith." Mr. Chambers hastened to receive him fittingly, but his guest, dispensing with all formality, said : "You are surprised possibly at my visit. There is nothing at all strange about it. The originator of the *Edinburgh Review* has come to see the originator of the *Edinburgh Journal*. After this informal introduction, the two men drew their chairs round the fire and chatted over the history of their lives and their work.

In 1849 Mr. Chambers purchased the estate of Glenormiston, in his native county of Peebleshire, which, from that fact, possessed special interest for him. He laboured to promote all public improvements, and in 1859 presented the town of Peebles with the *Chambers' Institution*. This consisted of a suite of buildings comprising public reading-room, a good library, a lecture hall, museum, and a gallery of art.

He took a most active part in agitating for the repeal of the paper duty, which pressed very severely on publishers. He had the satisfaction of seeing the tax abolished, October 1st, 1861. Previous to that, in 1853, the advertisement duty, eighteenpence each, had been removed, and the newspaper stamp in 1855, so that, with the repeal of the paper duty, the press was set free in all its departments. A remarkable advance from the time when the firm of W. & R. Chambers first started.

In 1865 the citizens of Edinburgh elected Mr. Chambers as their Lord Provost. During his term of office he devoted himself to the furtherance of social improvement, and was the means of passing, in 1867, "The Improvement Act," by which 2,800 unwholesome dwelling-houses were pulled down to make place for good ones. The beneficial effect of this measure was soon apparent in the decrease of the death-rate in the city. At the termination of his term of office he allowed himself to be re-elected, in order that he might continue his improvement schemes.

As the Lord Provost of Edinburgh, Mr. Chambers was, on the 2nd of May, 1866, presented at Court by Sir George Grey. Conflicting must have been his thoughts as he mounted the great staircase of St. James's. They would travel back to the time, when as a struggling youth in Edinburgh, he started business with five shillings capital. What a singular contrast to the stately dignitary arrayed in full official robes, and about to pass into the presence of royalty as the Chief Magistrate of that city which had witnessed his early struggles with penury and want! How natural that the Bible text, so peculiarly applicable to him, should flash across his mind: "Seest thou a man diligent in his business? he shall stand before kings!"

William Chambers was revered by men of the highest learning; the University of Edinburgh gave expression to this feeling by conferring on him, in 1872, the degree of LL.D. This was particularly gratifying to him, as it showed in what high appreciation his efforts to instruct the people were held.

The literary work of William Chambers was confined chiefly to articles for the *Journal* and the *Penny Magazine*. He wrote on a variety of topics, frequently taking excursions abroad, or to the English counties to gather materials. In 1838 he made a tour through the Netherlands in order to study the system of elementary education in that country. He found that the secular and religious education of the children were kept distinct. Each child received its religious instruction from the clergyman to whose church it belonged, whether Jew or Christian. Dr. Chambers was in sympathy with this custom, and had the satisfaction of seeing it established in the Edinburgh Industrial School. He prepared for the National Exhibition in Hyde Park, 1851, a little book entitled *Fiddy, an Autobiography*. It was beautifully got up, and exhibited as a specimen of the work of the firm of W. & R. Chambers. In 1864 he completed his *History of Peebleshire*, and in 1872 published a memoir of his brother Robert, who died March 17th, 1871. He also wrote in the same year *Ailie Gilroy*, a novel founded on facts.

Dr. Chambers lived to see the jubilee of *Chambers' Journal*. It took place in 1882. He was unable to be present on the joyful occasion, as his declining health obliged him to live almost the life of a recluse. but he rejoiced in it as the seal of success to his life's efforts. The publishers and booksellers of Edinburgh presented him with a congratulatory address. From the employés of the firm he received an equally gratifying tribute. The majority had served the firm from 30 to 40 years, while ten had been connected with it from 40 to 50; thus showing the kindly feeling which had ever existed between the employers and the employed in the firm of W. & R. Chambers.

Having the satisfaction that his life's work was done, Dr. Chambers passed peacefully away on Sunday morning, the 20th of May, 1883, full of years and full of honour. His last honour, that of a baronetcy, came too late. The patent was already on its way when he expired. To the city of Edinburgh he had been a munificent benefactor; his last work was the restoration of that ancient edifice—sacred to the memory of John Knox, and the centre of the ecclesiastical history of Scotland—the Cathedral of St. Giles.

LORD LAWRENCE.

LORD LAWRENCE possessed a happy blending of those traits of character which distinguish the natives of the British Isles. With Irish geniality and boldness was blended Scotch caution and English endurance. He inherited this diversity of character from his parents. His father, a native of Coleraine in the north of Ireland, had, when seventeen years of age, gone to India as an army volunteer. There, for fifteen years, he endured the privations and perils of active service. He distinguished himself in many engagements, but his valour was unrewarded. In 1809, weakened in body and with no higher rank than that of a regimental captain, he returned to England. His regiment was quartered at Richmond, a small Yorkshire town. Soon after his settlement there John Lawrence, his sixth son and eighth child, was born on the 4th of March, 1811.

There was nothing in the early years of John Lawrence to foreshadow the greatness which he was destined to attain as Governor-General of India. After his three brothers, Alexander, George, and Henry, who were also destined to become famous in India, left home, John became his father's chief companion. Many long rambles the father and son took together. The old veteran would fire the imagination of his youthful listener with the history of his military exploits. "We derived most of our mettle from our father," wrote John Lawrence, when referring to the careers of himself and his illustrious brothers. But his mother's influence also played its part.

Letitia Knox was the daughter of a clergyman in the north of Ireland, and a descendant of the great Scottish reformer whose name she bore. The Scottish traits of character were very strongly marked in her, and stood her in good need when she became the wife of Alexander Lawrence, and had, while following his fortunes as a soldier, to rear a family of twelve children on the scantiest means. Her illustrious sons, if they derived "their mettle" from their father, had to thank her for the management and skill which kept them a home, and enabled them to get education. This they gratefully remembered when, in after years, the "Lawrence Fund" was started by them for her benefit.

The early life of John Lawrence was passed successively at Richmond, Guernsey, Ostend, and Clifton. In 1819 he accompanied his brother Henry to a school at College Green, Bristol, kept by a Mr. Gough. Four times a day the brothers trudged to school over the hills separating Clifton from Bristol. This was the beginning of a companionship which was eventually to terminate in their being the joint rulers of the Punjab, that large tract of country ere long to be annexed to our Indian Empire. From the school at Bristol John passed in 1823, when twelve years old, to his uncle's school at Foyle, in the north of Ireland. He did not specially distinguish himself in his studies, but was fond of history, and read "Plutarch's Lives" assiduously. There were in the school a hundred boarders, whose delight it was to get up sports of an heroic and spirit-stirring character. John Lawrence joined in all these with zest, but the religious lectures which the sister of the head-master gave to the boys were not to his taste. Being her nephew he got an extra amount. Often he tried to slip past her door, but the worthy lady usually made him prisoner. This early dislike, engendered by having religious subjects injudiciously forced upon him, showed itself throughout the life of Lord Lawrence by his reticence on religion. His feelings on that subject were deep and sincere, but he seldom spoke of them, holding them too sacred to be commonly talked of.

In 1825 John Lawrence removed from his uncle's school at Foyle to one in North Wiltshire, about six miles from Bath. Wraxall Hall was the name of the school. There he had for companions Robert Montgomery, who afterwards succeeded him as Governor of the Punjab, F. B.

Ashley, afterwards Vicar of Woburn, Buckinghamshire, and Mr. Wellington Cooper. With these he contracted life-long friendships. The description given of a school adventure of John Lawrence, by Mr. Cooper, is interesting from the glimpse it gives of his early daring and determination. " We were fast friends," writes Mr. Cooper, " and in the kindness of his heart he would have done anything for me. I was very fond of bird-nesting. A swallow had built its nest at the top of our chimney, and I expressed a wish to get at it. ' I'll get the eggs for you,' said John, and went straight to the chimney, and began to climb up it inside. It soon became too narrow for his burly frame. ' Never mind, I'll get them yet,' he said, and at once went to the window. I and my brother followed him through, and, climbing a wall twelve feet high, which came out from one end of the house and formed one side of the court, pushed him up from its summit, as far as we could reach, towards the roof. He was in his night-shirt, with bare feet and legs; but, availing himself of any coign of vantage that he could find, he actually climbed up the wall of the house by himself. When he reached the roof, he crawled up the coping stones at the side on his knees, and then began to make his way along the ridge towards the chimney; but the pain by this time became too great for human endurance. ' Hang it all,' he cried, ' I can't go on!' and he had to give it up."

The person who possessed the greatest influence, throughout his life, on John Lawrence, was his sister Letitia. She was the eldest of the Lawrence family, and singularly adapted for friend and counsellor to her brothers and sister. She possessed the noble qualities of her famous brothers united to womanly gentleness. Possessing refinement and culture, she had also great discernment. When her five brothers were winning their honours in India, it was to their sister Letitia that they turned for counsel. It was her influence at the turning point of the life of John Lawrence that decided his career in the Indian Civil Service.

In 1827 an old family friend, who had procured appointments for the three elder brothers, Alexander, George, and Henry, in the Indian Army, offered John Lawrence an appointment in the Indian Civil Service. This was a great disappointment to the ardent boy, who had been all his life longing to distinguish himself in the army, as his father had done. "A soldier I was born, and a soldier I will be!" was his passionate exclamation, when the Civil Service was proposed. Well was it for the future history of India that the mild counsels of Letitia Lawrence prevailed with her impetuous brother, and he reluctantly but bravely yielded to her wish, and accepted the offered appointment.

To fit himself for his work he went to the East India College at Haileybury, July 22nd, 1827. There he remained for two years. He gained several prizes, and in the last term the gold medal for law. He valued not the honours for himself. Speaking of his prizes, he would say, "They are Letitia's books; they are all hers; I should not have had one of them but for her. I work with her in my mind; she shall have every one of them." When he passed out of Haileybury College no one prophesied a brilliant future for him; it was his brother Henry who attracted most notice. "He will be Sir Henry Lawrence some day," was the prediction of a friend. No one dreamed of seeing rugged, honest, downright John rise to be Lord Lawrence and the Viceroy of India. Circumstances had yet to prove his mettle.

On the second of September, 1829, John Lawrence, with his brother Henry, sailed from Portsmouth for India. They reached Calcutta February 9th, 1830. There they separated, Henry to join his regiment at Kurnal, a military station north of Delhi, and John to complete his study of the native languages at the College of Fort William. He was ill most of the time during his residence at Fort William. The climate did not agree with him. He disliked India, and longed for home. He often said, afterward, that if £100 per year had been offered him in England, during those dark days, he would have gone straight home.

He worked on, however, and passed the necessary examinations in the native languages. He was now ready for a post. He did not take the usual holiday before setting to work, but started immediately for his appointment at Delhi. The inhabitants of that district were turbulent and warlike, and for that reason John Lawrence chose to begin his work there. He disliked inactivity; the more arduous the task, the better he liked it. He arrived at Delhi, the imperial city of the Mogul empire, early in 1831. He now entered upon the work of the district, which was for thirteen years to be his training school, and twenty-five years later to witness his crowning achievement, when he recaptured it during the Indian Mutiny.

John Lawrence went to Delhi as one of the "assistants" to the Resident-Governor, Thomas Theophilus Metcalfe, a younger brother of Sir Charles. His first appointment was that of "assistant judge, magistrate and collector" of the city and its environs. He remained in this office for four years, working steadily on, with now and then a visit to his brother Henry, who was living at Kurnal, a short distance from Delhi.

In 1834 John Lawrence was transferred from his post at Delhi, to be collector of Paniput, a northern division of the Delhi territory. He was now thrown more upon himself, and rapidly showed his marked individuality by his management of this district. The principal work of a "collector" was the collecting of the land tax, which the natives paid to the Government. But there were a variety of duties besides that. The collector was also the magistrate; he had charge of the police, and to him every question of dispute was brought for decision. He acted as a king over his district. One part of his time was spent in the Cutcherry at the central station where the natives came to have their disputes settled. It was weary work sitting hour after hour thronged by people clamouring to state their grievances, and it required a sharp eye, and a powerful and sagacious mind to discharge such a duty. John Lawrence threw himself entirely into his work. He studied the habits of the natives, gathered them about him in an evening, as he sat in his shirt sleeves smoking, listened to their accounts of the crops, the state of the country, and the latest village news. The people soon learnt that they had over them a man who would enforce obedience. He was not to be trifled with. If the news of a robbery or a murder reached him, he was soon mounted and off with his men, sparing no labour until the culprits were brought to justice. Bad characters held him in wholesome terror, and reformed out of sheer despair at ever being able to perpetrate their bad deeds without the vigilant magistrate bringing them to justice. "*Jan Larens sub junta*" (John Lawrence knows everything) was the verdict of the people. The knotted stick which he carried with him they also called "*Jan Larens*," and believed that it was a magic wand. In favourable weather he made a progress through his dominions, pitching his tent outside the villages where he waited to discharge his magisterial duties. The news soon spread that the "collector" had arrived. The scattered population hurried to present their petitions to him. Sometimes it was a disputed boundary to decide, or a family feud to reconcile, and often the sick to relieve; for he always carried his medicine chest. Nearly half his time was passed in tents, as he travelled about among the people redressing their wrongs. He received comparatively small pay for his labour, but his wants were few as he seldom visited the Europeans, but lived a simple life among the natives. He was thrown so much upon them for society, that when his friends paid him a visit they had great difficulty to understand him, his talk was so interspersed with native words and phrases.

John Lawrence had the charge of the Paniput district for nearly two years. It was in bad order when he came to it, but greatly altered by his vigorous administration. He revised the assessment of the land tax, and succeeded in making the people pay it regularly. Where poverty and discontent had prevailed, order and contentment reigned. He was grieved to leave his work at Paniput, but was ever ready to obey orders. In 1837 he was recalled to Delhi, and shortly afterwards appointed to be joint magistrate, and deputy collector of Gorgaon, the southern division of Delhi.

He had now to deal with a people who were noted as the greatest robbers in Northern India. The difficulties of ruling them was increased by the drought and famine which came upon the district at that time; but his usual methods for maintaining order succeeded.

From Gorgaon he was summoned to Etawa in November, 1838, to act as "settlement officer." There he was brought face to face with the horrors of an Indian famine. The misery and destitution he saw among the people made him feel the necessity of rigid economy in the government

H

departments, in order that money may be forthcoming for the construction of roads, bridges, tanks, and canals, by which such fearful calamities may be avoided. These improvements he carried out when he became Governor of the Punjab. "Give India good roads and canals," he would say, "increase in every way the facilities of communication, and encourage the employment of capital on its resources, and then more will be done to obviate the recurrence of famines than in any other way that can be devised."

During his settlement at Etawa, John Lawrence was prostrated by an attack of jungle fever. His life was in danger, but he determined not to die, and calling for a bottle of Burgundy he drank it off. When the doctor called expecting to find him dead, John Lawrence was sitting at his desk making out his settlement accounts. But his constitution was thoroughly weakened and he was compelled to return to England for three years' rest.

So ends the first stage of John Lawrence's Indian life. It was one of toil and hardship, but an apprenticeship that well fitted him for future events. Many anecdotes are told of him during this period. While collector at Delhi, a chief, residing in a desert part of the country, refused to pay his land tax. John Lawrence with one servant rode off immediately, a distance of thirty miles, to demand payment. He found the village gates shut and barred against him. It was during the hottest part of the season, and he had no food or shelter, but, sending back his man to Delhi for guns, he seated himself under the shade of a babul tree opposite the principal gate. The chief was a little astonished to see his stronghold beleagured by a single man. But John Lawrence sat on through the burning sun until the evening, when a neighbouring chief came and offered to help him. In a short time the rebellious chieftain was forced to submit to pay his land tax and a fine as well. Years afterwards, when John Lawrence was Chief Commissioner of the Punjab, a list of rebel chiefs, sentenced to death, was brought to him. He quickly noticed among the names that of the chief who had helped him twenty years before on the day when he sat outside the closed village; instantly he struck his name from the list and spared his life.

On another occasion an Indian village was in flames and

an old woman, unable to lift her sack of corn, sat upon it determined to perish with it. John Lawrence ever on the alert, came up at the time and quickly carried off the old woman's sack to a place of safety. On returning to it next day, he found he was quite unable to lift it from the ground—such had been his access of strength in an emergency.

When John Lawrence started for India his mother's parting injunction was :—" Don't marry a woman who had not a *good* mother, and don't be too ready to speak your mind. It was the rock on which your father shipwrecked his prospects." The time had now come for him to remember the first part of his mother's advice. During his visit to his friends he determined to select a wife, or "the calamity," as he humorously put it. He had a high ideal of the woman he would like for a wife, but she was not readily found. After visiting his home at Clifton, he spent a fortnight with his sister Letitia (now Mrs. Hayes), at Bath. From there he went into Devonshire, but still his choice was not made. In June, 1840, he visited Ireland and renewed his acquaintance with a charming Irish maiden, whom he had met while visiting his friend Mr. Young, shortly after his return from India. His "search" among the girls was at an end. In Harriette Catherine Hamilton he found the wife he wanted. After a two months' engagement they were married on August 26th, 1841.

Miss Hamilton was the daughter of a clergyman in Donegal. Her life had been passed amongst the wilds of the north of Ireland. She knew little of the world beyond, but she was endowed with those high qualities which rendered her a fit help-meet for John Lawrence. He never regretted the choice he made. In after years, when sitting one evening in his drawing room with his sister Letitia and other members of his family, he found that Mrs. Lawrence had left the room. "Where's mother?" he asked of his daughter. "She's upstairs," replied the girl. Shortly after he put the same question, and received the same answer. Finding that Mrs. Lawrence did not return he made a third inquiry, which led his sister Letitia to exclaim, "Why really John, it would seem as if you could not get on for five minutes without your wife." "That's why I married her," said he.

Mr. and Mrs. Lawrence passed their honeymoon on the continent. While at Naples the news of the first Afghan war reached them. John Lawrence was impatient to return to India and take his part in the struggle that was going on. He hurried back to London to be ready for the start. He was, however, seized with a dangerous illness. The doctors forbade his return to India, but he resolved to run the risk, saying, "If I can't live in India, I must go and die there."

In November, 1842, John Lawrence and his young wife arrived at Bombay. They had an adventurous journey through central India, heard accounts of the war, and the terrible retreat of the army from Cabul. There seemed to be no opening for John Lawrence. Taking the advice of his brother George he went to Delhi in 1843 and received a temporary appointment, and at the end of the following year was made Magistrate and Collector of Delhi in his own right. The manner in which he discharged his duties and the valuable aid he gave during the rising of the Sikhs brought him under the notice of Sir Henry Hardinge, the Governor-General. After the defeat of the Sikhs, and the annexation of the Jullundur Doab, a territory in the Punjab, when a Governor was wanted for the conquered country, "Send me up *John Lawrence*," was the peremptory message of the Governor-General to the Lieutenant-General of the North-West Provinces. Accordingly on March 1st, 1846, John Lawrence was appointed to be ruler of the Jullundur Doab.

Emerging now into public life, he displayed his powers for administration. He inspired his assistants with his own energy; one of them writing at this time says :—

"It seems but yesterday that I first stood before John Lawrence, in April, 1846, at the town of Hoshiarpore, the the capital of a district in the Jullundur Doab. . . . I found him discussing with the Postmaster-General the new lines of postal delivery, and settling with the officer commanding the troops the limits of the cantonments. . . . Seated around the small knot of Europeans were scores of Sikh and Mohammedan landowners, arranging with their new lord the terms of their cash assessment. John Lawrence was full of energy—his coat off, his sleeves turned up above his elbows—and was impressing upon his subjects his principles of a just state demand, and their first elementary ideas of natural equity; for as each man touched the pen, the unlettered token of agreement to their leases, he made them repeat aloud the new trilogue of the British Government:— "Thou shalt not burn thy widow; thou shalt not kill thy daughters; thou shalt not burn alive thy lepers;" and old greybeards, in the families of some of whom there was not a single widow, or a female blood-relative, went away chanting the dogmas of the new Moses, which next year were to be enforced. Here I learnt my first idea of the energetic order and rapid execution which make up the sum total of good administration. . . ."

In addition to the mangement of his own district, John Lawrence acted twice for his brother Henry, whose health gave way, as Resident Governor of Lahore, a most important post.

On March 29th, 1849, after the second Sikh war, Lord Dalhousie, the Governor-General, declared publicly the annexation of the Punjab. The Mogul dynasty was to be deposed, the young Maharajah, Dhuleep Sing, was to receive £50,000 a year. All his territories, together with the crown jewels, including the peerless Koh-i-noor, were to be given up to the British. A board was appointed to govern the new annexation; at the head of it was placed Henry Lawrence, next in rank came his brother John, and the third member was Charles Greville Mansel.

At an early meeting of the Board the priceless Koh-i-noor, laid in a small box beneath many folds of linen, was handed to John Lawrence for safe keeping. He placed it in his waistcoat pocket, and becoming absorbed in business, entirely forgot the treasure. When he dressed for dinner the waistcoat containing it was thrown carelessly on one side. At a subsequent meeting of the Punjab Board Henry Lawrence suggested to his brother the advisability of taking measures to forward the Koh-i-noor to the Queen, whose crown it was to adorn. For a moment John Lawrence was mystified, he had forgotten that it had been placed in his keeping, but suddenly recalling the circumstance, he acceded with perfect composure to his brother's suggestion. Watching his opportunity he quietly quitted the council-room, and hurried home. He enquired eagerly of his man-servant if he had seen a small box which was in his waistcoat pocket, " Yes, Sahib," the man replied, " I found it and put it in one of your boxes." " Bring it here," said the Sahib. The old native accordingly produced it. "Open it," said John Lawrence, "and see what it contains." After removing the fold of linen, the old man said, " There is nothing here, Sahib, but a bit of glass." He was quite unconscious that he held in his hand the diamond which was destined to sparkle, as the most priceless gem, in the crown of England's Queen. John Lawrence drew a sigh of relief when he found the jewel was safe, and lost no time in forwarding it to England. The story is illustrative of the man. He was unaccustomed to the care of jewels, never wore them himself, and was always careless of conventionalities, his mind was so absorbed in his work.

The Punjab Board did not work smoothly. Henry and John Lawrence were very opposite characters. The one was emotional and regardless of expense, the other was stern, practical, and economic. Both had strong wills and hot tempers. It was difficult for them to work harmoniously together. John Lawrence took up the practical part of the administration, while Henry spent much of his time in visiting the different parts of the territory. Each was anxious to work for the public good, but they were drawing in different directions. Henry Lawrence was greatly in sympathy with the Jagheers and native aristocracy, and anxious to uphold them, while John was labouring to reduce the burdens of the lower orders. Finding it impossible to work together, both brothers resigned.

Lord Dalhousie, the Governor-General, determined to abolish the Board, and appoint a Chief Commissioner. To that post John Lawrence was elected, February, 1853. Henry, who had recently been knighted, was appointed Agent at Rajpootana. The parting between the brothers was very painful, each esteemed the other so highly. Sir Henry was so warm-hearted, generous, and impulsive, that all men loved him; John Lawrence had those sterner qualities, which command trust and respect. He inherited from his mother rare financial abilities. It was he who managed Sir Henry's affairs, and enabled him to provide for his wife and children in the event of his death. All his talents were now brought into play as Chief Commissioner of the Punjab.

During the time that he held that office John Lawrence carried out the schemes, already started by the Board, on his own lines. He brought forward measures for the construction of roads, bridges, viaducts, and the excavations of canals. He founded dispensaries and schools. Many barbarous customs were eradicated; the natives learnt to till the soil, and pursue their various avocations in contentment. Fine public buildings were rising up, both civil and military. The jails were improved, and the streets drained and paved. All this was effected in five years, and at the least possible expense.

John Lawrence manifested his discretion in the selection of his subordinate officers. Many of them were daring, reckless even, but the wise Commissioner overlooked trifling faults if he found a man had mettle in him.

One of the last acts of Lord Dalhousie, before his retirement, was to procure a K.C.B. for John Lawrence, whose abilities he so much valued. Lord Canning, the new Governor-General, conferred the honour of knighthood upon the energetic Commissioner of the Punjab soon after he landed in India.

In 1857 came the great crisis in the Government of India —the Mutiny. For some time murmurs of dissatisfaction had been heard among the native troops. They grew louder and louder, until the Sepoys burst out in open revolt at Meerut. There was no master hand to crush it. The mutineers secured Delhi, the imperial city of the Moguls, and enthroned the old King as Emperor of Hindostan.

On the 12th of March, 1857, Sir John Lawrence received the telegram announcing the insurrection at Meerut. He was staying with his wife and family at Rawul Pindi at the time. For weeks he had been suffering with neuralgia, but when that startling telegram arrived he leapt from his bed, regardless of bodily pain, and began to despatch letters and telegrams to all parts. When, later in the day, the news that Delhi was in possession of the mutineers reached him, his labours were redoubled. With his knowledge of the native population, he grasped to its full extent the fact that a vast political revolution had begun, which aimed at securing the Indian empire.

After sending off his wife to Murri, he began his stupendous task of securing the safety of the Punjab, and making it the means of re-taking Delhi. Montgomery, Edwards, and Nicholson were already at work in the province, proving the wisdom of John Lawrence in his selection of them as subordinates, by the manner in which they disarmed such regiments as appeared mutinously inclined.

During this crisis every department turned to John Lawrence for advice. Not only did he issue commands to the civilians, but the highest military authorities acted upon his orders. Robert Nicholson was raised, at his suggestion, from a simple captain to be a Brigadier-General. Well did after events prove the wisdom of this promotion.

John Lawrence now devoted all his energies in raising troops, and pushing them forward to Delhi, A small force was already encamped on the Ridge, a low line of hills outside the city. Within, the mutineers were strong in numbers and well supplied with guns. It was useless to attempt a bombardment of the city until more troops had been raised. Night and day John Lawrence laboured to organize regiments from among the natives whom he could trust as loyal to the British flag. He raised money in the Punjab to supply them with arms and ammunition, and quickly despatched them to swell the army on the Ridge. Disaffection sprang up in his own quarter, but the Sepoys were quickly disarmed, and with the least possible amount of bloodshed. He was ever merciful, and shrank from massacre unless every other means failed. He implored men and money from England, but knew full well that India for the next few months must depend upon her own resources. He it was who held the tangled threads, and unravelled them with a master hand. When the Punjab was drained of every trusted soldier he could send to the army before Delhi, there was this question to consider—suppose the mutineers gain the victory, what then? He had his plan. It was to hand over the Peshawur district territory to the Afghan King, thereby gaining him as a friend and ally in the event of our losing Delhi. This far-seeing policy was highly commended by Prince Albert, when, some years afterwards, Sir John Lawrence went to see the Queen and Prince at Windsor.

For two months John Lawrence worked at raising troops, with only one interval. At the risk of being shot any moment by concealed sepoys, he paid a hasty visit to his wife at Murri. He longed to be assured of her welfare. Finding her safe, he was back again at his work within twenty-fours hours.

Having completed his work at Rawul Pindi he pushed on to Lahore. There in August, 1857, the sad news reached him that his gallant brother Sir Henry had fallen at Lucknow. He burst into tears when the telegram was brought him. This was not the only time when the rugged features of John Lawrence were convulsed with emotion. Beneath his stern demeanour was a heart tender and loving.

Meantime the army before Delhi was preparing for the final attack. Now that the last recruit had arrived from the Punjab, there were only 11,000 men. Inside Delhi was an army of 40,000. The siege train reached the Ridge on the 4th of September. John Lawrence had now completed his work. He had sent regiment after regiment to Delhi, raised from wild tribes which only his power could subdue. So great a terror had the name of *Jan Larens* on the mutineers in Delhi, that they gave up all hope of gaining the victory. thinking that he was with the army on the Ridge. The commanders raised the courage of their men by parading through the streets of Delhi a stalwart fair skinned Kashmeri, whom they declared to the ignorant masses was the redoubtable *Jan Larens*, taken prisoner by them.

The siege began on the 7th of September; by the 12th the four batteries were ready, and began their work of destruction on the walls of Delhi. For forty-eight hours there was one ceaseless roar of artillery. On the morning of the 14th Robert Nicholson, at the head of the first column, as the thunder of the guns ceased, and midst a breathless pause, moved rapidly for the walls. Shouts of exultation, mingled with the cries of the slain, as he triumphantly mounted the first breach. The other columns followed, and soon the whole line of ramparts was in their hands. Upon the Cabul gate waved once more the British flag. The Lahore gate was still held by the enemy. Nicholson waved his sword above his head, called to his men to follow him, and advanced towards it. His noble stature was marked by the mutineers, who thronged every house-top and window. A "brute bullet" pierced his noble heart. He begged to be allowed to remain in the streets until Delhi was taken ; but his comrades carried him away to die in his old quarters on the Ridge. He lived to hear that the object for which he had given his life was gained—Delhi was recaptured.

John Lawrence was at Lahore waiting the result of the conflict. There the news of the fall of Delhi reached him, but there came also the news of Nicholson's death. He burst into tears when he heard it. "We have lost" said he to Neville Chamberlain, "many good and noble soldiers, but none of them to compare to John Nicholson. He was a glorious soldier; it is long before we shall look upon his like again."

Now that the mutiny was quelled, it remained for John Lawrence to restore order to the country. He treated the mutineers with clemency, and stopped, as far as he was able, all spoliation, making a special journey to Delhi for the purpose. He succeeded in protecting the mosques, palaces, and glorious historic buildings from the fury of the soldiers. Working with Sir Colin Campbell, who had arrived with men from England, he proceeded with his pacification policy: such regiments as had been true and loyal received back their arms, the faithful chieftains were rewarded, and the loan which had been raised from the Punjab was paid back with interest. The people returned to their peaceful employments, and the country gradually became tranquil.

India had become the possession of the British nation. It now passed from the East India Company to the Crown. Many well-intentioned people thought that it should be made Christian per force, and all its native customs abolished. Sir John Lawrence strove to consider the rights of the Indian nation. He advocated the reading of the Bible in the schools and colleges, but did not agree with its being forced upon the people. He argued, that grants which had been made to native religions should be continued, that caste should be respected, native holidays observed in the public offices, and native law adhered to as much as possible, except in the matter of polygamy and early betrothals, which he considered socially dangerous.

The Queen highly approved the policy of Sir John Lawrence, especially with regard to native religions. She remarked, that her attachment to her own religion would prevent her from interfering with the religions and customs of the natives of India, which were equally dear to them.

In the beginning of 1859 Sir John Lawrence left for England to take the rest which sixteen years of continuous labour had merited. Lady Lawrence, who had preceeded him, met him at Paris, and they proceeded to London to join their children.

Before leaving India Sir John received a farewell address, signed by the leading natives and Europeans. The East India Company granted him a pension of £2,000 per year in recognition of his great services.

On his arrival in London honours fell fast upon him. He was presented with the freedom of the City, and with an address in Willis's Rooms signed by 8,000 persons, including the leading men of the time. The Universities of Oxford and Cambridge conferred on him the honorary degree of D.C.L. He was invited to Windsor to receive the congratulations of the Queen and Prince Albert, and shortly afterwards was invested with the Order of the Star of India. His appearance at Court caused some anxiety to his friends. They wondered how the rough veteran would conduct himself. The Court *costumier* was in despair; Sir John would pin his numerous honours in the wrong places.

After a tour in Ireland and a visit to his old home at Clifton, now vacant by the death of his parents, he settled in a house in Upper Hyde Park. His sister, Letitia, now a widow, made one of his household. For a few years he enjoyed a happy home-life; romped with his children, played vigorously at croquet, gathered about him his old Anglo-Indian friends, and attended daily at the Indian Office as a member of the newly-formed Indian Board. But there was more work in store for him.

The death of Lord Elgin rendered the office of Viceroy vacant. On the morning of November 30th, 1863, Sir Charles Wood looked in at the Indian Office and told Sir John Lawrence that he was appointed to be Viceroy of India.

It was a sorrowful time for his family. Lady Lawrence felt greater grief at the breaking up of their happy home-life than joy at the honour conferred upon her husband. She thus describes the parting : " He had prayer with us all before he took leave, and a very solemn and impressive meeting it was. At last the parting came. Before parting, we all gathered for the last time round the drawing-room fire, and he made each child say a hymn to him, Bertie, who was little more than two years old, being in his arms. He left home about 7 p.m. to catch the mail train from Charing Cross; and thus, on December, 9th, 1863, closed one of the happiest chapters in our happy lives." On parting with his youngest child Sir John Lawrence burst into tears, saying, "I shall never see Bertie again," meaning that the prattling infant would be grown into a boy, ere he would see him again, and would not be the same Bertie.

Sir John was received in India with great enthusiasm. His first Durbar was held at Lahore, October, 1864. It was a week of universal rejoicing. There was the state dinner at Government House, the opening of the "Lawrence Hall" erected by the Viceroy's friends, and on the eighteenth the grand assembly of the native princes and chiefs. On a plain outside Lahore had been erected a huge canvas palace, around were the tents of 600 chieftians and their followers, besides princes and dignitaries, all assembled to do homage to the new Viceroy. The suspense was at its height on that memorable morning when Sir John Lawrence drove up to the tent. The band struck up, the troops presented arms, the royal salute was fired, and that vast assembly, characterized by all the gorgeousness of eastern splendour, rose to their feet as the Viceroy ascended his throne. Beside him were his old friends of the mutiny, Sir Robert Montgomery, Sir Henry Maine, Sir Donald Macleod, and the various officers of the Punjab. All felt that the honours of that day could have fallen on no worthier man. As the booming of the cannon died away, the rugged veteran, simply clad, but with all his orders on him, rose to address that vast concourse, which only his popularity could have drawn together. He spoke in Hindustani, and in the same simple, earnest manner, as in the days gone by, when in the cool of the evening the village chiefs had gathered round his tent, when he was the collector of Paniput. Now, as then, the verdict was the same, *Jan Larens subjunta* (knows everything). The speech ended, the princes and chiefs came forward and were presented to their ruler.

A few months later, Sir John Lawrence was joined by his wife and two eldest and two youngest daughters. He took up his winter quarters at Calcutta, doing the honours as Viceroy.

For the five years he governed India he laboured to make her peaceful and prosperous. He induced the Government at home to sanction a grand scheme of irrigation. New railways were made, the telegraph system re-organized, splendid barracks erected, and he gave untiring attention to sanitary reform. When he left India there were 19,000 State-aided schools, and out of the 700,000 pupils 54,000 were girls. He reduced taxation, and by his great financial schemes was able to hand over to his successor a country unencumbered by arrears of debt.

His Viceregal Court was pure as Victoria's. The impure, the profane, or the profligate, stood abashed in his presence. On one occasion a lady spoke sneeringly of the Bible at his dinner table. Sir John Lawrence fixed his searching grey eyes upon her and said, " How can you speak like that of God and of God's Book in the presence of these young men." He always treated the native population with the greatest respect. A young officer once spoke of them as " those niggers," in talking to Sir John Lawrence. " I beg your pardon," said the Viceroy, " of what people were you speaking?"

He took great interest in all institutions for promoting the welfare of the people. Hearing of the Moravian Mission, he invited one of the brotherhood to dine at Government House. The missionary arrived dressed like a veritable John the Baptist. The Viceroy's friends were obliged to lend him clothes to fit him to appear at dinner. Sir John Lawrence gave him the place of honour, and encouraged him to speak of the doings of himself and brother missionaries. In the course of his remarks the missionary informed the Viceroy that he and his brethren came out as single men, but in due time applied to the society at home for wives, which, in accordance with the practice of the Moravians, were chosen and sent out. The missionary sent to meet the brides, cunningly married the bonniest himself, taking first choice. " What families have you ?" said the Viceroy, following up the course of events. " Wan has wan (one), wan has two, and wan wants," gravely replied the missionary. This was too much for some young officers present; they burst out into uncontrollable fits of laughter, while

Sir John tried in vain to stop the hilarity and soothe the missionary.

After forty years of Indian service and five years as Viceroy, Sir John Lawrence returned to England. It was an impressive scene when he stood for the last time on the steps of Government House to receive his successor, Lord Mayo. He said to a friend, "It was a proud moment for me when I walked up the steps of this house, feeling as I then did, that without political interest or influence I had been chosen to fill the highest office under the crown, the Viceroy of the Queen. But it will be a happier moment to me wheh I walk down the steps with the feeling that I have tried to do my duty."

He landed in England on the 15th of March, 1869, and settled down with his family at No. 26, Queen's Gate, Kensington. The remaining ten years of his life were passed in the midst of his numerous family. He lived to see many of his sons and daughters happily married, and his grandchildren playing around him.

He was elected Chairman of the first Kensington School Board, and gave untiring labour to its work. Her Majesty conferred a peerage upon him for his Indian services. The title which he selected was, "Lord Lawrence of the Punjab and of Grateley." "Grateley" was an estate left him by his sister, Letitia, who had died during his residence in India as Viceroy. On April 19th, 1869, he delivered his maiden speech in the House of Lords. It was in support of a Bill for limiting a seat on the Indian Council to ten years.

The last few years of his life was saddened by approaching blindness. His vigorous consitution was undermined by forty years of Indian life, but to the last he was active. On the 19th of November, though ill and weak, he insisted on taking his place in the House of Lords. He had prepared a speech, but was too weak to deliver it. He succeeded in saying a few sentences to protest against the repeal of the cotton duties, which he thought to be a needless remission, and made more in the interests of English manufacturers than of India.

The next day, when walking with his lady secretary, Miss Gaster, he felt worn out, and could hardly stagger along. Seeing some strawberries in a shop window, he asked her to buy him some. The price was exorbitant, being 10s. per basket. "Spend 10s. on myself for such a purpose," he said, " I never did such a thing in my life," and walked away without them. Lord Lawrence never begrudged money to others, but gave largely to charities, and was most considerate for the comfort of all connected with him. He was unhappy because the old women, who kept the lodge gates of his country house were exposed to the inclemency of the weather when they came out to open the gates. He ordered knitted woollen bonnets for them, which were rain and frost proof.

But his eventful life was drawing to a close. After his last attempt to speak in the House of Lords, he gradually sank. His family gathered round him, waiting for the end. "Do you know me?" asked his wife. "To the last gasp, my darling," he whispered, and, as she stooped to kiss him, added, "I am so weary," and with those words on his lips, passed away to the land "Where the weary are at rest."

He was buried among the illustrious dead in Westminster Abbey. The simple tombstone of Sir Henry Lawrence, at Lucknow bore in accordance with his request, the inscription : "Here lies Henry Lawrence, who tried to do his duty." A friend suggested that a suitable one for Lord Lawrence's would be, "Here lies John Lawrence, who did his duty to the last."

ROBERT DICK.

ROBERT DICK, the Scottish naturalist, was the son of an excise officer, and was born at the village of Tullibody in Clackmananshire, January, 1811. He received his schooling at the Barony School of his native village. It was kept by a Mr. Macintyre, a very clever man. He soon found in Robert Dick one of his brightest scholars, and was so struck by his ready acquirement of Latin that he advised his father to send him to college to prepare for one of the learned professions.

The schoolmaster's advice might perhaps have been taken, but all hope of a college career for Robert ended at his father's second marriage in 1821. His step-mother blighted his life. She was very cruel to him and his little brothers and sisters. He bore it patiently, but the effects of this cruelty remained with him throughout his life, causing him to be sad and retiring, in fact quite a recluse.

His father removed to Dam's Burn, a hamlet a short distance from Tullibody, when Robert was about ten years old. They lived in a house at the foot of the soft green Ochil Hills; from the back green Robert could easily ascend the heights. Driven from home by his harsh step-mother he found solace in nature. He watched the birds, the insects, and the butterflies; gathered the ferns and the flowers, and the stones under his feet were not passed by unheeded. By a dyke at the back of the house he treasured his collection of felspar, porphyry, and greenstones, and turned them over and over, wondering what made one stone so different from another. His eyes were open to observe. What other boys passed by unnoticed he inquired the why and wherefore of. But these rambles wore out his clothes and his boots, and made his stepmother very angry. To prevent his going out she hid his boots, but the indefatigable young naturalist still climbed the hills and came back with bleeding feet.

At the age of thirteen he was apprenticed to a baker in Tullibody, and thus returned to his native place. He received no wages, only his food. A bed in a small room over the bakehouse was provided for him, He found his life as a baker very uninteresting. "Had my own mother been alive," he would bitterly exclaim, "I should never have been a baker." The only relief to the tedium of the bakehouse was going the rounds with the bread. Tullibody was in the midst of beautiful scenery, and right merrily did the young naturalist set off on his rounds with the basket of bread on his head, for these journeys gave him opportunity to study nature. On his way back he would wander through Menstrie Glen, observing the growth of the plants. He gradually learned to detect their differences, although, as yet, he had learnt nothing from books about their orders, classes, and genera. Each Saturday he returned home to stay until Sunday night. His step-mother would only allow him clean stockings once a fortnight, but his sister walked part of the way back with him to Tullibody and exchanged stockings. She washed and darned his, and had them in readiness for the following Sunday.

In 1826 his father removed to Thurso as supervisor of the excise. Four years later Robert Dick, then twenty years of age, came to Thurso also, and started in business for himself in a little shop in Wilson's Lane, nearly opposite his father's house. There was only one other baker in the place, and for some time he did a good trade. His sister kept his house until her marriage. He then engaged, as a housekeeper, Annie Mackay, a Highland woman, who remained with him throughout his life, devoting herself to his interests in the most faithful manner. In 1828 his father removed to Haddington, and from that time Dick began his solitary, eccentric life in Thurso.

Thurso is situated at the mouth of the Thurso river and at the southern end of Thurso Bay. It is the most northerly town in Great Britain, John o' Groats being a little more to the east. The Thurso river is the first salmon river in Scotland. The sight of the glorious, dashing sea beating round the Caithness cliffs was a great delight to Dick. There was nothing but the boundless ocean between Thurso and the coast of Labrador.

The county of Caithness was at that time one of the bleakest, barest, and most outlandish places in Scotland. Instead of hedges, Caithness flag-stones set on end separated the fields. In the northern parts it was scarcely possible to grow a tree. But to relieve this interior desolation, it had a most glorious coast scenery, Duncansby Head, Dunnet Head, Holborn Head, and Noss Head rise grim and giant-like around the coast skirting the Pentland Firth and North Sea. Caithness was originally peopled by the Scandinavians. These people had little to do with the other parts of Scotland, but found it easier to sail backwards and forwards across the North Sea to trade with Norway and Denmark. As a consequence Caithness remained in a very barbarous state. The country was one desolate morass without roads. There was not a wheel cart in the place before 1780. Goods were carried in cribbans or wicker baskets slung on each side of a pony from a wooden saddle. Six or seven ponies were formed into a file by tying the halter of one to the tail of the other. The driver led the front pony and the others were dragged forward. Caithness owes its improvements to Sir John Sinclair, who, on attaining his majority, employed men to make roads and bridges, and to bring the country into a state of cultivation.

It will be seen from this description that Caithness was not a very promising field for a naturalist. But Robert Dick succeeded in making a most valuable collection of insects, ferns, grasses, and fossils during his wanderings over the county. He became so engrossed in his studies that the good people of Thurso thought there was something "uncanny" about him. What could he want with beetles and grubs? did he put them into his bread? they queried. The boys flocked round the shop to see the "eccentric baker" sally forth. He dressed in a swallow-tail coat with brass buttons, jean trousers, and chimney-pot hat, and wore thick-soled boots with hob-nails in them. For refreshment he carried ship's biscuit, relying on the nearest burn for quenching his thirst, and also for wetting his stockings to give him ease in walking. Thus equipped, when his baking was over, he started on his excursions across the country; the small boys following his footsteps until they grew tired. In this way he travelled the length and breadth of Caithness, scaled its precipitous cliffs, descended its ravines, and made himself thoroughly acquainted with its botany and geology, pursuing his entomological studies at the same time. The distances he walked were very great. He often spent the whole night in searching for some little fern or sprig of heather in the moonlight. On one occasion he went to gather plants on Morven, the great mountain of Caithness, situated thirty-two miles from Thurso. He started at two o'clock in the early morning, and reached it a little before noon. After spending three hours in searching for plants, he returned to Thurso by three o'clock on the following morning. Concluding a description of this journey to his sister, he says, "I reached Morven top at eleven o'clock a.m., and left it at two p.m. It was now mid-day. The river of Berridale runs at the foot of Morven. The best way of getting over it is to wade through it; but what of that? The Highlandman walks best when his feet are wet, and so does the Lowlandman if he could only be persuaded to try. In going to Morven I had waded no fewer than six burns, and at least a score of marshes. My feet had not been dry since seven in the morning. It was all the same to me which way I took. 'Onward!' was the word, and yet the light of day was gone and the moon was up long, long before I gained a civilized road.

"The night became windy and stormy. Tremendous sheets of hailstones and rain impeded my progress, so much so that I thought, as Burns says, that 'the deil had business on his hand,' and that he was determined to finish my course with Morven. But no! In spite of hail, rain, wind, and fire (in fact, I had them all), I got home at three o'clock on Wednesday morning, having walked, with little halt, for about twenty-four hours. I went to bed, slept till seven o'clock, then rose, and went to my work as usual. Sixty miles is a good walk to look at a hill. Oh, those plants, those weary plants!'

During one of his midnight rambles Dick was espied by an energetic gentleman who was on the look out for salmon poachers. Seeing Dick's figure looming in the distance he went down on all fours and crept cautiously along, following the figure as it moved about. At last, seeing it disappear into one of the crevices and stoop down among the ferns, he rushed forward exclaiming, "Now I have caught you poaching!" But Dick turned round composedly and said, "No, Sir, I am not poaching; I am only gathering some specimens of plants," and opening his handkerchief he displayed his treasures. The gentleman was not a little chagrined to find that he had spent two hours crawling on all fours, and instead of a salmon poacher had only found, as he thought, a madman gathering ferns. These midnight rambles were of constant occurrence, as some of the botanical specimens he sought could only be seen at dawn when they opened their delicate leaves to the sun.

Dick lived very much to himself. He was too shy to make friends, and never thought of marriage; for he was wedded to science. His fame soon spread among the townspeople, and anyone who had found an insect, a plant, or a butterfly, went to the baker's shop to display his treasure. Dick was in the habit of rewarding the boys, when they brought him a good specimen, in order to encourage them in their researches.

One of Dick's discoveries among the plants of Caithness was that of the *Hierochloe Borealis*, or Northern Holy Grass. The inhabitants of Norway and Sweden were in the habit of strewing their churches with it, hence its name of Holy Grass. Dick found it by the side of the River Thurso, but was too retiring to make his discovery known. For twenty years he treasured it secretly. It chanced, however, that a young botanist noticed it, when looking over his collection, and at once communicated the fact to the Professor of Botany at Edinburgh University. That gentleman doubted that the plant existed in Great Britain, still more so in Caithness, the most northerly county of Scotland. The celebrated botanist, Don, had asserted that it grew in Britain, but his statement was not accepted by other botanists. The finding of it by Dick now settled the question. In July, 1854, he forwarded a specimen to Professor Balfour of Edinburgh, together with a paper for the Botanical Society, giving full information as to where, and at what season of the year it was to be found in Caithness. The Society returned him a special vote of thanks for his discovery. The Holy Grass has a beautiful spiral stem, and a rich golden seed. When trampled upon it emits a fragrant odour.

Robert Dick's one extravagance was books. All his scanty savings were spent upon them. His flour merchant at Leith bought for him such as he ordered, and forwarded them packed inside the flour bags. Their arrival was eagerly looked forward to; for he was a passionate student. Still he never took for granted what he read in books on scientific subjects until he had verified the facts by his own personal observation.

It had been asserted by eminent geologists that there were no fossil remains to be found in the Scotch Highlands. It was not long before Dick found this statement to be quite incorrect. During one of his botanical excursions in 1835 he discovered the remains of a fossil fish in the slaty rocks of the Caithness Cliffs. He had now the disputed fact before his eyes, and set to work to establish it. Long, long journeys he took over the length and breadth of the county, searching for fossil fish in the boulder clay. In every direction he found them, proving clearly that at one time the whole of Caithness had been under the sea. It had receded, leaving the fish behind embedded in the boulder clay. There they had become hardened into stone. In this way the Caithness flags had been formed, and so to use Dick's words, " Thurso was built of dead fish."

He started out on his geological excursions with his trouser pockets filled with chisels, in one hand a four pound hammer, and in the other a fourteen pound "smiddy fore hammer." In his chimney-pot hat he carried paper and twine. The good people of Thurso began to wonder what new freak the baker had taken. As soon as it became known that the fossils he found were valuable visitors came flocking to Thurso, and the people of the place tried to make a trade out of selling the fossil fish to tourists. When Dick walked abroad the boys dodged his path, and if he threw down a stone there was a rush among them to secure it, thinking that it might be valuable. This sudden awakening of the Thurso people to interest in his movements was a source of much annoyance to him. He had to jealously guard the places where he had seen a fossil, until in the dead of the night, with the help of a strong workman, he could remove the heavy stone to his house, and dig out the precious fossil.

He had a contrivance of his own for polishing his stones.

It consisted of a bench made by placing a flat stone on the top of a cask. On this he trimmed his stones by means of a piece of common saw, which he had fitted with a wooden handle, and some sand and water. He then polished them by rubbing their surfaces together. What is usually done by machinery he did by the strength of his arms.

When exploring the country he always carried his map and marked on it the dip of the strata. He usually found the map incorrect, and was able to rectify it by his own observations. This map of his was full of marks; "stuff," "nonsense," &c., where a loch or a river was indicated, meaning that there was no such thing. Underneath it he wrote, "I have been rambling over Caithness since 1830, and anything more unlike the truth than the above picture I have never seen." A book or a map was never relied on by him until he had proved it to be correct. "Let us have facts, real indisputable facts;" he said "there can be no science without them." When he was told that some scientific men doubted his views he replied, "Why can't they leave their books, and come here and see for themselves." He had a supreme disgust for those gentlemen who wrote about, or drew maps of a country having only studied it from a "gig." His disgust was complete, when towards the close of his life, the newly formed Natural History Society of Thurso, of which he was made an honorary member, made an excursion in "gigs" to Dunnet Hills. "I am very glad," he said, the next day, "that I did not consent to go a gowking to Dunnet Hills. The party went off in gigs single and double; and what they saw in crossing the sands I know not. Certes, no one ever heard of objects in natural history being collected *in gigs.*" To a man who would walk 50 miles, with hardly a halt, to search for a plant, or climb precipitous cliffs with the sea surging round him, that he might unearth a fossil fish, the idea of naturalists journeying in gigs was intolerable.

His geological studies brought him into contact with Hugh Miller, with whom he corresponded for many years, supplying him with most valuable information. "I am a quiet creature," he wrote to Hugh Miller, "and do not like to see myself in print at all." So for years his observations were given to the world through the medium of Miller's writings. "He has robbed himself," said Hugh Miller, "to do me service." But he was content to do so if he could in

any way further science. He was most unselfish in giving
his information, and worked day and night finding fossils and
making sketches of them for his friend. Miller's book,
The Footprints of the Creator, was written chiefly from
Dick's observations, which its author was ever ready to
acknowledge. In the following letter he thus describes to
Hugh Miller his first great find, that of the fossil fish,
Holoptychius, " I never wielded the hammer and chisel until
last spring—March, 1844; and the laying bare of the large
fossil (of which I send you the cast and the remaining fossils)
was one of my first exploits. It was about the vernal equinox.
The wind blew off the land. A merry sea tripped through
the Pentland Firth. The tide was about full. The waves
came dashing in on the rocky shore in long rolling billows,
scattering in spindrift.

" I had laid the large plate bare, and was resting in mute
astonishment at the size of the fossil—for I measured it with
the handle of the hammer and found it fully eighteen
inches in length—when I was roused from my reverie by
the waters dashing at my feet. The tide was now coming
in! What was I to do? To raise it stone and all was im-
possible, and I feared that it might be damaged or taken
away if I left it until next evening. There was no time to
deliberate. The tide was nearly up to the stone. I then
attempted to lift it whole out of its bed, little thinking in my
ignorance of the extremely brittle nature of petrified bones.
Alas! the bone was broken across! I gave a gasp, and cried
'Oh!' But I set to work and lifted the rest out, and put the
whole in my handkerchief. When I reached home they
were a mass of broken débris. I managed, however, to put the
bits together again, and of these I send you the plaster cast.
. . . . I have taken note of what you say, and will
endeavour to comply with your kind suggestion that I
should make further searches. . . . . I have been
along the shore once or twice already, and know of a job or
two—one of them rather promising—a bone, as long as my
finger, is standing out of an impure bituminous limestone,
but what the bone may be can only be known when it is
dug out." . . . .

Hugh Miller paid Dick a visit of a few days, and great
was the delight of these two congenial spirits to wander
about together, examining the rocks and digging out the

precious fossils. The untimely death of his friend deprived Dick of a most sympathetic companion. It was a very great grief to him; but in the year 1853 Charles William Peach, the famous Cornish naturalist, came to live in Wick, the principal fishing town of Caithness, and soon established a friendship with Dick, which somewhat compensated him for the loss of Hugh Miller.

Charles Peach was a coast-guard's man, and while on duty on the Cornish coast had been an ardent naturalist and collector. He had disproved the statement made by geologists that fossil remains did not exist in the Cornish rocks. He was busy finding them at the same time that Dick was making similar discoveries in Caithness. Peach had read about Robert Dick in the writings of Hugh Miller, and on his settlement at Wick took a journey to see him. He found Dick busy in his bakehouse. "I am Charles Peach of Ready Money Cove in Cornwall," said he, "and you are Robert Dick of Pudding Goe." "How are ye?" answered Dick, "Come into the bakehouse." And there these two ardent naturalists began their friendship. Many were the talks and disputations they had as the years went by. Sometimes the disputations rose so high that Annie Mackay, Dick's Highland servant, would say, "Eh, maister, ye're awfu' hard wi' Mr. Peach; he'll never come back again after sic rough usage." But Peach always did find his way back whenever an opportunity occurred.

Dick's bakehouse is well worth a description. It was ornamented with his drawings; for he was a clever draughtsman. Over the fireplace was a figure of the beautiful Greek boy drawing the thorn from his foot. On the side of one of the windows was a well-executed figure of an ape. The two figures met the eye of anyone entering the door in marked contrast. Dick was not a believer in the Darwinian theory of evolution, and when a visitor questioned him on the subject he merely pointed to the two contrasting figures, and said nothing. He thought them a sufficient answer. On the other walls were figures of Egyptian deities, for he had a passion for studying the manners and customs of the Egyptians.

Sir Roderick Murchison was on one occasion admitted, in company with Mr. Peach, into the sanctity of the bakehouse. The conversation turned on maps, and Sir Roderick complained of the badness of the maps which were published of Caithness. To this Dick most heartily agreed, saying, "If you will permit me, I will endeavour to show you a map of Caithness." So taking a few handfuls of flour he moulded a model of the geological structure of Caithness, showing its hills and dales, cliffs and rocks, its watershed, and in fact a complete outline of the county. Mr. Peach said afterwards, "I felt it to be a great privilege, indeed, to be present at the meetings of the baronet and Dick in the bakehouse. It was a treat to me to see the hills and dales, the rocks and cliffs, made up with flour, and a likeness of Caithness moulded in relief by his nimble fingers. He seemed to be familiar with every foot of the country, every hill and dale, every movement and flexure, every fraction and dislocation, and the readiness and ease with which he communicated the information greatly pleased and surprised the renowned geologist; and when he left the place he expressed his delight and astonishment at the amount of information he had received from the wonderful, and comparatively unknown, baker of Thurso."

At the British Association held in Leeds, September, 1858, Sir R. Murchison devoted the greater part of his address to eulogizing Robert Dick. After telling his audience of the scene in the bakehouse, he went on to say: "but this is not half of what I have to tell you of Robert Dick. When I became better acquainted with this distinguished man, and was admitted into his sanctum—which few were permitted to enter—I found there busts of Byron, of Sir W. Scott, and other great poets. I also found there books carefully and beautifully bound, which this man had been able to purchase out of the savings of his single bakery. I also found that Robert Dick was a profound botanist. I found, to my humiliation, that this baker knew infinitely more of botanical science—ay, ten times more—than I did; and that there were only some twenty or thirty British plants that he had not collected. Some he had obtained as presents, some he had purchased, but the greater portion had been accumulated by his own industry in his native county of Caithness. These specimens were all arranged in most beautiful order, with their respective names and habitats; and he is so excellent a botanist that he might well have been a professed ornament of Section D (Zoology and

Botany.) I have mentioned these facts," concluded Sir Roderick, "in order that the audience may deduce a practical application." Mr. Peach forwarded a paper containing a report of Sir Roderick's speech to Dick, and received in reply the following verses; for poetry making was one of Dick's accomplishments.

> "Hammers an' chisels and a',
> Chisels an' fossils an' a',
> Sir Rory's the boy, o' the right sort o' stuff,
> Hurrah! for the hammers sae braw.
>
> "It's good to be breaking a stone,
> The work now is lucky an' braw;
> It's grand to be finding a bone—
> A fish-bone the grandest of a'.
>
> "Hammers an' chisels and a', &c., &c.
>
> "May labour be crowned wi' success—
> May prudence promulgate the story—
> May scoffers grow every day less,
> Till the rocks are a mountain o' glory.
>
> "Hammers an' chisels and a', &c., &c.
>
> "Here's freedom to dig and to learn—
> Here's freedom to think an' to speak,
> There's nane ever grumbled to look at a stone,
> But creatures both stupid an' weak.
>
> "Hammers an' chisels and a'," &c., &c.

Robert Dick now grew suddenly famous. His bakehouse was besieged by visitors anxious to talk with him and see his collection. Thomas Carlyle, the Baroness Burdett Coutts, the Duke of Argyle, and many famous naturalists were among his visitors. The students from the college were frequently coming and going, and to them Dick was ever ready to give free access to his collection, and to impart his stores of knowledge. But newspaper correspondents, or any persons who came out of mere curiosity he would not see.

Although his fame as a naturalist was great, as a baker he was a failure. His bread was excellent, and as a biscuit maker there was not his equal in the place, and he had never neglected his work for his scientific pursuits. But a prejudice had grown up against him among the Thurso people, and they would not buy his bread. They could not understand his ways, thought him "uncanny," and worst of all, he did not attend church. That, in Scotland, was the unpardonable sin. No one could bring a single charge against Dick's moral character; he was kindness itself, and in reality a deeply religious man, but his neighbours could not give him credit for this, because he was careless of the outward observance. Dick had been a regular church goer as a young man, but a sermon from the minister stopped him. One day Dick had met in the street a barber named Geddie, who was a great talker and busybody. "That was a fine sermon o' the minister's yesterday," said Geddie; "Yes," replied Dick, " but he was perhaps a wee thocht indebted to 'Blair's Sermons' and 'Harvey's Meditations.'" "Ay, was he?" said the barber, and away he went to spread Dick's remark far and near. In time it reached the minister's ears. Now Dick was in the habit of taking an early morning walk each Sunday before going to kirk. Not long after the talk with the barber the minister, in retaliation, preached a sermon on Sunday walking, and of going forth in pursuit of science falsely so called, &c. Everybody in the congregation knew that the minister was preaching at the baker. It was too trying to a shy, timid man like Robert Dick to be thus held up to public reproof. He never entered the church again, but held a private service each Sunday morning in his own room instead.

From this cause many of Dick's customers left him. Added to this, there were six rival bakers in Thurso, while at the time he began business there was but one. To complete his ruin, a ship bringing him flour from Leith was wrecked. Through this disaster he lost upwards of £45. This reduced him to bankruptcy. His father had long been dead, and the only relative to whom he could apply for help was his sister. She lent him £20; but it was not enough. There was no other alternative for him but to sell his fossils —the patient and arduous collection of so many years. Mr. John Miller, F.G.S., who was a friend of Dick's, and took great interest in his researches, agreed to buy them for £45. How deeply he felt parting with them may be seen from a letter to his brother-in-law. "Unhappily," he said, " I have now no fossils. I have given them all away. Alas ! how often has my heart beat proudly, when looking over the figures of jaws in Duff's and Dr. Buckland's books, and saying, O yes, these are very fine ; but, humble as I am, I have finer than either! But that is over, and they are all away. They exist only in remembrance, and I never hope to find the like again."

Dick was enabled to keep on his business, but he had a hard struggle to live. Exposure during his long journeys had weakened his frame and brought on rheumatism. Sometimes he could scarcely move his arms. When he felt a little better he would still persevere in his researches. Walking off to Dunnet Cliffs to gather ferns, or else to some of the spots where the Holy Grass grew to gather it for his fellow-botanists; for he had letters from all parts requesting specimens. In return, Dick had a number of things sent him for his herbarium. He laboured hard to make another collection of fossils, but during one of his excursions he was seized with severe illness, from which he never recovered. He lingered for some time, receiving the greatest kindness and sympathy from his numerous friends. Mr. John Miller sent his housekeeper to nurse him and paid his doctor's bill. But all was of no avail, his constitution was thoroughly worn out by his prolonged exposure in the pursuit of science. He died on the 24th of December, 1866.

When it was known in Thurso that the poor baker was dead, all animosity was forgotten, and the people thought only of his blameless, unobtrusive life. There was a public funeral, and every shop and place of business was closed. He was buried in the new cemetery overlooking the banks of boulder clay, on which he had worked so laboriously to dig out the fossil fish, and near to the place where he had first discovered the Holy Grass.

He left behind him 229 books, beautifully bound, and principally relating to scientific subjects. These were sold to pay his debts. His herbarium was made over to the Thurso Scientific Society. It was a wonderful collection, consisting of 200 folios full of botanical specimens. Dick had arranged them with the greatest nicety. Not a single imperfect specimen was admitted. He strove to preserve them as nearly as he could in a state of nature. The grasses and ferns were arranged in their natural curves, and even the tiny hairs on the leaves and stalks were spread out at the correct angle. His entomological collection contained specimens of nearly all the insect tribes to be found in Caithness. He was most persevering in his studies. Of beetles alone he found 256 different specimens in nine months.

He contributed most valuable information to the scientific world, and never hesitated to attack what he knew to be a false statement. Writing to Hugh Miller in 1850, he said, "Nothing is more at fault than the idea sought to be established by Sir Roderick Murchison's section in the front of your volume on the *Old Red Sandstone*, that the general dip of Caithness rocks is all *in one direction*. No such thing! I candidly tell you, my masters must revise their views before I can feel the smallest respect for what they say about Caithness. I cannot resist the evidence of my senses. Take, for instance, the hill of Buckies, which you saw. The dip there is north-east, whereas at Thurso the dip is north-west.

"Of course, I am very far from wishing you to meddle with the findings of men driving along the public road and surveying the country from *gigs!* No. But it is my misfortune to laugh outrageously during my rambles to find the Caithness rocks dipping in every airt* of the compass, whereas it is stated in geological books that they dip only in one."

Robert Dick was one of those men who studied science from pure love of it. His researches never brought him riches. He died in extreme poverty, but he left behind him a name that holds an honoured place among the students of Natural History.

---

* Direction.

ANTHONY TROLLOPE.

ANTHONY TROLLOPE was a man chiefly characterized by marvellous industry. He started his career with few advantages; he was imperfectly educated, depressed by poverty, and without friends, yet, by his astonishing industry and perseverance gained a wide-spread fame as a novelist. A friend once told him "that the surest aid to writing a book was a piece of cobbler's wax on his chair." This maxim he put in practice; nothing was allowed to interfere with the daily task he set for himself. At the close of his life he could boast of being one of the most voluminous writers of his time, although, in addition to literature, he performed the duties of a Post Office official. Social duties were not neglected. He was a genial man, fond of the society of his friends, and an enthusiastic hunter. When old age came upon him, he still strove to follow the hounds, disdaining to take the road, but rode with the younger men over hedges and ditches.

His mother was a wonderful woman, and from her he doubtless received the impetus to a literary career. She did not begin to write until fifty years of age, and from that time supported her family by her pen, continuing to work until she was 76. In 26 years she produced 114 books. Many of them were written under most trying circumstances; her husband was in failing health, poverty pressing upon her, and three children dying with consumption, yet she wrote on steadily and cheerfully. She was at her desk by four o'clock in the morning, in order to do her writing before the daily round of domestic duties pressed upon her.

The youth of Anthony Trollope was a very sad one. His father, though a scholar and a chancery barrister in

Lincoln's Inn, never succeeded in life. Debt was always hanging over him; therefore his children were reared amid all the misery of a vain struggle to keep up appearances. Anthony seems to have suffered more than the others; upon his sensitive nature it weighed heavily.

He was born in the year 1815, at Keppel Street, Russell Square, London. Shortly after his birth he was taken to Harrow, where his father had rented a farm and built a house. When he reached the age of seven he was entered at the Harrow School.

His life at Harrow was a crushing and humiliating one. As a day-boarder, who claimed an entrance to the school because of residence in the parish, he was treated as an inferior by the aristocratic boarders. Awkward in appearance, shabbily clothed, without a coin in his pocket, he received only ridicule and neglect. Timid and sensitive, this treatment weighed down his spirits until he lost all ability to learn. He sat apart, uncared for by teachers and scholars, a woeful picture of boyish misery.

After three years at Harrow he was sent to a private school at Sunbury, and from thence to Winchester. But his experience of school life was bitter at each place. He felt himself inferiorly placed to his fellow-scholars. Writing of his life at Harrow, Mr. Trollope thus expresses himself:—
"I remember well, when I was still the junior boy in the school, Dr. Butler, the head master, stopping me in the street, and asking me, with all the clouds of Jove upon his brow and all the thunder in his voice, whether it was possible that Harrow School was disgraced by so disreputably dirty a little boy as I! Oh, what I felt at that moment! But I could not look my feelings. I do not doubt that I was dirty;—but I think that he was cruel."

In 1827, while Anthony Trollope was at Winchester school, his father's affairs became worse and worse. His mother started to America, taking her son Henry and two young daughters with her. She hoped to be able to establish her son in a business at Cincinnati. Poor Anthony remained behind to share his father's broken fortunes.

If his life was miserable before, it now became doubly wretched. His father had ceased to be a barrister, and had removed to a tumbled down farm-house in Harrow. There he spent his time in writing an ecclesiastical history. Anthony led a solitary life; his father was too engrossed to notice him, and companions he had none. He was sent again to Harrow School, this time under more trying circumstances than formerly. His shabby clothes were rendered worse by the muddy lanes through which he tramped twice a day to school. In this wretched plight he had to take his seat beside the sons of peers and endure their disdain. He profited little by his schooling. At the age of 19 he left Harrow, after an attendance of 12 years, with little knowledge beyond a smattering of Greek and Latin.

Mrs. Trollope had returned from America, and by her writing was able to maintain her husband and family in comfort. In 1834 she left for Belgium, took a house just outside the walls of Bruges, and continued to make books. While there she buried successively her husband and three of her children. Anthony obtained employment as usher in a school at Brussels, but shortly left for London, where he had been offered an appointment in the General Post Office.

In London Anthony Trollope began his struggle for existence. His salary at the Post Office was only £90 per year; on it he had to keep up the appearance of a gentleman. He was not a favourite with the officials and only retained his situation through the intercession of his friend Mr. Clayton Freeling, the Secretary. His defective education was continually showing itself. He strove to do his duty, but circumstances were against him; he was constantly in trouble. On one occasion he had put a private letter containing bank notes on the table of the Secretary, Colonel Maberly. On the Colonel's return to the room, after a brief absence, the letter was missing. He, in angry tones, accused Anthony Trollope of having taken it, as he was the only person who had been in the room besides himself. Trollope indignantly replied that the Colonel must have taken it himself, striking, as he said it, his fist heavily upon a desk on the table. This action sent the contents of an ink bottle on to the face and shirt front of his irritated accuser. A clerk ran to the assistance of his superior and, with a quire of blotting paper, strove to mop up the ink. But the Colonel in his agony hit through the blotting paper at the unoffending stomach of the poor clerk. Just then the Colonel's private secretary entered with the missing letter, and Trollope was allowed to beat a retreat.

In 1841 he went to Ireland as clerk to a Post Office Surveyor. The position was not regarded as an enviable one, but he was glad to leave London. He afterwards looked upon this step as his first success in life. His salary was £100 per year, with 15/- for every day he was from home, and 6d. for every mile he travelled, making in all about £400 per year. He landed at Dublin on the 15th of September, and proceeded to Banagher, on the Shannon, which was to be his head-quarters. From there he took inspecting tours into Connaught and an occasional visit to Dublin.

For about the first time in his life Anthony Trollope gave satisfaction. He did his work well, made a few friends, and bought a hunter. From that time forward hunting was his favourite pastime. He never lost an opportunity to follow the hounds. It was his relaxation amid his busy life as a Post Office Surveyor and as a literary man.

He married in 1844. Twelve months afterwards his first novel, "The Macdermots of Balleycorn," was published. The tale was conceived by him one day when walking with his friend John Merivale. They came upon the ruins of a country house. It was a desolate spot. The avenue was overgrown with weeds and a look of loneliness and neglect apparent all around. As Trollope mused upon the scene the idea of writing a novel struck him; he returned home and wrote the first chapters of "The Macdermots."

The book was not a success, and he received nothing from the publishers. "The Kelleys and the O'Kelleys" was a failure also. His next attempt, "La Véndée," an historical novel, brought him £20. He did not gain anything more by literary work for several years afterwards; still, to be an author, and one of some repute, was his ambition; no amount of disappointment turned him from his purpose.

In the year 1851 Anthony Trollope was sent by the Post Office authorities to travel throughout the southern counties of England to establish good rural posts. The work suited him well. His visits of inspection were often paid on his way to the hunting field. The good people in the hamlets were occasionally startled by seeing a gentleman in a red coat dashing up to their doors, saying, "I am a surveyor of the Post Office, how do you get your letters?" and after making hasty notes of their replies galloping off. For two years he worked hard at this surveying; it resulted in the establishment of a very efficient rural postage. Previously people living in lonely farm-houses and out-of-the-way places had great difficulty in getting their letters delivered.

One midsummer night his journeyings led him to Salisbury. As he wandered round the purlieus of the cathedral the idea of writing a novel on clerical life and the doings of a cathedral city struck him; the result was "The Wardens." The graphic manner in which Mr. Trollope describes the life of a cathedral town has led many people to suppose that he had spent some period of his life amidst such surroundings. He had, however, no intimate acquaintance with the ways of a Close, or the life of the clergy. His "Archdeacon" was said to be life-like, yet at the time he wrote "The Wardens" he had never even spoken to an archdeacon. It was all the result of his vivid imagination and his musings beside Salisbury Cathedral on that midsummer night.

Mr. Trollope liked to repeat favourite characters such as the "Archdeacon" and "Mrs. Proudie." An amusing incident occurred in connection with this habit of his. When in London he passed his mornings at the Athenæum Club. There he might be seen scribbling away in a cosy nook at the end of the long drawing room. One morning two clergymen seated themselves near his retreat and, each having a magazine containing chapters of a tale by Trollope, they fell to criticising. "Here's that 'Archdeacon,'" exclaimed one, "whom we have had in every novel he, has ever written." "And here," said the other, "is the old 'Duke' whom he has talked about until everybody is tired of him. If I could not invent new characters, I would not write novels at all." Then one complained of the repetition of "Mrs. Proudie." Mr. Trollope was unable to contain himself. Springing from his seat, he confronted the astonished clergyman, declared himself the culprit, and, unheeding their profuse apologies, said, "As to 'Mrs. Proudie,' I'll go home and kill her."

In connection with his Post Office duties, Mr. Trollope had to take long railway journeys. To avoid wasting time he prepared a tablet on which he wrote while travelling, much to the amusement of his fellow-passengers, who looked with curious eyes on the absorbed individual in the corner of the carriage incessantly writing,

His first real success was "Barchester Towers," for which he received £100 in advance. From that time his fame was established and he was able to make his own terms with his publishers. Up to the end of 1857 he had only received £55 for the hard work of 10 years.

His industry was marvellous; he did not allow anything to interfere with his book-making. When he began a new book a diary was prepared, divided into weeks, and carried on for the period which he had allowed himself for the work. Each day he entered the number of pages he had completed, so that if he was idle the record of it faced him in his diary and was an incentive to make up for lost time. His usual number of pages per week was 40; occasionally he wrote as many as 112. This was extra work to his regular Post Office duties and had to be done at odd times. During his later years he adopted his mother's method of early rising. He paid his man-servant extra salary to wake him each morning at half-past five. After a cup of coffee he settled to his work. The first half hour was spent in reading what he had written the previous day; the remaining two hours and a half in writing his daily task, at the rate of 250 words per quarter of an hour. His watch lay before him as he wrote. In this way his literary work was completed before breakfast. He used to say that he owed his success to his faithful servant for waking him punctually at half-past five.

Mr. Trollope did not believe in waiting for moments of inspiration. He wrote on day after day, applying himself to his desk as a tradesman might to his business. He finished a novel one day and began another the next; never took time to contemplate, any more than a shoemaker who had finished one pair of boots would have sat down to receive inspiration for making the next. Whether at home or abroad, crossing the Atlantic or in a railway carriage, on he wrote. He prided himself on always having his sheets ready for the publishers, and one or two novels laid by as stock. By following out these methods he achieved pecuniary success, and was able to boast of having written more books than any of his contemporaries. But he did not anticipate that he would live through the fame of his writings after he himself had passed away.

His aim, in his writings, was to paint life naturally ; to show the daily round of commonplace life as it really was. He was actuated by a sincere desire to benefit mankind. Vice was always shown as vice, virtue as virtue ; and he strove above all to make his books pure as well as entertaining.

In 1857, having disposed of the "The Three Clerks," which contained many of his experiences while at the General Post Office, for £250, he started with his wife for a continental tour ; during which he visited his talented mother in Italy. This wonderful old lady had ceased writing herself, and was much gratified to find her son following in her footsteps.

While at Milan Mr. Trollope made use of the newly established telegraph to send a message for beds to the hotel at Verona, whither he was proceeding. When he reached the railway station of that town, a cry arose along the platform for Signor Trollopé. Signifying his identity, he was waited upon by an important looking personage elaborately dressed, and attended by half-a-dozen others equally gay. It was the landlord of the Du Torre hotel. He enquired for the Signor's people. Mr. Trollope, utterly amazed at this imposing reception, pointed modestly to his wife and brother ; he had no retinue. The hotel-keeper looked unutterable things, but proceeded to escort his visitors home. Three carriages, each with a pair of greys, were standing in readiness to take them to the hotel, which was lighted up in quite a gala manner. The same ceremony was observed when they alighted, and during the whole of their stay ; attendants with lighted candles followed them wherever they went. Gradually the affair was explained : the hotel-keeper had never before received a telegram, and was so impressed by it that he imagined the sender must necessarily be a great personsage, and provided for his reception accordingly.

After his return from the continent Mr. Trollope received a commission to go to the West Indies to enquire into the Postal system. His pen was busy during the voyage noting down all he saw. He published on his return "The West Indies and the Spanish Main."

His home had hitherto been in Ireland, but now that his literary fame was rising he longed for the society of men of letters. He applied to the Post Office authorities for an appointment in the south of England. In 1859, having had his request granted, he settled at Waltham Cross, Essex. There he led the life of a country squire, enjoying his favourite sport, and could sometimes boast of having six hunters in his stables. He was within easy distance of London, and for the first time in his life enjoyed the charm of literary society. He numbered among his friends G. H. Lewes, George Eliot, Millais the painter, Thackeray, and many other distinguished authors. He was engaged to write for the *Cornhill Magazine*, then under the editorship of Mr. Thackeray. He wrote for it "Framley Parsonage," for which he received £1,000. Millais illustrated it.

He felt that the popularity he had longed for since those miserable Harrow days, when he sat an outcast and thought how nice it was to be admired, had really come. His income, including his Post Office salary and the proceeds from his literary work, amounted to £4,500 per year. Long and sharp had been the struggle, but at last his efforts were crowned with success; he was accorded the fame he had sighed for in 1843 when he wrote "The Macdermots." He was too shrewd a man not to know that there was something in a name. To test the worth of public opinion he adopted a different style and published anonymously. But his secret was discovered and exposed by a critic before he had time to judge of the result.

In 1867 Mr. Trollope decided to resign his position in the Post Office. For 33 years he had worked hard, and was really attached to his labour; but he wished for freedom and more time to devote to literary work. During all these years he had never allowed his book-making to interfere with his postal work, having conscientious scruples about receiving pay which he had not justly merited. Through his active inspection an efficient rural post had been established throughout the country, the pay of the letter-carriers and sorters was increased, and their hours of labour better regulated. He was also the originator of the pillar boxes.

A short time after Trollope entered the Post Office his uncle asked him, "What destination he would like best for his future life." He replied, "To be a Member of Parliament." His uncle said, with a touch of sarcasm, "That as far as he knew few clerks in the Post Office became M.P.'s." This had long rankled in Mr. Trollope's mind, and now that he had some leisure he determined to contest a Parliamentary seat. In 1868 he became a Liberal candidate for Beverley, in the East Riding of Yorkshire. In company with his fellow-candidate, Mr. Maxwell, eldest son of Lord Herries, he went to spend a fortnight there before the election. A miserable fortnight it was. He had not the gift of oratory, neither did he care to conceal his real views merely for party purposes. The Beverley people cared nothing about his political opinions, but regarded him as an instrument for beating the Conservative candidate. The position was an odious one. He felt as he had done when he attended one of the May Meetings at Exeter Hall to report for a magazine. The first of those tedious sittings was enough; he refused to go through the ordeal again. The election at Beverley went against him, and he determined never to again put up for an M.P.

One of Mr. Trollope's sons had settled in Australia as a sheep farmer. In 1871, accompanied by Mrs. Trollope, he went to visit him. Having resolved to settle in London on his return, he broke up his home at Waltham Cross before setting out. The day after he sailed from Liverpool he began "Lady Anna," and completed it during the voyage of two months. After inspecting the Australian Colonies, he returned home by way of America, and paid a visit to Salt Lake City. Brigham Young was most ungracious to his visitor; he received him on his doorway, without asking him to enter the house. Eyeing Mr. Trollope curiously, he enquired if he were a miner. On receiving an answer in the negative, he asked if he earned his bread. "Yes," said Mr. Trollope. "Oh, then, I know you are a miner," replied Brigham. On being assured that he was not, he pressed his enquiry further, and asked how he earned his bread. "By writing books," said Mr. Trollope. "Oh, then, I am sure you are a miner," replied Brigham Young, and turned on his heel and closed the door.

After his Australian trip Mr. Trollope settled in a house in Montagu Square, London, but he still followed the hounds as perseveringly as when in his country house at Essex. He wrote as assiduously as ever until a few years before his death, when his failing health prevented him from accomplishing quite as much as formerly. In 1877 he visited South Africa and wrote a book on the colony. The following year he went on an expedition to Iceland in the "Mastiff," accomplishing the journey in 16 days. Upon his return he published, "How the Mastiffs went to Iceland."

In 1880 he left London and settled in Harting, a village in Sussex. He became ill with asthma, and sought relief by a visit to the more humid climate of Ireland. His recovery was only temporary; on the 3rd of November, 1882, he was seized with paralysis, and died on the 6th of December, four weeks after his seizure. At the time of his death he had completed a novel, "An Old Man's Darling;" another one, "The Land Leaguers," was unfinished. He left behind him an example of how far it lies within a man's own power to make for himself a name by persistent application to work.

SIR WILLIAM FAIRBAIRN.

SIR WILLIAM FAIRBAIRN belonged to a class of men who came into existence about the middle of last century, the Civil Engineers. Previously the term "engineer" had been applied only to persons in the military profession who had the management of engines, or the artillery of an army. To distinguish themselves from these, the men who devoted their mechanical skill to the designing of roads, bridges, water-works, docks, harbours, mills, and machinery, took the name of Civil Engineers. They defined their profession as, "The art of directing the great sources of power in nature for the use and convenience of man." An older engineering society adopted as its motto a more concise definition, "We conquer by art the difficulties offered by nature."

William Fairbairn was born at Kelso, February 19th, 1789. His father was descended from a respectable class of yeomen, and was a man of intelligence and great integrity of character. His mother was a handsome commanding woman, who could boast of descent from the noble house of Douglas. She was, too, a woman of marvellous industry. She spun the whole of the clothing for her husband and family, as well as the sheets and blankets. For twenty years she did this in addition to the numerous domestic duties which a large family and small means entailed upon her. Her hours of spinning were brightened by the companionship of Mrs. Curl, the aunt of Sir Walter Scott. This lady occupied a part of the house where the Fairbairns lived, and used to bring her spinning-wheel into Mrs. Fairbairn's room to work and chat with her. Young William was an attentive listener to their talk. Often the subject was of the doings of Walter Scott, then an advocate in Edinburgh.

One summer he spent two months in Kelso collecting materials for his "Border Minstrelsy," or, as his aunt said, "foolishly spending his time amongst all the auld wives of the country." During that visit he noticed William Fairbairn as a bright, quick child, and rewarded him for reading aloud.

In the autumn of 1799 the home at Kelso was broken up, and the Fairbairns removed into Rosshire, where Mr. Fairbairn and his brother had taken a farm called the Moy. During the two years spent there William, then a boy of 11 years old, had no instruction whatever. His time was spent in taking charge of his younger brothers and sisters. His first mechanical invention was made at this time in the shape of a little wooden waggon to draw about his young brother 15 months old. From this he proceeded to more complex things; boats, ships, wind and water-mills, which he constructed out of the roughest materials with a knife. Sometimes he had five or six mills working at once.

He had received his first instruction at the day-school of Kelso, and then at the parish school in the same place. During his father's unsettled wanderings he had little instruction beyond a short term at Mallochy school, and three months with an uncle, a schoolmaster of some proficiency. There he learnt arithmetic, book-keeping, and land surveying, and was making considerable progress when it became necessary for him to earn something to help the family at home. In August, 1803, he was sent back to Kelso and obtained work as a mason's boy. In a few days an accident compelled him to give it up.

His father now obtained a situation as steward of a farm belonging to the owners of Percy Main Colliery, North Shields. William, then 14 years old, had work given him at the colliery. Among the "pit lads" he had a very rough time. His Scotch accent and manner made him the subject of much ridicule. He was constantly getting drubbings from some of the noted pugilists of the pit.

On March 24th, 1804, his circumstances changed for the better. He was bound, for seven years, as an apprentice to Mr. John Robinson the millwright, or engineer at the Percy Main Colliery. His wages were to begin at 5s. per week, and increase to 12s. He had now started at a trade which was well suited to him, and soon became passionately fond of it, and fired with an ambition to pursue his education. During the first winter of his apprenticeship he arranged the following course of study for himself:—

Monday evening	...	Arithmetic, mensuration, &c.
Tuesday „	...	Reading, history, and poetry.
Wednesday „	...	Recreation, reading novels and romances.
Thursday „	...	Mathematics.
Friday „	...	Euclid and trigonometry.
Saturday „	...	Recreation, sundries.
Sunday ...	...	Church, Milton, recreation.

His father presented him with a ticket for the North Shields Subscription Library. From this time forward reading, and the acquisition of knowledge, became a passion with him.

An attachment to a young girl, who attended the same place of worship, led him to study the art of composition. In the "Town and Country Magazine" he came upon the correspondence of two lovers, Frederick and Felicia. He read one of Frederick's letters, shut up the book, and then wrote to his beloved in the same polished strain. Great was his mortification when comparing his effusion with the copy to find it inferior in grace of expression. However, he laboured on, and doubtless charmed the heart of the fair one by these his first attempts at composition.

Music was added to his other studies. On an old fiddle, which he had purchased for 2s. 6d., he drove his family to distraction with his scrapings. His progress in the art was not successful, as will be seen from the following anecdote. Some years afterwards when his engineering work took him to Alsace, he was entertained at a great dinner. During the meal he had been expatiating to a Mr. Gros, who spoke a little English, on the nature of home-brewed ale. After dinner Mr. Gros performed on the violin, and seeing Fairbairn interested, asked him to favour the company. Continuing the account, Mr. Fairbairn writes, " I had no alternative but one of my best tunes, the " Keel Row," which the company listened to with amazement, until my career was arrested by Mr. Gros calling out at the pitch of his voice, " Top, top, Monsieur, by gad, dat be home-brewed music."

After working for several years in the millwright's shop, Fairbairn was appointed to the charge of the pumps and

steam engine of Percy Main Colliery. He was heartily
glad to be free from the irksomeness of the workshop, and
delighted at having a place of trust and responsibility. The
duties were very severe. Often in winter time he was
suspended by a rope for seven or eight hours at a stretch
with the water pouring upon him as he examined and
repaired the machinery. But to counterbalance these hard-
ships, the new post gave him leisure time for reading. He
frequented the Shields Library every other night, and during
the day-time walked in the fields with his books. He had
erected a flag-staff over the sheers of the pit. When any-
thing went wrong the flag was hoisted, and Fairbairn
hastened from his meditations in the fields to his engine.

At this time he made the acquaintance of George
Stephenson, who had charge of an engine about two miles
from Percy Main Colliery. In the summer evenings he
walked over and tended the engine for his friend, thus
enabling poor Stephenson to earn a little extra money by
heaving ballast out of the collier vessels. The friendship
between these celebrated men, begun in this way, lasted
through life.

His apprenticeship over, Fairbairn obtained employment
as a millwright—first in Newcastle and then at Bedlington,
where he met his future wife, Dorothy Mar. When the
works on which he was engaged were completed, he deter-
mined to seek his fortune in London.

On December 11th, 1811, he embarked on board a
collier ship at North Shields for the metropolis. Hogg, a
fellow-workman, agreed to accompany him. Fairbairn's first
experience of London was anything but encouraging. The
ship having anchored at Blackwall Reach, he went on shore
with the captain, who had made free with the bottle before
he started, and led his companion into some of the worst
slums. At last Fairbairn refused to follow him any longer,
and asked a watchman to direct him to a house of shelter
for the night. Having procured a comfortable bed, he was
soon sound asleep. Early in the morning he was awakened
by a great noise outside the house. A large and excited
mob had assembled. He soon learnt that during the night
a whole family had been murdered in the house next door.
He quickly made his escape with feelings of thankfulness,
and a very unfavourable impression of London.

He had, however, greater difficulties to face yet. He and his friend Hogg engaged a garret in Duke's Court, St. Martin's Lane, and began their search for work. They only possessed £6 between them. This they carefully portioned out. But, owing to their difficulty in gaining admission into the Millwrights' Society, the days passed by and no work could they get. At the end of a month their money was spent, and they were on the eve of starvation. In desperation they set out to tramp the road to Hertford. They arrived there, wet to the skin, without food, and with only thirteen pence in their pockets. A master millwright to whom they applied for work said they were nice young men, and offered them half-a-crown to assist them on their way. Fairbairn's pride could not tolerate that; he indignantly refused the proffered money, and resumed his journey. Hogg bitterly reproached him for doing so, and was so overcome at their miserable condition that, while passing through the churchyard, he sat down on a tombstone and sobbed. Fairbairn kept up his spirits, and dragged his companion to the outskirts of the town, where he was told that a mill was being built at Cheshunt, and the master was in want of " hands." On they pushed, and to their great joy, obtained work for a fortnight. During that time they met with a friend, who gave them information how to enrol themselves in one of the London Millwrights' Societies. This done, they obtained employment at a Patent Ropery which was being built at Shadwell.

Fairbairn spent two years in London, during which time he subscribed to the Ratcliffe Library, and continued his various studies. At the house of a relative he made the acquaintance of a Mr. Hall, a clergyman, and a writer for the magazines, who introduced him to the Society of Arts, and into the company of some distinguished persons. Mr. Hall was interested in agriculture, and proposed to Fairbairn to join him in constructing a machine for digging by steam power. The machine was exhibited before the Duke of Norfolk, then President of the Society of Arts, but it met with a good deal of opposition. The making of it had cost Fairbairn all his savings—£20—and now that his engagement at the Patent Ropery was ended, he found himself again in very bad circumstances. Mr. Hall was too poor to help him, or even to bear his share of the machine expenses.

Fairbairn was in a destitute state, but obtained an order from a pork-butcher in Tottenham Court Road to make a sausage-machine. This proved a successful undertaking. He was able to meet his debts, and had £7 in hand. After a roving tour through the South of England, he worked for a time at the Phœnix Foundry in Dublin, and finally settled in Manchester, the city which was to witness his marvellous success.

On the 16th of June, 1816, Fairbairn married Dorothy Mar, to whom he had been attached for some time. He had saved a small sum out of his weekly earnings for setting up house. He thus describes their beginning: "We spent several months in that town (Macclesfield), and then removed to Manchester, where I took a small cottage of two rooms, and fitted it up in a style of neatness of which we were both of us justly proud. The first articles of furniture which came into the house were three oil paintings and three mahogany knife-cases, which I bought at a sale. These purchases appeared no better in the eyes of Mrs. Fairbairn than the bargain of the green spectacles, made by Moses in the 'Vicar of Wakefield.' They were articles not for immediate use, but they looked handsome: the first on the walls and the latter on a neat mahogany table. Shortly afterwards the pictures became, and have continued to be, the most favoured articles in the house, and they decorate the walls of my dining room at the present moment."

On the 30th of March, 1817, their first child was born. Mrs. Fairbairn's life was despaired of, and, while she lay in a very critical condition, the nurse accidentally set fire to the bed-curtains; fortunately, Fairbairn was at home. He snatched his wife and child from the burning bed in time to save their lives. The accident and Mrs. Fairbairn's prolonged illness threw the young couple into great straits. It was a hard task to make both ends meet, but they struggled through that trying year without getting into debt beyond the loan of £5 from a friend.

About this time a new bridge was being projected over the River Irwell, which divides Manchester from Salford. Premiums were offered by the authorities for the best designs. Fairbairn, who was then working as a draughts-man with a Mr. Hewes, entered the lists as a competitor, and prepared a design for the intended bridge. Before sending it in he thought it courteous to show it to his master. He soon found, however, that Mr. Hewes was himself offering a design. The rivalry occasioned by this made Fairbairn's position a very uncomfortable one. At the end of the week he gave notice to leave his situation. This was a turning point in his career. He felt how utterly impossible it was for him to rise in the profession as long as he remained the servant of another. For five years he had worked as a journeyman, during which time he had laboured hard to acquire knowledge in the various subjects relating to engineering. He now determined to start business for himself.

In November, 1817, having severed his connection with his old master, he applied at the firm of Messrs. Hulme and Sons, Clayton, near Manchester, for work on his own account. Mr. Hulme gave him the order to construct an iron conservatory. Having prepared the drawing, which was highly approved, Fairbairn looked about for a partner in the undertaking. Mr. James Lillie, an old shopmate, consented to join him. Thus began the firm of Fairbairn and Lillie, manufacturing engineers. But it was not all smooth sailing yet; no sooner was the conservatory commenced, than a disturbance arose over the infringement of a patent, and the work was obliged to be abandoned. Fairbairn found himself again thrown without work and without money. Lillie wanted to retire and give up the venture altogether, but ultimately yielded to Fairbairn's determination to carry on. They hired a miserable shed in the High Street and set up a lathe, which they had made with their own hands. It was turned by their one workman, James Murphy. One or two small orders came in, and were executed so well, that they received an offer from Mr. Murray, a cotton spinner, to make extensive alterations in his factory. Before the contract was made, Mr. Murray expressed a wish to visit their shop and assure himself that they had the necessary means for carrying out the order. Considering their one lathe and miserable shed, the enterprising partners were rather fearful of the visit. "This proposition," says Mr. Fairbairn, "was anything but encouraging, as both of us were aware of the poverty of the land, and the risk we should incur by such an exhibition. There was, however, no alternative; come he would, and immediately on our return we set to work to put the 'house in order' for his reception. On the following day he came punctually to the time, and, after looking round, he observed that there was no approach but through an entry about four feet wide, and that having only one tool we should never be able to execute a work of such magnitude. We earnestly assured him to the contrary; and, having made an agreement with him, we commenced, with glad hearts and willing minds, what we considered our first and best order as men of business. One of the conditions was to execute the alterations without stopping the machinery, or only such portion as we might require for the time being. This we accomplished satisfactorily; and having worked from five in the morning till nine at night, we completed the order within the specified time, and in such a manner as to satisfy Mr. Murray and his friends."

The alteration at Mr. Murray's mill gave Fairbairn an excellent opportunity for studying its machinery. His quick perception discovered many defects, which he at once improved, and with such success that Mr. Murray recommended him to the notice of other cotton spinners. This resulted in fresh orders, and gradually the firm of Fairbairn and Lillie became widely known as enterprising engineers and millwrights, who were able to introduce improved methods in the construction of machinery. At the end of five years they found themselves well established business men, with good works in Mather Street, and with stock and machinery amounting to £5,000 in value. This had all been obtained through persistent work, and by men who had started without a farthing of capital.

In 1824 the firm received an order to construct, on Fairbairn's new principle, the water-wheels at Catrine Cotton Works on the banks of the Ayr. Simultaneously with this came an important order from abroad to erect a mill and water-wheels for Mr. G. Escher, of Zurich. Mr. Fairbairn visited Switzerland, and gave such satisfaction with his improved machinery that an extensive continental trade resulted. "In 1830," writes Mr. Fairbairn, " our stock-book showed a balance of nearly £40,000 in our favour, and left us sufficient capital to enable us to build a foundry, and increase our works in other departments to the extent of giving employment to upwards of 300 hands." At this time Mr. Fairbairn enrolled himself a member of the "Institution of Civil Engineers."

The firm which had carried on so successfully for fifteen years was dissolved in 1832, Mr. Lillie drawing out his capital and leaving Mr. Fairbairn sole proprietor of the Canal Street Works. Thus left to himself he started in a fresh branch of manufacture, viz., iron ship-building and the construction of steam-engines.

The opening of the Liverpool and Manchester Railway gave great alarm to the canal boat proprietors. They felt that this new mode of transit would ruin their trade unless they could find some means of competing with it in swiftness. Mr. Fairbairn was applied to, and constructed a small iron steamer, the "Lord Dundas." It was considered a great success, but did not quite equal the locomotive in speed. Still the canal proprietors welcomed the idea, and orders for iron steam-ships came in so rapidly that Mr. Fairbairn was obliged to open separate works for this branch of the trade. He selected London as being the most important port, and established his new works at Millwall, on the Thames, in 1835. They were continued for thirteen years, during which time upwards of a hundred vessels were made. Among them were vessels for the Admiralty, the East India Company, and iron steam-yachts for the Emperor of Russia and for the King of Denmark.

Mr. Fairbairn took out two patents for improvements in this branch of the trade—one, in 1841, for "Certain improvements in the construction and arrangement of steam-engines," and, in 1846, "An improvement in the mode of driving the screw propeller by the application of a large wheel with internal teeth."

The competition in iron ship-building was very great, and in spite of Mr. Fairbairn's popularity as a mechanical engineer the works at Millwall were a heavy loss. It amounted during the thirteen years they were carried on to £100,000. But this was compensated for by the immense profits accruing from the Manchester works. It was in connection with these that Mr. Fairbairn's great commercial success came. But he was not a man who strove to amass money; he sought rather the popularity of an inventor or originator. Any novel idea he would take up and work out without ever considering its commercial value. In fact, mere money-making was far from his thoughts. It was not until his sons entered into partnership with him that he made a fortune.

The building of locomotives formed an important branch of Mr. Fairbairn's works. They were constructed on Watt's principle with some slight alterations. The tank engine, which does without a tender by carrying the fuel and water on the engine itself, is supposed to have been invented by Mr. Fairbairn.

Boiler-making, too, was undertaken by him, although it had usually been considered a separate trade. When his workmen in this department "struck" in 1837, he resolved to make himself independent of them. With the aid of his foreman, Robert Smith, he constructed the rivetting machine. The patent for it was taken out in February, 1837. Referring to his invention, Mr. Fairbairn says, "The new machine effected a complete revolution in boiler-making and rivetting, and has substituted the rapid noiseless work of compression for the eternal din of the hammer ; besides making the work infinitely superior in quality and strength. The introduction of the rivetting machine gave great facilities for the despatch of business. It fixed, with two men and a boy, as many rivets in one hour as could be done with three men and a boy in a day of 12 hours on the old plan ; and such was the expedition and superior quality of the work, that in less than 12 months the machine made boilers were preferred to those made by hand in every part of the country where they were known."

The alarming number of boiler explosions led Mr. Fairbairn to enquire into the cause of them. He believed that by far the greater part resulted from the imperfect construction of the boilers. Late in life he took out a patent for improvements in their make. He was also instrumental in starting a society for enquiring into the causes of steam-boiler explosions and reporting on them. This inspection proved to be a great check on careless employers. As a consequence the explosions considerably diminished, and great loss of life was prevented.

In 1839 he received an order from the Sultan of Turkey to construct a number of Government works. This occupied him for some years in manufacturing the necessary machinery. At their completion Mr. Fairbairn received from the Sultan a Turkish decoration, set in diamonds, as a mark of his appreciation.

The rapid advance of railways necessitated the erection of bridges. Mr. Fairbairn turned his attention in that direction, and in 1846 took out a patent for making Tubular Bridges. He was engaged, in conjunction with Mr. George Stephenson, in constructing the Tubular Bridge over the Menai Straits. Mr. Fairbairn's tubular bridges became so famous that he was inundated with orders; before 1851, he had erected more than 100 of them.

In 1852 he received the order from the Government to design and construct the mechanical part of the small arms factory at Enfield. About the same time he completed his largest work in mill construction, the great woollen works of Mr. (afterwards Sir Titus) Salt, at Saltaire in Yorkshire. These immense works, covering $6\frac{1}{2}$ acres of ground, were planned entirely by Mr. Fairbairn, excepting the architectural parts.

Mr. Fairbairn's fame as a mechanical engineer was so great that he was consulted from all parts of the world. He visited the court of Prussia, dined with the King, and gave his advice on the construction of a proposed bridge across the Rhine. The Czar of Russia received him, as Mr. Fairbairn expresses it, "like an old school-fellow; shook me cordially by the hand, and listened with great interest to everything I had to say about the bridges." King Oscar of Sweden conferred a high distinction upon him, and during his visit to France in 1854, he had an interview with the Emperor Louis Napoleon, who presented him with a gold snuff-box set with diamonds. He was none the less honoured at the British Court, and had many interesting conversations with the Prince Consort.

The various scientific societies, both at home and abroad, showered their honours upon him. In June, 1850, he was elected a member of the Royal Society, London, and the following year was elected a member of the National Institution of France. For many years he was connected with the Manchester and Philosophical Society, and in 1855 became its President.

Having realized a fortune, Mr. Fairbairn withdrew from

business in December, 1853. But he continued to take the most active interest in all engineering improvements. His literary contributions on the subject are too numerous to mention. He wrote paper after paper, treatise upon treatise, for the reviews and scientific papers. He also published a number of books, the first one being "Remarks on Canal Navigation, illustrative of the advantages of the use of Steam as a Moving Power on Canals." In 1849 he published another important one, "An account of the Construction of the Britannia and Conway Tubular Bridges, with a complete history of their progress."

In 1860 Mr. Fairbairn received the Gold Medal of the Royal Society, and in the following year was made President of the British Association. About the same time the degree of LL.D. was conferred upon him by the Edinburgh University, at the instance of Lord Brougham, the Chancellor The University of Cambridge gave him the honorary degree of D.C.L. in 1869. But the crowning honour of Mr. Fairbairn's life came in 1869, when he had attained his 80th year. Mr. Gladstone announced to him that it was her Majesty's desire to confer upon him the honour of the Baronetage. Sir W. Fairbairn was inundated with congratulations. In replying to one such letter he says, "As regards the name, I liked the old one, 'William Fairbairn of Manchester,' better; I am well known by it, and I fear both my friends and the public will be slow to recognize me by any other, But, be this as it may, I am becoming every day more reconciled to the new title, and 'My Lady' takes to it with more grace and dignity than her husband."

In Manchester Sir W. Fairbairn was greatly loved and honoured for his uprightness of character, and his many works of benevolence. "There's Fairbairn," the people said to each other, as they saw his commanding figure and venerable white head approaching. In taking his daily walk to the Canal Street works, he always crossed the streets at certain parts. He would allow nothing to interfere with his habit. If a friend was with him, he gave him a gentle push into the mud when they came to one of these points in the road and made his usual crossing. He was for many years an active member of Cross Street Chapel, and formed a close friendship with its ministers, the Rev. J. G. Roberts and the Rev. W. Gaskill.

In private life he was exceedingly social. His house, the Polygon, was seldom without visitors. It was his delight to gather round him his family and other congenial spirits in the evenings for long chats, He particularly enjoyed a good story. After his household had retired for the night, he betook himself to his library, and wrote far into the small hours of the morning at some literary work, or in answering the letters of his numerous correspondents. He never neglected to answer any letter that was sent to him. This entailed a great amount of writing, for, besides his numerous friendly and scientific correspondents, everyone who thought he had made a discovery, wrote to "Fairbairn" to ask his advice.

Full of years and full of honour, this remarkable man passed away August 18th, 1874, at Moor Park, Farnham, the house of his daughter, Mrs. Bateman. His funeral took place in Manchester, and was of a most imposing character. The number of people present was estimated at from 50,000 to 70,000. In the following year a statue was erected to his memory in the Town Hall.

Sir W. Fairbairn has left behind him a world-wide fame. It was he who abolished the ancient millwright, and substituted in his place the skilful mechanical engineer. He was one of the founders of the British Association, and to almost every branch of his profession contributed some useful improvements; his most important being in connection with the construction of mills and water-wheels. An eloquent tribute to his memory appeared, shortly after his death, in the "Engineer." "No man, living or dead, has done so much to make mechanical engineering, in two important branches, so nearly perfect. Fairbairn found millwrighting a second-hand trade. He abolished the millwright and introduced the mechanical engineer; and for this achievement alone he would deserve to be honoured. In a word, it is difficult to discover a branch of the art of mechanical engineering to which Fairbairn has not contributed something. His footprints may be found in every path which the engineer can tread, and the sands of time can never efface them."

ROBERT TANNAHILL.

ROBERT TANNAHILL, the weaver-poet, was born at Paisley, on the 3rd of June, 1774. His father had settled in Paisley as a weaver of silk gauze, and had married, in 1762, Janet Pollock, daughter of Matthew Pollock, a small landed proprietor of Boghall, Ayrshire. Robert was their fourth child.

He received a limited education, and at an early age was sent to work at the loom. There he distinguished himself by his perseverence and industry. He strove to cultivate his mind and make up for his defective education.

During his early years he had contributed to the amusement of his companions by his rhymes, and his employment as a weaver did not interfere with his cultivation of the muse. He had, attached to his loom, a rude desk which he could use without rising from his seat. While at work he hummed over old and neglected airs, which it was his delight to collect, and as appropriate verses came into his mind, jotted them down at his desk.

His first poem appeared in one of the Glasgow newspapers ; it was a set of verses in praise of Ferguslie Wood, one of his favourite resorts near Paisley.

His life passed smoothly along until he was twenty-six years of age, when an unsuccessful love affair rendered him melancholy and sad. The lady had received his addresses favourably at first, but in the end jilted him for a wealthier suitor. This so stung his pride that he refused to reconcile himself to his fickle love, even when she professed repentance. This was his only love passage, he remained a bachelor for life.

In the year 1800 he and his brother Hugh removed to Lancashire. His brother settled at Preston, while he fixed his abode at Bolton. After a stay of two years he was summoned to his father's death-bed, and after that parent's decease devoted himself to his widowed mother. He touchingly refers to this in his poem, "The Filial Vow." Throughout his life his attention to his mother was very marked. She was a noble woman; possessed of more than ordinary intelligence. Her early life had been passed with an uncle who was celebrated, in his locality, as a rhymer. Possibly she inspired her son with a love of poetry from the stores of her memory.

After his father's death Tannahill settled down with his mother in Paisley, and continued to work as a weaver. He refused the place of overseer in a manufacturing establishment, as he preferred to remain at an occupation which placed more time at his disposal. He was contented as long as he had a modest sufficiency, and a few congenial friends. In his song, "Though Humble my Lot," he thus expresses his sentiments:—

> "Though humble my lot, not ignoble's my state,
> Let me still be contented though poor;
> What destiny brings, be resigned to my fate,
> Though misfortune should knock at my door.
>
> I care not for honour, preferment, nor wealth,
> Nor the titles that affluence yields,
> While blithely I roam in the hey-day of health,
> 'Midst the charms of my dear native fields."

To the list of his friends was added, about this time, the name of Robert Archibald Smith, a musical composer. Mr. Smith had achieved some fame by his musical ability, and by the manner in which he had overcome the difficulties which beset him. The friends were kindred spirits, and delighted to spend their Saturday afternoons together. In bad weather the time was passed in Smith's rooms in reading and reviewing their compositions; at other times they took long country rambles. During one of these strolls Mr. Smith played a joke upon his friend. Tannahill had a mistaken idea about those above him in social position. He thought that a rich man was naturally cold and unsympathetic; for this reason he avoided the society of the upper classes, and never sought for their patronage. Mr. Smith wishing to dispel this erroneous idea, devised a scheme for introducing him to a family of distinction in the neighbourhood of Paisley. The ladies of the family had engaged Mr. Smith to procure a song suitable for a favourite air—" Lord Balgownie's Favourite." He applied to Tannahill, who wrote for it, "Gloomy Winter's noo awa." The lady was so pleased with it that she expressed a wish to see the author. Mr. Smith, knowing Tannahill's dislike to rich people, determined to entrap him. When the time came for their Saturday afternoon ramble, Mr. Smith told his friend that he had some music to leave at a certain gentleman's house. The poet, unsuspectingly, accompanied him, but remained modestly outside while Smith went it. In a little time, to the great consternation of Tannahill, a lady came forward and invited him by name into the house. He had no alternative but to follow her. She led him to the music room, where, to use Mr. Smith's words, " He sat, as it were, quite petrified." The music, however, banished his uneasiness. He talked with his host until dinner time, when he again showed signs of timidity. Mr. —— insisted that his friends should remain to dinner. Tannahill's misery was complete. Many a rueful glance he cast at his friend, who would not appear to notice his various dumb signs of anxiety to escape. The cheerful meal reassured him, and he became fairly communicative. In after time he dwelt on this visit with pleasure, and it tended to modify his opinion of the upper classes.

The fame of the weaver-poet now began to spread. He was requested to contribute to a leading London magazine. In 1805 he sent to it '· The Braes of Gleniffer," the "Ode to Sincerity," "The Dirge," and "The Portrait of Guilt." Encouraged by the success which these met, he published, in 1807, a collection of poems and songs with the following modest preface:—" The author of the following poems, from a hope that they may possess some little merit, has ventured to publish them ; yet. fully sensible of that blinding partiality with which writers are apt to view their own productions, he offers them to the public with unfeigned diffidence. When the man of taste and discrimination reads them, he will no doubt find many passages that might have been better, but his censures might be qualified with the remembrance that they are the diffusions of an unlettered mechanic, whose hopes, as a poet, extend no farther than to be reckoned respectable among the minor bards of his country." His poems met with a hearty reception. He attained a popularity which had not been accorded to any author since Robert Burns. He had a deep love for nature, and delighted to sing in his native dialect of the charms of fair Scotia. "The Braes of Gleniffer" is about the finest of his songs; the lines thrill with pathos.

> "Then ilk thing around us was blithesome and cheery,
> Then ilk thing around us was bonnie and braw;
> Noo naething is heard but the wind whistling dreary,
> And naething is seen but the wide-spreading snaw.
>
> The trees are a' bare, and the birds mute and dowie,
> They shake the cauld drift frae their wings as they flee,
> And chirp out their plaints, seeming wae for my Johnnie,—
> 'Tis winter wi' them, and 'tis winter with me."

There is very little humour in his writings; the nearest approach to it is in "The Trifler's Sabbath Day." He draws a picture of the various ways in which the "trifler" endeavours to kill time, and pass the weary hours of the Sabbath. Driven to a last extremity he baits the mouse-trap, chases his victim round the floor, and finally,

> "He swims it in a water tub—
> Gets glorious fun till Four."

His songs attained a greater popularity than his poems. He heard them sung in almost every company he entered. Writing to a friend he says: "Perhaps the highest pleasure ever I derived from these things [his songs] has been in hearing, as I walked down the pavement at night, a girl within doors rattling away at some one of them." On another occasion, while taking a solitary walk, his musings were interrupted by the voice of a country girl singing to her companions one of his songs, "We'll meet beside the dusky glen, on yon burn side." This incident formed the subject for Mr. D. W. Stevenson's statue of Tannahill, which was unveiled in his native town of Paisley, October, 1883. The sculptor has represented the gentle poet dressed in the ordinary dress of the beginning of the century. He appears to be making a pause during a walk; one hand hangs carelessly by his coat collar, while the other holds his low-crowned hat. Mingled surprise and pleasure are depicted on the face of the poet in his listening attitude. In bas-relief appear bronze figures of three country girls—one is singing while her companions listen with delight.

In common with all Scotch poets love is one of Tannahill's favourite themes. "Jessie, the Flower of Dunblane" gave rise to many stories regarding the subject of the song. Tourists have frequently been shown the cottage where "Jessie" lived. The poet, however, denied that a real "Jessie" existed, the poem was simply one of the imagination. "Gloomy Winter's noo awa'" is an exquisite song.

> "Gloomy Winter's noo awa',
> Saft the westlan' breezes blaw ;
> 'Mang the birks o' Stanley shaw
>   The mavis sings fu' cheerie, O.
>
> Sweet the craw-flower's early bell
> Decks Gleniffer's dewy dell,
> Blooming like thy bonnie sel',
>   My young, my artless dearie, O.
>
> Come, my lassie, let us stray
> O'er Glenkilloch's sunny brae,
> Blithely spend the gowden day
>   'Midst joys that never weary, O.
>
> Tow'ring o'er the Newton woods
> Lavrocks fan the snaw-white clouds
> Siller soughs, wi' downy buds,
>   Adorn the bank, sae briery, O.
>
> Round the sylvan fairy nooks,
> Feath'ry breckans fringe the rocks ;
> 'Neath the brae the burnie jouks,
>   And ilka thing is cheerie, O
>
> Trees may bud and birds may sing,
> Flowers may bloom, and verdure spring,
> Joy to me they canna bring ,
>   Unless with thee, my dearie, O."

Tannahill had a great passion for collecting old and neglected airs and making verses to suit them. His enthusiasm may be seen in a letter to his friend Mr. Clarke, the band-master of the Argyleshire Militia, and a man of some musical ability. The letter, dated 28th of May, 1808, runs thus :—

"My dear friend, I hope you have been blessed with your usual share of good health since I heard from you. I am now going to beg you, as a very particular favour, that you would send me, as soon as you can, any fine Irish airs, of the singing kind, which you may chance to know. I don't mean any of those already very common, such as "The Lakes of Killarney," "Shannon's Flowery Banks," &c. What makes me so importunate with you is, that if I can accomplish songs worthy of being attached to them, I shall have the pleasure of seeing them printed in, perhaps, the most respectable work of the kind that ever has been published in Britain. Now, dear Jamie, as this is placing me on my very soul's hobby, do try to oblige me. Should you favour me with any, they must be *rale* natives of the dear country, for I believe there are many imitations composed on this side of the water. I am sure I have heard some very pretty Irish airs played as retreats; try to recollect some of them. . . ."

It was to Mr. George Thompson's "Select Melodies" that Tannahill was anxious to contribute. He had some correspondence with Mr. Thompson on the subject and forwarded some of his songs, but they did not meet with approval.

Upon being asked by Mr. Clarke to write an ode for the Burns' Anniversary in Ayr, Tannahill replied:—" My dear friend, there is not a man in the world whom I would wish to oblige before yourself, and I am sorry that I cannot comply with your flattering proposal that I should write an ode for your ensuing anniversary. A few days prior to the receipt of yours, Wylie was chosen for our next year's President, and in a moment of enthusiasm I came under a promise to furnish him with something of that kind for what he calls *his night*. I shall attempt something ; however, I tremble when I think of it. To do justice to the subject would require the abilities of a Campbell, or a Scott, and I almost despair of being able to produce anything half so good as what has already been, by different hands, given to the public; besides I know that the society are determined to have a blazing account of our meeting sent to some of the newspapers ; of course, my rhymes are designed to be attached as a train to the dazzling luminary, or as a *lang* wigle-waglin' tail to a callant's dragon [boy's kite]. . . ."

The ode written for the anniversary showed his great appreciation of Burns; the last verse runs thus :—

> "Alas! our blest, our dearest Bard,
> How poor, how great was his reward;
> Unaided he has fix'd his name,
> Immortal, in the rolls of fame.
>   Yet who can hear without a tear
> What sorrows wrung his manly breast;
> To see his little helpless filial band,
> Imploring succour from a father's hand,
>   And there no succour near?
> Himself the while with sick'ning woes opprest,
> Fast hast'ning on to where the weary rest;
> For this let Scotia's bitter tears atone,
> She reck'd not half his worth till he was gone."

At the beginning of the year 1810 Tannahill became very gloomy and despondent. His weak bodily health aggravated this. Several harsh criticisms on his poems preyed upon his mind and deepened his melancholy. He determined to try and establish his reputation as a poet by publishing his songs set to the airs which he had laboured to collect. His friend Mr. Smith, arranged them with a pianoforte accompaniment. This new collection was offered to Mr. Constable, the eminent publisher. That gentleman was from home at the time, and, as he had many new works on hand, poor Tannahill's manuscript was returned. This was a heavy blow; it added greatly to his depression.

He received about this time (1810) one tribute to his genius in a visit from his brother poet, James Hogg, the Ettrick Shepherd. The two friends spent only a short time together, but it was balm to Tannahill's wounded spirit. He accompanied the "Shepherd" on foot half way to Glasgow. Bidding him adieu, he grasped his hand, and with tears in his eyes, said: "Farewell! we shall never meet again! Farewell! I shall never see you more!"

Writing to a friend at this time, he thus describes his state of mind :—

"I am an ungrateful wretch in not writing to you before to-day. My conscience has been upbraiding me these ten days past for delaying it. I hope this will find you and your two Annie's as well as I wish you. My spirits have been as dull and cheerless as winter's gloomiest days. . . . . What has the world to do with, or who cares (take the mass of mankind), for the feelings of others? Am I right? Happiness attend you.

"R. TANNAHILL."

One painful feature of his melancholy was that he imagined his best friends were wishing to injure him. He also felt a jealous fear of his claims to genius being disputed.

While in this unhappy state he paid a visit to his friend, Mr. Borland, who thought that his mind was affected, and brought him back to Paisley. On the night of his return he went to bed apparently more tranquil than usual. In a short time it was found that he had stolen out. His friends searched all night until the dawn, when they found his coat lying by the side of a stream. This confirmed their worst fears; the unhappy Tannahill had drowned himself in despair. His death occurred on the 17th of May, 1810; he had only reached his 36th year. His mother remained to mourn his loss.

Tannahill was chiefly characterized by a beautiful spirit of gentleness. His devotion to his mother has already been referred to, and the same kindness of behaviour pervaded his intercourse with his friends. He was sober and frugal, but could enjoy conviviality within bounds. Writing to a friend he says:—"A social night passed in moderation is life to me; but the roar of inebriation I never could, nor never shall be able to bear."

For many years there was not even a stone to mark the poet's grave; but, owing to the exertions of Dr. Daniel Richmond and other gentlemen, a granite obelisk was erected in 1866 in the West Relief Churchyard, Paisley. Tablets have since been placed to mark the house where he was born, also his residence and workshop. The last tribute to his memory was the statue already referred to. Paisley has done well in honouring one who by his simple lyrics has touched the hearts of his countrymen, and inspired them with sympathy for all that is good and true. Not one coarse word or expression marred his poems. His mind was simple and pure. Though his life was brief and sad, it was not in vain. His words still live.

JAMES GARFIELD.

JAMES GARFIELD was born in a log cabin in the backwoods of America, on the 19th of November, 1831. His parents were pioneers, cultivating their little plot of land in the woods of Ohio for a livelihood. He lost his father when only 18 months old, and was, with his brother and two sisters, left to the care of his mother. "I have planted four saplings in these woods; I must now leave them to your care," were the dying words of that father to the wife he was leaving to battle her way in that desolate region. Well did Mrs. Garfield fulfil her trust. With her own hands she laboured on the farm—sowing corn, making the fences, and tending everything with only the help of her eldest boy Thomas, a lad of nine years old. When the corn grew scarce she stinted herself to live on one meal a day, so that her little ones might have plenty.

Placed in such circumstances James Garfield had very few advantages in his early days, but the influence of that brave mother, united to the spirit of self-dependence, engendered by having to rely upon his own efforts, more than compensated for the loss of social advantages, and made him the hard worker, the brilliant scholar, the intrepid soldier, and the wise governor—he eventually became.

When four years old he was taken to school by his sister, who carried him on her back over the three miles to the school-house, because he had no shoes, and his mother could not afford to buy him a pair. He was a bright little fellow, and soon learnt to read. "Yes mother," said he, "I have heard it," was his remark when he spelled out in his first book—"The rain came pattering on the roof." From that time he understood that words expressed thoughts, and books contained words. His ambition was fired by his teacher telling him that if he learnt well he might grow up and be a general. But school life was not all smooth sailing to him ; he could not sit still. His bright inquisitive eye was ever roaming from his lesson book. He wished to be obedient, and he tried, but only to transgress again. His teacher complained to Mrs. Garfield, " Oh James," was all his mother said, but it went to the little fellow's heart, and laying his head on her lap he sobbed out—" I *will* be a good boy ; I *mean* to be a good boy ; I *will* sit still." The next day found James as usual, eyeing everything in the school. The teacher having had his eyes opened by Mrs. Garfield saying that perhaps he could not sit still, wisely left him alone. From that day there was not a brighter scholar in the school than James Garfield. His own lessons were always perfect, and he would often repeat what he had heard the older scholars reciting. He acquired a wonderful amount of information, for nothing escaped his watchful eye.

This restless habit attended him throughout his life. On one occasion when sleeping after a terrible battle, he kicked off his bed clothing as he used to do when a child. " Tom, cover me up," he murmured. An officer pulled the blanket over him, awakening him in the act. When told what he had said, he turned over and wept, for his thoughts travelled back to the days of his childhood in the little log-house in the woods of Ohio, and the kindness of his good brother Thomas.

When he was eight years old James Garfield gave up regular schooling in order to assist his brother with the farm. He took lessons, however, during the winter months. His bright lively disposition made him a favourite with the neighbours, and he delighted to listen to their conversation when they grouped round the fire in an evening. His mother belonged to a sect called the " Disciples ;" members of it were constant visitors at her house. James would listen to their talk on politics and religion. The rite of adult baptism was a favourite theme with them ; between this and the virtues of Whigs and Tories the boy got rather confused. " Jimmy, what are you, Democrat or Whig ?" asked a sportive neighbour. " I'm Whig ; but I'm not *baptized*," gravely answered James.

His leading characteristic was a determination never to be beaten. " Can't " was a word he did not understand ;

"I can" was ever on his tongue. Mr. Thayer, his biographer, tells a humorous story to illustrate this. He was after hens' eggs in the barn, with his playmate, Edward Mapes. It was just about the time when he was eight years old, perhaps a little older. Edwin found a pullet's egg, rather smaller than they usually discovered.

"Isn't that cunning?" said Edwin, holding up the egg.

"I can swaller that," was James's prompt answer.

"Whole?"

"Yes, whole."

"You can't do it."

"I *can* do it."

"I dare you to swaller it," continued Edwin, eager to see the experiment tried.

"Not much to dare me to," responded James. "Here it goes;" and into his mouth the egg went, proving larger than he anticipated, or else his throat was smaller, for it would not go down at his bidding.

"No use, Jim," exclaimed Edwin, laughing outright over his failure. "This egg is small, but it won't fit your throat."

"It's going down, yet," said James, resolutely, and the second time the egg was thrust into his mouth.

"Shell and all, I s'pose," remarked Edwin. "S'pose it should stick in your crop, you'd be in a pretty fix."

"But it won't stick in my crop," replied James; "it's goin' down. I undertook to swaller it and I'm goin' to."

The egg broke in his mouth, when he almost unconsciously brought his teeth together, making a very disagreeable mash of shell and meat. It was altogether too much of a good thing, and proved rather a nauseating dose. His stomach heaved, his face scowled, and Edwin roared; still James held to the egg, and made for the house as fast as his nimble limbs could take him, Edwin following after to learn what next. Rushing into the house, James seized a piece of bread, thrust it into his mouth, chewed it up with the dilapidated egg, and swallowed the whole together.

"There!" he exclaimed; "it's done!"

After a few years at farming he became filled with a restless longing for the sea. He obtained a rather unwilling consent from his mother, and set out to seek employment on a Lake Erie vessel. The first captain he applied to for a berth completely scared him by his profane language; but eventually he engaged himself as mule-driver to a canal boat. The captain of the boat was his cousin, who expressed great surprise that a lad of James's abilities should take up with such employment. It was not to last for long; his work on the tow-path was brought to an end by an attack of ague, which compelled him to return home. During his illness he resolved, when he had recovered, to devote himself to learning. He had made trials of several trades, and none suited his tastes. Before going on to the tow-path he had worked at carpentering, and had served some time with a black-salter, always gaining the confidence of his employers by his industry and obliging manners. But now the turning-point of his life had come. Through the advice of Mr. Bates, a young teacher who visited him, he resolved to enter Geauga Seminary, a Free-will Baptist institution.

He was accompanied to the seminary by his two cousins. They set out loaded with their provisions and cooking utensils, as they intended to hire a room and board themselves for the sake of cheapness. The appearance of James when he presented himself at the seminary is thus described:—

"He was shabbily clad in coarse satinet trousers, far outgrown, and reaching only half way down the tops of his cowhide boots; a waistcoat much too short, and a threadbare coat, whose sleeves went only a little below the elbows. Surmounting the whole was a coarse, slouched hat, much the worse for wear; and as the lad removed it, he displayed a heavy shock of unkempt yellow hair, that fell half way down his shoulders."

Rigid economy was the practice of James Garfield; for some time he lived on a milk diet to enable him to pay his school expenses. He also did carpentering in odd hours, and so managed to pay his way without appealing to his mother for help.

Amongst his fellow-students he was known as an indefatigable worker. He did everything with a will and a determination which overcame all obstacles. At the head of his classes, and as the steady workman in the carpenter's shop, he drew universal respect. His companions felt no jealousy at his success because they knew how perseveringly he worked. The frank kindliness of his disposition won all hearts. He was the best speaker in the school debating society, studying up each subject thoroughly, so that he could speak with ease and confidence.

During the first vacation he busied himself to build his mother a frame barn in place of the old log one. That finished, he worked for a farmer during harvest time, and so earned money to pay all debts and buy a new suit of clothes; but he had only a solitary ninepence in his pocket when he returned to the seminary. It did not stay there long, for on the following Sunday, when the contribution box came round, in went his ninepence.

He now, applied himself more vigorously than ever to his studies, in the hope that he would be able to teach school during the next vacation. The principal of the seminary encouraged him in the idea, saying: "You will govern a school well, I think, without much trouble. A young man who is popular with associates in study usually makes a good teacher." His scholarship was well established by the end of the term. After paying all his bills with the money he had earned in the carpenter's shop he had seven dollars left.

Hastening home he began to look out for a school. He found it wearisome work. Two days he walked from place to place, but without success. He returned home weary and discouraged. The next morning he was roused from his sleep by hearing a voice under his window utter the magic word "school." In a moment he was up, and eagerly enquiring from his mother who was talking to her. It was a man enquiring for a teacher for the school at the Ledge. James Garfield accepted the post with alacrity, and started to it at once. The school was the most unruly one in the district, but he determined to bring it into order. The boys learnt to respect him, and at the close of the term both parents and pupils were unanimous in saying that "he was the best teacher they had ever had." He went amongst the scholars as "Jim," but left the school as "Mr. Garfield."

After another successful term at the seminary, he engaged to teach the school at Warrensville during vacation. It was a more advanced school than his former one. He was paid sixteen dollars a month. In order to teach an advanced pupil geometry he bought a text book and studied it himself, keeping well in advance of his pupil, who never suspected that his ready teacher had only just begun the study. In after years, when addressing a public audience, he said : " A young man should be equal to more than the task before him ; he should possess reserved power." James Garfield was always equal to an emergency.

During his third term at Geauga Seminary a Miss Lucretia Rudolph joined the classes ; she was the first young lady who attracted James Garfield, and eventually became his wife.

His fame as an orator was rapidly rising. From the addresses he delivered at the " Disciples " meetings everyone prophesied that he would become a great preacher. At the end of the session he was requested to make an oration at the annual exhibition. It would be his last effort at the Institution, and he laboured hard to make it a success. He was rewarded by the plaudits of his listeners, who were amazed to hear such eloquence from the lips of a raw youth.

Still bent on acquiring knowledge, James Garfield decided to enter the Eclectic Institute, in order to prepare himself for college. Before going he yielded to his mother's persuasion to accompany her on a visit to some relatives living at Zanesville. The journey proved an instructive one ; for the first time he rode in the railway cars, and at Columbus saw the Legislature in session. Little did he think, as he gazed upon that assembly, that he was destined to hold the proudest place among them. When he expressed to his mother the benefit he had derived from seeing these sights, she wisely replied, " It does boys, who think much, good to see things which set them to thinking."

He obtained employment, during his visit to Zanesville, to teach the school at Harrison, receiving twelve dollars a month pay. At the end of three months he returned home with his mother, and began his preparations for going to the Eclectic Institution at Hiram.

It was the last day of August, 1851, when James Garfield reached Hiram, and presented himself before the Board of Trustees for admission into the Institution. He explained his poor circumstances, and applied for the post of janitor to enable him to earn money to pay his classes. The duties of a janitor consisted in ringing the bells and sweeping the floors. "How do we know that you will perform your work well?" asked one of the trustees." "Try me for a fortnight," replied James, " and if it is not done to your satisfaction I will retire without a word." The first bell had to be rung at 5 o'clock in the morning ; on the mark precisely was James Garfield's rule, and he never deviated from it during the time that he filled the post of bell-ringer. He swept the floors just as conscientiously, never losing caste among his fellow-students, because poverty compelled him to earn money in this menial way. He dignified the office by his own high character.

At the end of the first year he ceased to be janitor and became assistant teacher of the English department and of ancient languages. We thus find him working hard as teacher, student, and carpenter, for he had still to support himself by manual labour.

The esteem in which he was held in the Institute is shown by a conversation which took place regarding him between Miss Booth, who was studying at the Institute, and the Principal.

"He is the most remarkable young man I ever met," said Miss Booth; "there must be a grand future before him."

" Truly, if he does not fall out of the way," answered the Principal.

"I scarcely thought that were possible when I spoke. His Christian purpose is one of the remarkable things about him. His talents, work, everything, appear to be subject to this Christian aim. I feel sure that he will make a power in the world."

His three years at Hiram were a brilliant success. At the end of the time he was fit to enter college two years in advance. He had mastered in three years the work of six. Four years was the usual time taken for the preparatory studies for college ; he had mastered that together with two years of college studies in advance, besides earning money for his expenses—first by janitor work, and then by teaching and carpentering.

Before he left college he had become engaged to Miss Lucretia Rudolph, the young lady who attracted his attention at Geauga Seminary, and who was a pupil in his

Greek class at Hiram. He was 22 at the time of his engagement and the young lady 21.

His oratorical powers became widely known during his residence at Hiram. One evening he was on the platform of the weekly prayer meeting along with the pastor of the "Disciples" church, Father Bentley, when a messenger came to ask him to go at once to address a political meeting. As he passed down the aisle Father Bentley called out, "James, don't go!" then suddenly altering his mind, he said to the congregation: "Never mind, let him go; that boy will yet be President of the United States."

At the close of the summer term he presented himself for admission to Williams College. His appearance is thus described: "He was a tall, awkward youth, with a great shock of light hair rising nearly erect from a broad, high forehead, and an open, kindly, and thoughtful face, which showed no trace of his long struggle with poverty and privation. His dress was thoroughly western and very poor at that." For these things he cared little; his aim was to get an education. His brother Thomas lent him the money to meet his college expenses, so that he was able to dispense with manual labour and devote himself entirely to study. He would not accept the loan, however, until he had insured his life and thus secured a sum of money to his brother in case he should die before he was able to repay him.

His college career was a brilliant one. At the end of his course he graduated with highest honours, and left with the praises of masters and pupils. During the time spent in college he had been able to gratify his love of reading from the rich stores of the college library. As a debater and orator he was unrivalled. On one occasion he startled his companions by the eloquence of his address. It was at the time when the news reached Williams College of the dastardly attack of Brooks upon Charles Summers. Preston Brooks, of South Carolina, was enraged against Charles Summers for his attacks on slavery. Assisted by some southern ruffians he beat him with a heavy cane as he sat at his desk in the United States Senate, and almost succeeded in killing him. An indignation meeting was held amongst the students. James Garfield made a most powerful speech. His companions listened breathlessly as he poured forth his torrent of eloquence in defence of the slaves. As he concluded, applause loud and long rang through the building. "The uncompromising foe to slavery," exclaimed one of his admirers.

He graduated in 1856, and received many flattering offers of appointments. Before leaving Hiram he had promised to return as professor when his college course was ended; therefore, putting aside all more advantageous offers, he became Teacher of Ancient Languages and of Literature at Hiram Institute for a salary of 800 dollars a year.

He was welcomed back with great enthusiasm. At the end of the first year he was placed at the head of the Institution as "Chairman of the Board of Instructors," and one year later was made Principal. On the 11th of November, 1858, two years after settling at Hiram, he married Miss Rudolph.

Mindful of his own early struggles, he was ever on the alert to discern ability in young men and help them forward. One of his favourite occupations was "boy capturing." Often he was pained to see promising youths taken from school just when they were beginning to develop into scholars. He took great trouble to "re-capture" such boys by talking to their parents and persuading them to study their son's welfare and allow them to continue at the Institute. When want of money was made the objection, he would talk to the boys themselves, show them how they might earn money out of school hours, as he had done, and so dispense with help from their parents. All his pupils admired and loved him; one of them has said:—
"A bow of recognition or a single word f om him was to me an inspiration."

His lectures, which he delivered on a variety of topics, were eagerly listened to. An extract from one on "The Turning-Point of Life," will illustrate his high teaching:—
"The comb of the roof at the court house at Ravenna (capital of Portage County, of which Hiram was a town) divides the drops of rain, sending those that fall on the south side to the Gulf of Mexico, and those on the opposite side into the Gulf of St. Lawrence; so that a mere breath of air, or the flutter of a bird's wing, may determine their destiny. It is so with your lives, my young friends. A passing event, perhaps of trifling importance in your view, the choice of a book or companion, a stirring thought, a

right resolve, the associations of an hour, may prove the turning-point of your lives."

He would never pass by anything without understanding it, and tried to instil the same habit of observation into his pupils. Sometimes, in the midst of giving a lesson, he would break out with a sudden interrogation, such as: "How many windows are there in this building?" "How many boot-scrapers are there at the doors?" Once, when walking with a friend, Mr. Garfield suddenly darted down a cellar, over the door-way of which was the sign, "Saws and Files." "I think this fellow is cutting files," said he, on hearing a clinking sound, "and I have never seen a file cut." So he spent ten minutes there, and found out all about the process.

Mr. Garfield's influence as a Christian was very great. He frequently preached at the "Disciples" Church in Hiram, and was in request at other towns both as a preacher and as a ecturer. On one occasion he distinguished himself in a debate with Alphonso Hart on the slavery question. The debate took place in the "Disciples" Meeting-house. Crowds flocked to hear. Mr. Garfield entirely discomfited his opponent amidst the applause of his fellow-citizens.

In 1859 the faculty of Williams' College honoured him by inviting him to give the master's oration on Commencement Day. A warm welcome awaited him, and his oration created universal delight. On his way home he was met by a delegation of citizens, who asked him to become a candidate for the office of State Senator. In 1860 he was elected by a large majority, and for seventeen years served his country as a faithful legislator, never swerving from the path of right and honour.

His remarkable powers were destined to be displayed in yet another field. In 1861 the war broke out between the North and South States. The Southern States had formed themselves into a Confederacy for the purpose of separating from the North, in order that slavery might become perpetual. The Northern States joined together to put down the infamous traffic. James Garfield was quickly pressed into their service. As a soldier he displayed remarkable courage and foresight. The men under his command were among the best drilled in the army. If there was danger to face he was ever to the front. On one occasion it was necessary for General Thomas to be informed of the disaster which had befallen General Rosecrans at the battle of Chickamauga, in order that he might meet the rebel leader, General Longstreet, victoriously. Garfield volunteered to take the fearful ride. "As you will General," said Rosecrans, and, taking Garfield by the hand, he added, "We may not meet again; good-bye; God bless you!" General Garfield set out upon this perilous journey, accompanied by Captain Gaw and two orderlies to guide the way. To avoid the enemy they had to make a wide detour, which led them through eight miles of tangled forest. On they rode until a shower of bullets warned them that the enemy was at hand. They had ridden into an ambuscade of skirmishers and sharpshooters. The balls fell fast around them, laying the two orderlies lifeless, wounding one horse and killing the other. Garfield had a cotton field to pass and a hill to climb before he could descend into the valley and be safe from the shots. It was an awful moment; but, putting his lips firmly together, he said to himself, "Now is your time; be a man, Jim Garfield," and started full gallop across the cotton field, riding zigzag to escape the bullets which showered around him. The cotton field passed, he had still to ride up an incline of one hundred yards before he could pass the crest and be in safety. As he rode up the hill, tacking from side to side, another volley was fired, and his horse was wounded, but he passed the summit safely. In the valley General Dan McCook met him, saying, "My God! Garfield, I thought you were killed certain. How you have escaped is a miracle." He had still four miles to ride before he reached General Thomas. Pushing forward at a breakneck pace he was soon in sight of him, and in a few minutes more was at his side unscathed, but his noble horse fell dead. This terrible ride of General Garfield saved the army of the Cumberland from disaster.

The first victorious battle that James Garfield fought was that of Middle Creek. He had a body of the Hiram students under him, whom he inspired with his own courage. When President Lincoln heard of the glorious victory, he turned to a distinguished officer, who was present, and said, "Why did Garfield, in two weeks, do what would have taken one of your regular officers two months to accomplish?" "Because he was not educated at West Point," replied the

West Pointer, laughingly. "No," said Mr. Lincoln, "that was not the reason. It was because. when he was a boy, he had to work for a living."

General Garfield displayed the same power over men in peace as in war. When, on the 14th of April, 1865, President Lincoln was assassinated, the excitement in New York was intense. The people seemed on the eve of a revolution, but in the midst of the tumult a voice was heard exclaiming: "Fellow Citizens: Clouds and darkness are round about Him! His pavilion is dark waters and thick clouds of the skies! Justice and judgment are the habitation of His throne! Mercy and truth shall go before His face! Fellow Citizens: God reigns, and the Government at Washington still lives." The speaker was General Garfield. The effect of his words was instantaneous; the tumult was stilled.

In 1880 he was elected to a seat in the United States Senate. Five months afterwards the National Republican Convention assembled to nominate a President for the United States. After 34 ineffectual ballots, the vote was cast for James Garfield. Instantly one of the delegates marched forward and placed his flag over the head of the patriot. Another and another followed his example, until 700 delegates waved their banners, and joined with the 15,000 spectators in the gallery, in declaring JAMES A. GARFIELD PRESIDENT OF THE UNITED STATES.

Unfortunately for his country, President Garfield did not live long to hold the office he was so competent to fill. The four months of his Presidency showed his admirable capabilities. He strove to elevate the people morally, socially, and commercially; and to mitigate existing evils, especially the system of patronage. It had been the custom of the President to give all offices to the nominees of the Senators of each State. This Mr. Garfield refused to do, but his upright conduct cost him his life. Guiteau, a disappointed place hunter, made a murderous attack upon him as he was entering the waiting-room of the Potomac railway station. He was shot in the arm and body, and fell bleeding upon the floor. For a few hours it was thought that he could not survive; but, by the skill of the physicians and the nursing of his devoted wife, his life was prolonged until the 19th of September.

During those weeks of suspense the American people

hoped and prayed that his life might be spared, but it was not to be. When expectations ran highest that he would rally, the beloved and honoured President passed peacefully away. His body was embalmed and removed to Washington, where it lay in state for two days, after which it was interred in the cemetery of his native place, Cleveland.

The whole civilized world joined with the American people in mourning the premature death of a man so truly great. With him to see his duty was to do it; no matter at what personal cost. "I would rather be beaten in right than succeed in wrong," he would frequently say. His honesty of purpose was ever manifest, and drew men to him as by magnetic force. When honours fell fast upon him he never forgot, or strove to hide his early struggles, but gloried in the fact that what he was, he had become through his own efforts. "I never meet a ragged boy on the street," he often said, "without feeling that I owe him a salute, for I know not what possibilities may be buttoned up under his shabby coat."

JANET HAMILTON.

JANET HAMILTON was one of the most remarkable women of her time. Although she never moved out of the humble sphere of life in which she was born, her fame as a poetess was known throughout Scotland. When in declining years and smitten with blindness, she lived in her humble cottage, visitors of all kinds delighted to make her acquaintance. Those who had the privilege of visiting her, left feeling that they had enjoyed communion with a mind of surprising intelligence. She could delight by her Scotch stories, enter into the political questions of the day, had sound, practical views on all social questions, besides a varied acquaintance with literature. But her visitors felt that the greatest treat was to hear her repeat some of her own exquisite verses. Her career was one of remarkable industry and singular uprightness and piety. She battled with poverty, hard work, and many troubles, but rose, triumphant, above them all.

Janet Hamilton was born at the hamlet of Carshill, in the parish of Shotts, Lanarkshire, in October, 1795. Her father was a shoemaker, respectable, but very poor; her mother was a very godly woman, descended from a noted Covenanter, John Whitelaw. This ancestor was engaged in the battle of Bothwell Bridge, and, on the defeat of the Covenanting army, rode from the slaughter, hotly pursued by the king's soldiers. Entering his house breathless and fainting, he snatched a hasty meal and went into hiding. For four years he successfully evaded his pursuers, visiting his wife and family by stealth. On these occasions his daughter sat on the roof of the corn-kiln, with her spindle and distaff, and, while she spun, kept a sharp look-out for the dragoons, who were constantly searching for fugitives. On one occasion the alarm was given, and John Whitelaw, with a friend, dashed into the adjacent moss, a waste tract of land, where they lay almost covered with water. The dragoons searched the house and demanded from Mrs. Whitelaw, who lay in bed with her newly-born infant, where her husband was hiding. On her refusal to tell, they plunged their swords into the bed-clothes, and dragged the pillows from her head. Snatching a piece of burning peat from the fire, they placed it on the thatched roof, and rode off, exulting in the thought that the cottage would soon be in flames. Their purpose was defeated; the peat was removed before any harm was done. After many hairbreadth escapes, John Whitelaw was captured, tried in Edinburgh, and executed in front of the old Tolbooth, on the 12th of November, 1683.

Janet Hamilton has related this incident in verse. During her childhood the stirring events in connection with the Covenanters, were the frequent theme of conversation between her parents and grandparents. Her mind was well stored with records of those times of persecution.

Her grandparents were rather remarkable characters. They had lived through the terrible famine of 1739-40, when the poor of Scotland were wandering about famished and desperate, glad to eat the refuse from the dung-hill, or boil down the leaves of the beech tree for food. More than 2,000 persons perished from cold and hunger during those terrible times.

Many a lesson of carefulness was taught the young Janet as her grandmother talked of those famine days. At other times the old dame would tell wondrous tales of fairies, and relate the legends of the district, firing the imagination of her young listener in the same way as Robert Burns had been stirred by the tales of an aged crone.

Janet had very little opportunity for learning in her youth, not being sent even to the village school. By the time she was five years old, she could, owing to her mother's teaching, read Bible stories, and children's half-penny books. Writing she did not learn until after she was 50 years of age.

Her parents removed, when she was seven years old, to

Langloan, where the remainder of her life was spent. It was a hamlet near Coatbridge, a small town on the high road between Glasgow and Edinburgh. At the time when Janet's parent removed there, it could boast of some rural beauty. She delighted to play by the streams, gather wild flowers, and listen to the singing of the birds. Nature was her favourite study all through her life, and even when blindness came upon her, she loved to listen to her own ballads on nature, and, as her daughter read, would lean forward in her chair exclaiming: "I see it! I see it a'! Its like a crystal o' light set in my very heart."

Latterly, Langloan lost its rural beauty, and became dirty and smoke-begrimed from the colleries started in the neighbourhood. In her poem " Oor Location," the poetess thus describes it:

> " A hunner funnels bleezin', reekin',
> Coal and ironstone, charrin', smeekin';
> Navvies, miners, keepers, fillers,
> Puddlers, rollers, iron millers;
> Reestit, reekit, raggit laddies,
> Firemen, enginemen, an' paddies;
> Boatmen, banksmen, rough and rattlin',
> 'Bout the wecht wi' colliers battlin';
> Sweatin', swearin', fechtin', drinkin',
> Change-house bells an' gill-stoups clinkin."

During the first two years of her life at Langloan Janet had to take charge of the house while her parents were engaged in field work. Besides the house-keeping, she had to prepare two hanks of sale yarn each day; that was the task allotted her by her mother.

Her home life was a very strict one. Particular observance of the Sabbath, according to the custom of Scotland, was rigidly enforced. Saturday evening was spent in preparation for the coming day. The house was cleaned, the Sunday clothes put ready, and the vegetables prepared, so that there might not be any cooking upon the sacred day. Loitering in bed was not allowed on Sunday morning. Janet had to be up early, read her daily chapter from the Bible, and learn her appointed task. This, generally, consisted of a psalm or hymn, a page of " Brown's" and two or three of the Shorter Catechism. These were repeated to her mother in the evening. At church she was forced to listen attentively, knowing that, on her return, she would be required to repeat the text and the heads of the discourse. The house door was always kept bolted on the Sabbath, and the shutters of the front window closed to give a solemn dimness to the apartment. During the afternoon Janet read "Pilgrim's Progress" or "Watt's Divine Songs for Children," while her father and mother sat in silent meditation. The day concluded with a simple supper and family worship, after which she went to bed followed by her mother, who repeated solemnly in her ear: "Ha'e ye gi'en yersel' tae God the night, Jenny?"

These godly lessons were deeply imprinted on the mind of Janet Hamilton. She did not, however, enforce the same rigid observance on her own children. Her views gradually widened, and although she maintained the sanctity of the Sabbath, her good sense taught her that too strict a religious discipline made sacred things hateful to children.

When she was eight years old her love for reading became intensified by finding a copy of "Paradise Lost," and of Allen Ramsay's Poems on the beam of a weaver's loom. In her poem, "A Wheen aul' Memories," she thus refers to it:—

> "And the looms they war rattlin' an' blatterin' awa,
> For in that wee shopie the wabsters war twa—
> Jock Jameson, an' Jamie, a son of the house,
> An wow but thae callans war cantie and crouse.
>
> It was there my young fancy first took to the wing;
> It was there I first tasted the Helicon spring;
> It was there wi' the poets I wad revel and dream,
> For Milton and Ramsay lay on the breast beam."

She was well supplied with books from a circulating library. Amongst those she read were, "Plutarch's Lives," "Ancient Universal History," "Raynal's India," "Pitscottie's Scotland," "The Spectator," "The Rambler," and, as a special treat, Ferguson and Burns. She did her reading in odd moments—her daily task was never neglected.

After they had been two years in Langloan her parents gave up field labour, and her father re-commenced his trade as a shoemaker. Janet was put to work at the tambour-frame, then a very profitable employment for girls.

At this time she became acquainted with a very respectable young man, whom her father had hired to assist him in his work. In the year 1809 this young man became her husband. She was only thirteen years old at the time of her marriage, and her husband was eighteen. It was a cold February morning when the youthful couple started, on foot, to Glasgow to be married. They told their errand to an acquaintance in Glasgow, who directed them to the Rev. Dr. Lockhart, of College Church. The good Doctor asked if they had any witnesses. " None," they answered. He good-naturedly summoned the porter and Betty, the housemaid, and in their presence the knot was tied. In the dusk of the evening they reached their village home, where a few of the old neighbours welcomed them to a cup of tea. Never had either of them to regret the step they had taken. A married life of sixty-five happy years was theirs. The love never faltered. At eighty old John looked with as much love on his blind wife as he had done on the day she became his child-bride. After their humble home was paid for, a Spanish dollar was all the money they had. With that, and their two pair of hands, they started life. Many trials awaited them, and the care of a family of ten children. But their trust was in God, and their courage never left them.

Now that the cares of married life came upon her, Janet Hamilton had little time for reading. Such, however, was her thirst for knowledge that she would sit at her books through the night until two o'clock in the morning. She exhausted the stores of the village library, much to the astonishment of the librarian who had never met with such an instance before. He expressed a fear that she would read herself blind, which prophecy was sadly fulfilled. Her faithful gudeman had now to trudge to a more distant library. Time after time he returned with his armful of books until that library was exhausted, and the librarian was led to exclaim that, " he had never met with such a case of fell reading before." Being desirous that her neighbours should share her pleasure, she started a small circulating library. It was not a successful undertaking; books were lost or not returned, and she was forced to give it up. Her domestic duties were never overlooked except on one occasion—when Shakespeare first came into her possession—then she was charmed into forgetfulness of everything. She attributed her knowledge of grammar to the reading of Shakespeare. " Shakespeare was my teacher," she would often say, " and besides all this, God has given me a good tack [gift] of natural grammar."

She obtained the loan of "Blackwood's Magazine" from a friend, as it was issued. That and Shakespeare she kept in a niche in the wall beside her chair. She read at these precious books as she nursed her children, but if a neighbour came in they were quickly placed in the convenient niche, as she did not care to arouse the prejudice which was then felt in the village against such books.

Her children were all taught to read at five years old. As she sat at her tambour-frame, the little urchins in their patched clothes stood round her and repeated their lessons. In this way she made them all good scholars. In her beautiful poem, "The Mother at Home," she dwells on the education of children:—

"A voice deep and solemn is sounding abroad!
O mothers of Britain, each humble abode
Should echo the burden with which it is fraught—
Our children they must be instructed and taught.
* * * * *
"Your cares are full many, your leisure is small,
But the souls of your babes are more precious than all;
While you toil with your hands you should watch, teach and pray,
For where there's a will there is ever a way!
* * * * *
"The statesman, the patriot, the Christian have found—
Though grants, schools and teachers increase and abound—
For juvenile ignorance and vice there must come,
Bes't help, truest cure, from the Mother at Home."

While she tried to make her own home all that was good and pure, she sought through her writings to instil the same principles in the women around her:—

"There is an element of power
That suits the needs of every hour;
All wants to which our state gives birth—
The life, the mind, the home, the hearth.

"'Tis woman. From the mother's breast
The babe draws life and strength and rest;
She soothes its pains, its wants supplies,
With yearning love in heart and eyes.
* * * * *
"And who shall teach the infant mind
The way of truth and peace to find?
Who teach in wisdom's paths to tread,
But she who gives his daily bread?

> "A guiding star to shed and shine
> Soft radiance on the household shrine,
> And from her sphere—a span of earth—
> Pour light and love on home and hearth.
>
> "And such should woman ever prove—
> The pole-star of domestic love,
> To which the youthful circle tend,
> As mother, guardian, teacher, friend."

Janet Hamilton wrote her first poems when she was between 17 and 19 years of age. After the birth of her third child, she ceased composing until she was 54. At that age she first learnt to write. Her self-invented handwriting was of a very peculiar kind, hardly readable by a stranger. Most of her poems were written by her son at her dictation. She wrote for Cassell's "Working Man's Friend," and subsequently her poems were collected into a volume. They are chiefly in the Scottish dialect and full of national humour and pathos. Dearly she loved " auld " Scotland and her mother tongue :—

> "Na, na, I winna pairt wi' that,
> I downa gi'e it up;
> O' Scotland's hamely mither tongue
> I canna quit the grup.
>
> "It's 'bedded in my very heart,
> Ye needna rive an' rug;
> It's in my e'en an' on my tongue,
> An' singin' in my lug.
>
> *   *   *   *   *
>
> "Thy hamely worth, thy couthie speech,
> Are dear, hoo dear to me!
> An' next to God, my John, an' bairns,
> Thy place sall ever be."

The ballad of "Effie" is, perhaps, her finest poem. Garibaldi was her favourite hero. She loved to dwell on his struggles for Italian liberty, and would talk with great pride and emotion on the visit paid her by one of the general's sons. She would tell how he had actually lifted her "in his great strong arms" from her seat by the kitchen fire to her arm-chair in the best room. Her poem on "Freedom for Italy" is full of stirring power :—

> "'He is the freeman whom the Truth makes free;
> All else are slaves,' I cry aloud to thee,
> O Garibaldi! in the fateful hour.
> Think not 'tis in mere human might or power,

> Nor even the might of such an arm as thine,
> To compass freedom, lasting, true, divine—
> Not the keen edge of thy all-conquering sword
> Can cut the Gordian double-knotted cord
> That ignorance and superstition winds
> With deadening strain round captive human minds.
> Slaves of the Papacy! when will ye know
> That, to be free, yourselves must strike the blow?
> * * * * * *
> Awake!
> For truth, for freedom, for your country's sake!
> Awake from your enchanted sleep! Arise!
> Shake off the accursed spell; unclose your eyes.
> The Word of Life, the Sun of Truth has risen;
> To read, to hear insures not now a prison.
> No more Madais in dungeon cells immured
> By priests intolerant. Ye are secured from wrongs
> Like these. To every hearth and home
> The Word of God may safely, freely come.
> And he who runs may read, if read he can,
> How God gives freedom to enslavèd man."

She was ever active with tongue and pen in denouncing the horrors of strong drink. In her "Welcome to J. B. Gough," when he first came to this country as a temperance lecturer, she concludes thus:—

> "God shield thee in the fight!—
> His [alcohol] forts and towers of strength, raze, raze, them quite!
> Accept the deepest, dearest thanks of those
> Who, sharing not the sin, yet share the woes
> And shame incurred by lost degraded ones—
> Intemperate fathers, mothers, husbands, sons!
> 'Who winneth souls is wise'—in God's own might
> Go on; thy path shall like the morning light
> Wax brighter, till the noon of perfect day
> Shall blind, and scorch, and scare the fiend away!"

The essays of Janet Hamilton are full of interest from the graphic description she gives of Scottish life and character. Having her mind well stored with the tales and legends she had heard from her grandparents, she was able to write of the life and manners of Scotland during the last century. The famine time she has described with all its horrors, and has told many a curious tale of her grandfather's experience when he was a herd-boy on the banks of the Clyde. In those days salmon was so plentiful, and so general an article of food in the farmer's houses, that servants made it a part of their hiring stipulations, that they should only eat salmon once a day. Potatoes were a luxury, and much surprised was the herd-boy when a few of these precious articles were given him to plant. Each potato he planted in a separate mound made of manure and a little earth. The crop was plentiful. It was an eventful day in the farmhouse when the potato was first used as an article of food. The good wife, stationed in front of the pot, dived into its depths with a wooden spoon, and at each dive brought carefully out one potato, which was laid before each person, on a piece of pea-scone, and eaten as a great delicacy,

At sixty years of age, the poetess was smitten with blindness. She bore her affliction very patiently. Indeed it was difficult for a stranger to realize that she had lost her eyesight, so wonderfully were her other senses developed. It did not interfere with her work. She composed her poems as blithely and cheerily as ever, living in the comfort of her little cottage, her children about her, and her own gudeman by her side. She delighted to talk with visitors of her early days, and her many struggles. If the conversation turned on poetry her memory was well stored with quotations. Her manner of talking was very striking. She was always composed and dignified, and her words followed each other with ease and grace. "The grand old Woman," *Punch* has styled her. Her neighbours looked to her for counsel, and she was the apostle of temperance and social reform amongst the rough colliers around her. Without having gone further from her village home than Glasgow, she possessed a world-wide sympathy with all measures for progress, Her knowledge was gained from books. Her insight into human nature was gathered from the lives of the humble peasants with whom she mingled. She has built up a character strong, noble, and pious, which her countrymen may be proud to contemplate.

"She has well earned a niche in the temple of fame;
This fine old Scotch worthy, our sympathies claim;
They honour themselves who honour the name
Of rare Janet Hamilton."

She passed away at the age of 76 in October, her favourite month, and was full of the spirit she prayed for in one of her poems:—

"Spirit of meekness—brooding in the air—
On thy soft pinions waft my lowly prayer,
That I may meet—calm, meek, resigned, and sober—
My life's decline—my solemn last October."

CHARLES DICKENS.

CHARLES DICKENS was born on the 7th of February, 1812, at Landport, near Portsmouth. The son of a clerk in the navy-pay office he had many changes of residence during his early years, according as his father was moved from place to place. When five years old Chatham became his home. The few years spent there were the happiest of his peculiarly unhappy and neglected childhood.

Of education he had but little. His mother taught him the rudiments of English and a little Latin. During the last two years spent at Chatham he attended the school of Mr. Charles Giles, a Baptist minister. This gentleman appears to have discerned something of the budding genius in the small, sensitive, delicate, and imaginative boy, placed under his care. He pronounced him to be a "boy of capacity," and, when in after years his then famous pupil was bringing out "Pickwick," sent him a silver snuff-box inscribed to "the inimitable Boz." At this school Charles Dickens distinguished himself in a recitation about Dr. Bolus, taken from the "Humorist's Miscellany." He received a double encore from his admiring listeners.

In 1821 these happy days at Chatham came to an end. Dickens was taken by his parents to London. The parting from his Chatham friends was a sad one. In after years he recalled with emotion how on the night before he came away his "good master came flitting in among the packing cases" to give him Goldsmith's "Bee" as a keepsake.

Arriving in London, the elder Dickens with his family settled in Bayham Street, Camden Town. This was one of the poorest London suburbs. Charles had no companions, was not sent to school, and was, as he expressively put it, a "not-over-particularly-taken-care-of-boy." "As I thought," he once said, "in the little back-garret in Bayham Street, of all I had lost in losing Chatham, what would I have given, if I had had anything to give, to have been sent back to any other school; to have been taught something anywhere!" Left to his solitary musings the wistful imaginative boy busied himself in observing his surroundings. The washerwoman, who lived next door, the Bow Street officer across the street, and many other figures passing before him in their poverty and misery, fascinated him. He was unconsciously drinking in the manner in which the London poor lived. More than that, his heart was being trained to pity and compassion for these down-trodden, struggling, sorrowful people. In after years his graphic pen was to startle the world into laughter and into tears before his pictures—such as no other man ever drew—of the struggling poverty which had fixed itself on his boyish memory.

An elder cousin, James Lamert, lived with the Dickens' family in Bayham Street. He took pity on poor, lonely, delicate Charles, and lent him books. He also made and painted him a little theatre, and started some private theatricals, in which Charles took a creditable part. To the end of his life acting was a favourite pastime. He found another friend in a bachelor uncle, Mr. Thomas Barrow. An old barber, a quaint, odd character, often came to shave his uncle when Charles was present. He made a careful observation of the barber's peculiarities, and wrote a description of him, not, however, daring to show it to anyone. "Gil Blas" was a favourite book with him, and in imitation of the story of the canon's housekeeper, he wrote an account of an old woman who used to wait on his mother, and make delicate hashes with walnut ketchup. These were the beginning of his character sketching.

He was soon roused from dreamland to the stern realities of life. His father's affairs were in a very bad state. He could barely provide for his family. Mrs. Dickens tried to exert herself, and taking a house, No. 4, Gower Street, announced on the door-plate, "Mrs. Dickens' Establishment." Referring to this time Dickens writes: "I left at a great many other doors, a great many circulars calling attention to the merits of the establishment, yet nobody ever came to school, nor do I recollect that anybody ever proposed to come, or that the least preparation was made to receive anybody. But I know that we got on very badly with the butcher and the baker; that very often we had not too much for dinner; and that at last my father was arrested." Mr. Dickens, unable to meet his payments, was taken to the Marshalsea, the debtors' prison. His wife and five children were soon forced to take up their abode with him, while Charles was left to earn his living.

A more miserable existence than that passed by prisoners in the Marshalsea cannot well be imagined. In a miserable room, with scarcely the necessaries of life, families lived on month after month without any hope of getting away unless some stroke of good fortune befell them and enabled them to pay their debts. In "David Copperfield," Charles Dickens has described what passed before his eyes in the Marshalsea during his father's confinement.

At the suggestion of his cousin, James Lamert, Charles was taken into his warehouse, where the celebrated Warren's Blacking was made. It was at 30, Hungerford Stairs, Strand. His work was to cover the pots of blacking paste, first with oil paper, and then neatly tie on the outer paper. Six shillings a week was to be his pay. As he was the master's relative, Charles was distinguished from the other working boys by being placed by himself on a seat in the window recess. He served as an advertisement to the passers by, who gazed in admiration at his deftness in covering the blacking pots. However, this kind of isolation was intolerable. He yearned for sympathy and companionship, and left the window recess to join the other boys in the cellar below. The two boys who worked beside him were Bob Fagin, whose name he afterwards used for the Jew in "Oliver Twist," and Paul Green, commonly called Poll, which name he gave to *Mr. Sweedlepipe* in "Martin Chuzzlewit." Paul Green's father was fireman at Drury Lane Theatre, and his sister did the imps at the pantomimes. "No words," wrote Dickens, "can express the secret agony of my soul as I sunk into this companionship; compared these every day associates with those of my happier childhood; and I felt my early hopes of growing up to be a learned and distinguished man crushed in my breast. The deep remembrance of the sense I had of being utterly neglected and hopeless; of the shame I felt in my position; of the misery it was to my young heart to believe that, day by day, what I had learned, and thought, and delighted in, and raised my fancy and my emulation up by, was passing away from me, never to be brought back any more; can't be written."

Dickens at this time lodged with a "reduced old lady," living at Camden Town, who took in children to board. Little did the old body imagine when she took in the small, sickly boy that he would make her immortal as *Mrs. Pipchin* in "Dombey and Son." Out of 6/- wages Dickens had to provide his food. Each week he divided his money into separate parcels and labelled them for each day in the week. Sometimes his weakness for pastry would get the better of him and his day's money would go, on his way to work, in stale pastry exhibited for sale in Tottenham Court Road. At other times, seized with a longing to appear grand, he would treat himself to a meal at a superior coffee shop. On one occasion—his birthday or some festive time—he entered a public house in Parliament Street and in his most magnificent style enquired what the price of the *very* best ale was. "Twopence per glass," replied the landlord. "Then just draw me a glass of that, if you please, with a good head to it." The landlord was so astonished at the assumed grandeur of the small boy before him that he called his wife to look at him. The motherly heart yearned to the lonely child. She stooped and kissed him, half admiringly, half compassionately. These glimpses into Dickens' early days show how bitterly his impoverished, crushed-down condition pressed upon him. He longed to be somebody in the world; to be able to hold himself erect among his fellows.

Another incident occurred about this time illustrative of the agony which Dickens endured from his father's imprisonment in the Marshalsea. During his work he was seized with acute pain in his side. Bob Fagin filled some empty blacking pots with hot water and applied them until the pain was relieved. But Dickens was so weak from the attack that his companion insisted on seeing him home. He was too proud to let Bob Fagin know that his parents were in the Marshalsea, so after repeated attempts to get rid of him, he bid him good-bye on the steps of a house near Southwark Bridge, as though that was his father's house. To complete the deceit he rung the front door bell, and when the woman answered it, by way of saying something, asked if Mr. Robert Fagin lived there. By that time Bob was out of sight and Dickens made his way to the miserable Marshalsea. This shows only too sadly the weight of sorrow and shame pressing on that young, sensitive heart. It made him resort to deceit to hide his misery. When at the height of his fame the memory of those sad days haunted him like a spectre. He could never endure to pass by the blacking warehouse, so painful was the memory of his degradation.

He was thoroughly wretched with the old lady in Camden Town, and pleaded to his father, with tears in his eyes, that some other place might be found for him. Accordingly a back attic was taken in Lant Street, in the Borough, and a bed made up for him on the floor. He thought it a paradise, but his delight arose from the fact that he was near to the Marshalsea, and could take his meals with his parents and the rest of the family. This back attic he made famous as the lodging of *Bob Sawyer* in " Pickwick."

An unexpected legacy enabled the Dickens' family to leave the debtors' prison. Shortly afterwards Charles was taken from the odious blacking pots to attend school in the Hampstead Road, kept by Mr. Jones, a Welshman, and called " WELLINGTON HOUSE ACADEMY." There he remained for two years. During that time he does not appear to have acquired much knowledge, but the happier circumstances acted favourably on him, and he became a merry handsome boy; was the ringleader in all the school pranks; joined with distinction in the theatricals got up by the scholars, and contributed tales to be circulated by the school-club.

When fourteen years old he left "WELLINGTON HOUSE ACADEMY," and became clerk or office-boy to Mr. Edward Blackmore, attorney, Gray's Inn. He had an ambition to rise above this, and devoted himself assiduously to learning short hand, in order that he might fit himself to become a parliamentary reporter. His father had taken up that employment, and Charles was anxious to follow in his footsteps. Besides working at his short hand studies he spent much of his time in the British Museum Reading Room.

In 1831, when Dickens was nineteen years of age, he procured a berth as parliamentary reporter for the *True Sun*. He was afterwards engaged for the *Mirror of Parliament*, and in his 23rd year became reporter for the *Morning Chronicle*, the paper on which his father had been employed.

Shortly after this his first published writing saw the light. Having written his little sketch he dropped it stealthily one evening into the letter-box in Fleet Street. What was his delight when he saw it in print in the *Old Monthly Magazine* exhibited in a shop window in the Strand. "On which occasion," he writes, "I walked down to Westminster Hall, and turned into it for half-an-hour, because my eyes were so dimmed with joy and pride that they could not bear the street, and were not fit to be seen there."

During the two years that elapsed before he abandoned the press for literature his experiences were most exciting. Having to travel many miles at all times and seasons to out of the way places to report for the *Chronicle*, he had endless adventures in the stage-coaches, and at the old inns where they changed horses. Referring to the mishaps which befell him, and which were charged to the proprietors of the *Chronicle*, he says: "I have had to charge for half-a-dozen break-downs in half-a-dozen times as many miles. I have had to charge for the damage of a great coat from the drippings of a blazing wax-candle, in writing through the smallest hours of the night in a swift-flying carriage and pair. I have had to charge for all sorts of breakages fifty times in a journey without question, such being the ordinary results of the pace which we went at. I have charged for broken hats, broken luggage, broken chaises, broken harness, everything but a broken head, which is the only thing they would have grumbled to pay for." Reckless as this life seems, Dickens was gathering information, from the places he visited and the people he met, which was to prove invaluable for the writing of his books. The habits formed during his reporter days never left him. He always loved adventure, and often when at a banquet his friends saw his hand gliding along the table cloth as if taking down the speeches.

After his first paper appeared in the *Monthly Magazine* it was followed by nine others. These were collected into two volumes and published as "Sketches by Boz," 1836. They were illustrated by Cruikshank. The name Boz was taken from Dickens' younger brother Augustus. He was called Moses, in honour of the "Vicar of Wakefield;" this came to be Boses, and finally Boz.

On the 2nd of April, 1836, Dickens was married to Catherine, the daughter of Mr. George Hogarth, an old friend and fellow-worker on the *Chronicle.* About the same time was issued the first number of the famous "Pickwick Papers."

Dickens, whose "Sketches by Boz" had attracted so much attention, was asked by Chapman and Hall, then a new publishing firm, to contribute to their Library of Fiction. The "NIMROD CLUB" was first suggested, which it was proposed to bring out in monthly parts, treating on country pastimes and sports, suitably illustrated by Mr. Seymour. Dickens objected to this proposal, and after much discussion the "Pickwick Club" was decided on. It was to be illustrated by Seymour, and brought out in monthly parts. It is, however, to Dickens that the ever memorable figure of *Pickwick* is due. "Mr. Seymour's first sketch," writes Mr. Dickens, "was of a long thin man. The present immortal one he made from my description of a friend of mine at Richmond, a fat old beau, who would wear, in spite of the ladies' protests, drab tights and black gaiters. His name was John Foster."

The first numbers of "Pickwick" were not much noticed; "Sketches by Boz" attracted more attention. But as the story advanced public excitement became intense. Everybody was looking forward to the next number of "Pickwick. Thomas Carlyle tells a story illustrative of the excitement:—"An archdeacon with his own venerable lips," wrote Mr. Carlyle, "repeated to me the other night a strange profane story of a solemn clergyman, who had been administering ghostly consolation to a sick person, having finished, satisfactorily as he thought, and got out of the room, he heard the sick person ejaculate: 'Well, thank God, "Pickwick" will be out in ten days, anyway!' This is dreadful." People suddenly found that they were reading of real characters, full of the same joys and sorrows as the people about them. It was this perfect realism, this genuine humanness, the intense sympathy with all mankind which Dickens had, that made his works immortal, His chequered career had shown him life in a great variety of forms, so that his facile pen could paint the sayings and doings of out-of-the-way characters with an exactitude which was startling. He touched the hearts of poor and great alike by his intense human sympathy. The very ostlers in the inns got out of their beds and came crowding round the doors to hear Robert Burns speak. The same power which charmed the ostlers melted jewelled duchesses into tears. So with Dickens; the highest and the lowest in the land wept and laughed over his pages.

"Pickwick" was followed by "Oliver Twist" and by "Nicholas Nickleby." Besides giving amusement, Dickens had a distinct aim in these his first three books, as in his later ones. In "Pickwick" all the horrors of the debtors' prison were exposed. The time was fresh in Dickens' mind when his own father had passed his miserable days in the Marshalsea. Its other wretched inmates had become known to him during his visits there. In describing the experiences of *Pickwick* and the faithful *Sam Weller* in their imprisonment, the facts and many of the scenes were taken from his personal knowledge; in "Oliver Twist" he dealt a blow at the abuses in connection with parochial management; and in "Nicholas Nickleby" all the horrors of the Yorkshire schools were exposed. Before beginning that book he went to Yorkshire, accompanied by Mr. Hablot Brown, the artist who was to illustrate it, for the purpose of inspecting the cheap schools, and found that cruelties, of which the public little dreamed, were being practised in them. His description of Dotheboy's Hall was the result of this tour of inspection. Sydney Smith, writing of this book, said :—"'*Nickleby*' *is very good*. I stood out against Dickens as long as I could, but he has conquered me." By his books Dickens proclaimed these social wrongs throughout the length and breadth of the land. He lived to see them swept away.

The sale of his books was enormous. In a few years he was in receipt of a large income, and comfortably established in a house in Devonshire Terrace. Friends gathered around him; chiefly artists and literary men for whom he always had a preference. He chose the society of congenial spirits before those of high rank. When jaded and overworked he sought change and relaxation at Broadstairs, which was his favourite watering place.

In 1839 Dickens, with his wife, his friend and biographer, John Foster, and the artist Maclise, paid a visit to Landor at Bath. Three happy days these friends passed together, and during that time Dickens first conceived the story of little "Nell." It came to him while celebrating his birthday at 35, St. James's Square. Landor was so charmed by it that he declared it his intention to purchase the house and burn it to the ground, " to the end that no meaner association should ever desecrate the birthplace of *Nell*." He did not however carry this into effect.

Little Nell came before the public in 1840, when the first number of the "Old Curiosity Shop" was brought out. The pathos of the story affected the author as much as any of its numerous readers. He felt for her, clung to her, as though he could not give her up, and cried like a child when he wrote the chapter on her death. Writing to Mr. Foster at the completion of the story he says, " After you left last night, I took my desk upstairs; and writing until 4 o'clock this morning finished the old story. It makes me very melancholy to think that all these people are lost to me for ever, and I feel as if I never could become attached to any new set of characters." These creatures of his fancy were as real to Dickens as the men and women about him. He laughed with them, cried with them, and followed them to their graves with the keenest sorrow. The droll little figure of the *Marchioness*, in the " Old Curiosity Shop" was taken from the maid who waited on his parents in the Marshalsea.

In 1841 Mr. Dickens received quite an ovation in Edinburgh, when on his way to the Highlands. There was a general rush to get tickets for the public dinner in his honour. But his Scotch reception was far exceeded by the lionizing which awaited him in America. From the time he landed, in 1842, until he embarked for the homeward journey, he was beset by visitors, and ovations of every description. Writing of it he says, "I can do nothing that I want to do, go nowhere where I want to go, and see nothing that I want to see. If I turn into the street I am followed by a multitude. If I stay at home the house becomes, with callers, like a fair. If I visit a public institution, with only one friend, the directors come down incontinently, waylay me in the yard, and address me in a long speech. I go to a party in the evening, and am so hemmed about by people, stand where I will, that I am exhausted for want of air. I dine out, and have to talk about everything to everybody. I go to church for quiet, and there is a violent rush to the neighbourhood of the pew I sit in, and the clergyman preaches *at* me. I take my seat in the railway car and the very conductor wont leave me alone. I get out at the station, and can't drink a glass of water without having a hundred people looking down my throat when I open my mouth to swallow. Conceive what all this is! Then by every post letters on letters arrive, all about nothing, and all demanding an immediate answer. This man is offended because I wont live in his house; and that man is thoroughly disgusted because I wont go out more than four times in one evening. I have no rest or peace, and am in a perpetual worry." Gratifying, in one respect, as this American homage was, it soon became irksome, and it was with a sense of relief that Dickens found himself again in the quiet of his home at Devonshire Terrace. A dinner, with a company of his nearest friends, celebrated his home coming.

Soon after his return he published the "American Notes." They were not favourably received across the Atlantic. Dickens was still fresh from the boredom to which curiosity had subjected him, and wrote rather harshly of the Americans and their manners.

Shortly after his return from America he visited Cornwall, in company with his friends Foster, Maclise, and Stanfield. During that trip the outline of "Martin Chuzzlewit" was decided on. The complete book was published in 1844, and dedicated to Miss Coutts (afterwards the Baroness). A very warm friendship existed between this lady and Dickens. They were one in their sympathy for the poor. Miss Coutts was ever ready to devote her wealth to charitable purposes. Dickens was able to direct her charity into the right channels; for no man knew better than he the ins and outs of the London slums. It was to them he went to study character, and gather information for his books. He took with him a sympathetic heart, and would relate the misery he saw to Miss Coutts, who devised, with his co-operation, various schemes for the amelioration of the condition of the poor. In return for this Miss Coutts undertook the education of Dickens' eldest son.

In 1843, "The Carol," the first of Dickens' Christmas stories, was brought out. "Blessings on your kindly heart," wrote Lord Jeffrey to him, "you should be happy yourself, for you may be sure you have done more good by this little publication, fostered more kindly feelings, and prompted more positive acts of beneficence, than can be traced to all the pulpits and confessionals in Christendom since Christmas, 1842." Letters came in from people of all classes, telling Dickens of the joy with which the "Christmas Carol" had been received in their homes, and of the good it had done by prompting feelings of kindliness and good-will.

Mr. Dickens, with his family, visited Italy in the summer of 1844, and remained there through the following winter. It was an idle time, for he could not write without the stimulus of the crowded London streets. "My figures seem to stagnate without crowds about them," he wrote from Italy; and again, "The absence of any accessible streets continues to worry me, now that I have so much to do, in a most singular manner. It is quite a mental phenomenon. I should not walk in them in the day time, if they were here, I dare say; but at night I want them beyond description. I don't seem able to get rid of my spectres unless I can lose them in crowds." When in London, it was his habit to walk miles along the crowded streets at night, and into the remotest corners, to study the people. It was his whole aim to paint life as it really was.

Sitting one morning unable to fix on a subject for his Christmas book his reverie was disturbed by a loud clang of bells which pealed from one of the Genoa churches. He decided at once to call his book "The Chimes." When it was finished he yearned to read it to his friends far away in England. For that express purpose he journeyed to London in the middle of the winter. At a select gathering in Mr. Foster's house he read aloud his touching story. Maclise drew a picture of the memorable group as they sat round the table after dinner and listened to Dickens. By his side sat Thomas Carlyle, thoughtful and meditative; Stanfield and Maclise bent eagerly forward in rapt attention; Douglas Jerrold gazed upwards; Laman Blanchard, Fox, and Foster sat solemn and attentive; while Harness and Dyce were melted to tears. It was a memorable group; each one moved in his characteristic way by the story of *Trotty Veck* and his fellow-characters in the "Chimes." When he finished it Dickens confesses to have had "a real good cry." He stayed but a week in London, and then went back again to Italy, returning some months later to Devonshire Terrace.

About this time he engaged frequently in public theatricals, giving them for the benefit of charitable institutions. In 1846 he visited Switzerland, and began to write " Dombey and Son." Regarding the popularity of this book the following story is told. Mr. Dickens was in Paris, and was hastily summoned home by the illness of one of his children, who was left in the care of its grandmother, Mrs. Hogarth. An old charwoman in the employ of Mrs. Hogarth was told that Mr. Dickens was expected. "Lawk, ma'am," she said, "is the young gentleman upstairs the son of the man that put together 'Dombey?'" On being assured that it was so, she said, "Lawk, ma'am; I thought that three or four men must have put together 'Dombey!'" Her mistress knew that she could not read, and pressed her further regarding her knowledge of 'Dombey.' The woman told her that she lodged at a snuff-shop, kept by a man named Douglas. There were several other lodgers, and on the first Monday of every month there was a tea, and after it the landlord read aloud the month's number of " Dombey."

"David Copperfield," one of the most interesting of Dickens' works, from the fact that it is in a great part an autobiography, was begun in May, 1849, and continued to be issued in monthly parts until November, 1850. Many of the incidents in the career of *David Copperfield* are identical with those of Charles Dickens; more especially those relating to his early years. The character of *Micawber* was taken from Dickens' father. When just completing the book he wrote to Mr. Foster. "Oh, my dear Foster, if I were to say half what *Copperfield* makes me feel to-night, how strangely, even to you, I should be turned inside out. I seem to be sending some part of myself into the Shadowy World." This book reached the highest sale of any of his books, " Pickwick " excepted.

Mr. Dickens left his house at Devonshire Terrace, which had been associated with so much of his career, in November, 1851, and settled at Tavistock House. There "Bleak House" was written, in which the abuses of the Court of Chancery were exposed. His numerous family were growing up around him, and into their sports he entered with all the natural gaiety of his disposition. He got up children's theatricals for their amusement, and contributed in every way to their pleasure. On one occasion his two young daughters had been teaching him the polka step, which he had promised to dance for their amusement on the approaching birthday of one of them. He woke up suddenly during the night with the thought that he had forgotten it. Out of bed he jumped, and went through his steps on the bedroom floor in the middle of a cold winter night. It was very characteristic of the man; he was full of frolic and swayed by sudden impulses. Differing widely from the majority of literary men, he delighted in life and company. He could not even fix on the title for a book without consulting his friends. He yearned for sympathy.

While taking part in the amusements of his children, he was ever anxious that they should have the highest religious training. The life of Christ was the example he held ever before them. To adapt it easily to their understanding he compiled for their use a simple narrative from the gospels. In a letter to his son, about to sail for Australia, he says:—"I therefore exhort you to persevere in a thorough determination to do whatever you have to do as well as you can do it. I was not so old as you are now when I first had to win my food, and to do it out of this determination, and I have never slackened in it since. Never take a mean advantage of any one in any transaction, and never be hard upon people who are in your power. Try to do to others as you would have them do to you, and do not be discouraged if they fail sometimes. It is much better for you that they should fail in obeying the greatest rule laid down by our Saviour, than that you should. I put a New Testament among your books for the very same reasons, and with the very same hopes that made me write an easy account of it for you when you were a child: because it is the best book that ever was or will be known in the world; and because it teaches you the best lessons by which any human creature, who tries to be truthful and faithful to duty, can possibly be guided. . . ."

In 1859 Mr. Dickens left Tavistock House for Gadshill, a mansion on the main road between Rochester and Gravesend.

He had first seen this house when a small boy as he passed from Chatham with his father. It had attracted his youthful fancy, and his father, amused at his admiration of it, jokingly told him that he might perhaps live in it himself when he came to be a man if he worked hard enough. Dickens never forgot that, and on hearing that Gadshill was for sale became its purchaser. It was a beautiful residence with spacious grounds. In the shrubbery was placed a Swiss châlet, presented to him by his friend, Mr. Fletcher, one room of which he used as a study during the summer months. It was in this châlet that the last page of his last book, "Edwin Drood," was written. It was his habit to have a number of favourite ornaments ranged on his writing-table. He could not write without them. Wherever he travelled these ornaments were taken to be placed on his table. Everything had to be put just to please his fancy before he could write a word. Flowers he invariably had beside him.

Mr. Dickens had never been a robust man, and about this time there were indications of his health giving way. The long walks, which were his favourite recreation, had greatly tried his strength. His nervous system was impaired; his prolific imagination began to fail him, and writing became a labour. He was seized with a restless spirit, and unhappy domestic affairs added to it. He sought refreshment in foreign travel, and visited the Continent and afterwards America, where he gave readings from his own books in the principal cities. These were a great success. The ticket offices were besieged during the small hours of the morning by the eager crowds. People fortunate enough to secure tickets got fabulous prices by re-selling. Many even paid for standing room outside the ticket office to any person willing to give up his place.

He returned from his American tour in 1868, much improved in health. After a few months' rest, he began another series of readings in England and Scotland. The nervous excitement occasioned by it was a source of anxiety to his friends; but he would not desist. He seems to have had a peculiar delight in reading his own productions, and laughed at their humour, and was moved by their pathos, as much as if they were some other man's creation.

His health became gradually worse from this time.

He lived on quietly at Gadshill, receiving his friends and spending his mornings in his beautiful châlet, busy with writing "Edwin Drood." On the 8th of June, 1870, contrary to his custom, he passed the *whole* of the day writing in the châlet. On the evening of that day he was taken seriously ill at the dinner-table. The doctors pronounced his illness to be effusion on the brain. He lingered until the following evening and then passed away. He was in his 58th year.

It had always been his wish to be buried without any ceremonial; but public feeling ran too high to allow of the remains of so remarkable a man being placed in any less honourable place than the venerable Abbey of Westminster. There he was laid to rest on the 14th of June, 1870. The greatest simplicity was observed in accordance with his wish, but it was impossible to restrain the crowds of voluntary mourners who thronged the road to the Abbey. All felt that there had passed away a man the like of whom would not soon brighten the world with humour, nor touch the heart with so sweet a pathos. "No death since 1866," wrote Thomas Carlyle, "has fallen on me with such a stroke. No literary man's hitherto ever did. The good, the gentle, high-souled, ever friendly, noble Dickens— every inch of him an honest man."

THOMAS EDWARD.

THOMAS EDWARD, the Scottish naturalist, has rarely been equalled as a worker. So great was his ardour in his pursuits that for years he devoted night as well as day to them; taking only an hour or two's sleep as he lay in the open air, or under the shade of a rock, watching to capture some animal to add to his collection. A shoemaker by trade, he was engaged at his work from six o'clock in the morning until nine in the evening; so that his only opportunity for pursuing his passionate study of natural history was at night.

He was born during the troublous time of the Napoleonic wars. His father was in the Fifeshire Militia, quartered at Gosport, Portsmouth. At that place Thomas Edward was born on Christmas day, 1814. The following year the battle of Waterloo restored peace to the country. The Fifeshire Militia was no longer needed at Portsmouth to keep guard over the French prisoners; so were ordered back to Fifeshire, and took up their quarters at Cupar. Shortly afterward they were disbanded, and John Edward was enabled to return to his peaceful calling as a hand-loom weaver. He settled with his family in the small village of Kettle, near Cupar.

The young baby, Thomas, soon began to show his parents, and their neighbours, the stuff he was made of. A more restless, unmanageable child could scarcely be imagined. Feet, legs, and arms always on the move. When only four months old he sprang from his mother's arms to catch some flies which he saw buzzing on the window pane, and was only saved from falling by his mother clutching at his long clothes. He learnt to walk at a very early age, and found his chief delight in watching a neighbour's sow, called Bet, and her litter of pigs. As he could not get inside the pigstye, he gazed through the palings at the interesting family. In vain did his mother, fearing the ferocity of the old sow, carry him away, and forbid him to return. It was of no avail. Whenever she asked "Where's Tam?" "Oh! he's awa wi' the pigs," was the invariable answer. One day the incorrigible "Tam" was missing altogether. His parents and the neighbours searched in vain. They thought the gypsies must have stolen him. A deputation of neighbours visited the camp to enquire. The gypsies denied ever kidnapping children, and the women of the tribe beat and pelted the intruders until they were forced to retreat. They returned to the village smarting from their ill-usuage. Another body of men were about to search in another direction, when the woman who owned the sow came in screaming with "Tam" in her arms, and threw him into his mother's lap. The story was soon told. The child had passed the night with the pigs. He was at this time only 12 months' old.

Shortly after this the family removed to Aberdeen. Young Thomas was now in his glory. His parents' house was in the Green, one of the oldest parts of the town. The Den burn flowed at the bottom of the street. Near at hand were the Inches, at the mouth of the Dee, where the tide came in daily. This was a delightful place for the baby naturalist. There was no end to the eels, crabs, worms, horse-leeches, tadpoles, and frogs to be found. The place where the town's manure heap was kept abounded in beetles, rats, sparrows, and innumerable flies. In the midst of these "Tam" was happy: not so his mother. The house was filled with his beasts. The fishes and birds could be kept securely, but the horse-leeches found their way into the neighbours' houses, fastened on their legs, and threw them into innumerable frights. The beetles, moles, and rats were seen crawling out of their hiding places to the terror of the good people. Tom was scolded, threatened, beaten, his beasts thrown out of doors, but still he persevered and brought home more.

His mother, in desperation determined to confine him to the house. Scantily dressed he was tied firmly by the leg to the table, and his wrists bound together. His little sister was set to watch him. No sooner had his mother gone out than "Tam," with manœuvres worthy of a conjurer, extricated his hands, and with his sister's assistance, whom he had cajoled into helping him, dragged the table to which his legs were tied close to the bars of the grate, and set the cord on fire. At that moment he heard his mother's hand upon the latch. He sprang behind the door and ran out as she came in. The good woman's horror can be easily imagined. The burning cord had set fire to the table, and soon the whole cottage would have been in flames, Tom spent a glorious day out of doors with his pets, but his homecoming was not quite so pleasant.

His father thought to break in the incorrigible boy by taking away his clothes altogether, so carried them with him to his work. Tom's mother covered his nakedness with an old red petticoat tied round his throat and left to hang about his body. Having occasion to go out for milk she left the house. He quickly fastened a string round his waist, girdle fashion, to confine the red petticoat, and stationed himself behind the entry door. His unsuspecting mother returned, and as she came in Tom bolted out into the street, and away to the sticklebacks, leeches, and crabs. When he returned home his father, who was prepared to give him a good thrashing, could only laugh when he saw his droll little figure in the red petticoat all bespattered with mud.

The result of this escapade was a fever which kept him between life and death for many weeks. He slowly recovered, but when he did, returned again to his old haunts and was as incorrigible as ever. On one occasion he, with a party of boys, espied a wasp's nest. Tom must have it. The other boys, afraid of being stung, declined to take part in the capture. He persevered, regardless of stings, and detached the nest from the tree. What was he to carry it home in? He bethought himself of his shirt. Hastily putting down the nest, he disrobed himself of that article and carefully wrapped his treasure in it. Arrived at home, he perceived through the keyhole his father sitting at the fireside. He dared not take in the nest so he placed it in an old pot at the side of the stair. After supper he prepared cautiously to undress. The quick eyes of his brother perceived his nudity and he sang out, "Eh, mother, mother, look at Tam! he hasna gotten on his sark!" The statement was too true. The bed-clothes were turned down and there lay "Tam" in a state of nature. His father threatened the strap if he did not confess what had become of his shirt. He was forced to admit that it was in the old pot outside. "And what have you got in it?" asked his father. "A yellow bumbees' byke." "A what?" asked both parents; "a yellow bumbees byke." "Didn't I tell you, sir," said his father, " only the other day, and made you promise me not to bring any more of these things into the house, endangering and molesting us as well as the whole of our neighbours. Besides, only think of your stripping yourself in a wood to get off your shirt to hold a bees' byke!"

"But this is a new ane," said the little culprit, "it's made o' paper." "Made o' fiddlesticks!" "Na, I'll let ye see it." "Let it alone; I don't want to see it. Go to bed at once, sir, or I'll give you something (shaking his strap) that will do you more good than bees' bykes!" Tom's shirt was put in a bowl and boiling water poured over it. When his parents ventured to open it there they found the wasp's nest.

Tom being now four years old he was sent to a dame school, kept by an old woman named Bell Hill. But alas! he often played truant, and stopped on his way to school at the fish-market to question the fishwives about the fish on their stalls. His grannie undertook to drag him to school by the "scuff o' the neck." But the old dame was outdone; Tom would elude her grasp like an eel, and run off to his favourite haunts, grannie giving chase, but generally to no purpose.

He could not resist bringing his beasts to school with him, and consequently became a dread and an annoyance to the school children. They were always getting stung or bitten by some of "Tam Edward's things." He promised Bell Hill that he would transgress no more, but circumstances soon led to his breaking his promise. He had a jackdaw, called Kae, but it made so much noise that his mother declared she would not have it in the house any longer. Tom thought the matter over. He could not part with his pet, so he must take it to school. He thought of an ingenious method for hiding it. His trousers were very wide and buttoned over his vest, so he thought them a convenient place for hiding his bird. He put it safely in before entering school. All went well until the schoolmistress gave the order for prayers. Tom found the kneeling position rather awkward with the jackdaw inside his trousers. The bird was uncomfortable at his altered position, and strove to thrust his bill out at the top of the pants. Tom gave it a vigorous push back, but the bird persisted, and at length putting out his head began a cre-craw, cre-craw. "The Lord preserv's a' ; what's this noo?" cried the school dame, starting to her feet. "It's Tam Edward again!" shouted the children, "wi' a craw stickin' out o' his breeks." The enraged Bell Hill pulled him by his collar and thrust him out at the school door. So ended his first school days.

He was next sent to a school near the old bridge of Aberdeen. It was kept by an old man who believed in the vigorous use of the "taws."* Tom progressed rapidly with his studies, but his besetting sin soon brought him into disgrace. One day the schoolmaster's attention was attracted by a loud scream from one of the scholars. "What's this?" he cried. "It's a horse-leech crawling up my leg!" "A horse-leech?" "Yes, sir, and seè," pointing to a bottle by Tom's seat, "there's a bottlefu' o' them!" "Give me the bottle," roared the schoolmaster, and, turning to the culprit, he said, "You come this way, Master Edward!" When Tom reached his desk, the schoolmaster held out the bottle and said, "that's yours, is it not?" "Yes." "Take it, then, and that is the way out," pointing to the door ; "go as fast as you can, and never come back ; and take that, too," bringing the taws down heavily upon his back.

A few days afterwards Tom's mother brought him to the school door, and was about to ask the master to take him back. But before she could speak a word the schoolmaster said, " Don't bring that boy here ! I'll not take him back—not though you were to give me £20! Neither I, or my scholars, have had a day's peace since he came here."

He was next sent to the Lancaster School in Harriet Street. The under master, in whose department Tom was placed, gave him strict orders not to dare to introduce any of his " beasts " into that school. Tom made his promise, and doubtless meant to keep it. But one day in passing to

---

* A leather strap about three feet long, cut into three tails at the end.

school he spied a sparrow's nest in the corner of a spout. He secured it by mounting a ladder which some workmen had left standing against the house. The nest contained five young birds. Marching off with his treasures he took them into school, and placed them below the form on which he was sitting. In about half-an-hour a chirrup was heard, which grew louder as all five little fledglings joined in the chorus. Before the master could well ask what was the matter the young birds fluttered about the schoolroom, the scholars giving chase. The schoolmaster was very angry, but forgave Tom for that first offence with due warning as to what he might expect if he transgressed again. Not long afterwards, however, he got his dismissal. The master was bitten by an insect. Tom was accused of having brought it, and, although he protested his innocence, after a severe thrashing, he was sent home with orders not to return. Thus ended his school-days.

He was only six years old, but his parents thought that settled employment would keep him out of mischief. Accordingly they sent him to work at a tobacco factory. He earned fourteen-pence a-week, and was very happy with his master, who was a bird fancier, and encouraged him to bring birds, and also allowed him to keep rabbits in the back yard.

After staying in that situation for two years he and his brother went to a factory at Grandholm, situated on the Don, about two miles from Aberdeen. Tom was enraptured with the beautiful scenery, and during meal hours rambled in the woods amongst the birds, insects, and wild flowers, many of which were quite new to him.

When 10 years old his parents took him away from the factory to apprentice him to a regular trade. He was bound to a shoemaker named Charles Begg for six years. With this master he had a most miserable existence He was a coarse, brutal, drunken man, who gave him all kinds of ill-treatment, and would not permit him to keep any pets. One afternoon, having finished his work, Tom was sitting waiting for his master. He had on his knee a little pet sparrow which he had taught to do a number of tricks. Presently Charles Begg returned in a drunken state. He struck Tom a violent blow laying him flat on the floor, and stamped his foot on the pet sparrow. The poor boy managed to escape from his violence, and picking up his little favourite, which was still breathing, carried it home in his bosom. He told his mother what had happened while tears fell fast on the little sparrow. " I wouldn't have cared so much for myself," he said, "if he had only spared my bird."

To avoid returning to his cruel master he went down to the harbour and tried to get work on some ship as a cabin boy, but without success. He next tramped all the way to Kettle—a distance of 100 miles—to visit an uncle, hoping that he might help him in his difficulty. He received a cool reception, so had no alternative but to return home. Finally an arrangement was made by which a different master was found for him, and he returned again to the shoemaking.

In course of time work became scarce, and he was dismissed. The idea of emigrating occurred to him. He thought he might manage to do it as a stowaway ; for he had no money to pay his passage. One of the sailors agreed to admit him into a hole near the bow of the ship, where he might hide until the vessel was far out at sea and it would be impossible for the captain to send him back. When the day fixed for the ship to sail came Tom crept into his hiding place, taking with him some biscuits and water. But the ship did not sail as advertised. For five days it was delayed. On the morning of the fifth day, just as the ship was being loosed from its moorings, Tom was startled by the voice of his sailor friend begging him to go ashore as the vessel was being searched for stowaways. Reluctantly he obeyed, and so ended his scheme for emigrating.

He next enlisted in the Aberdeenshire Militia. He was 18 years old at the time. One day during drill he saw a butterfly flitting past. Away he went in pursuit. Just as he was about to secure it he was gripped by the neck, and found it was his corporal with four Militia men who had come to arrest him for breaking away from the ranks during drill. The corporal secured him, and with two Militia men in front and two behind, marched him off toward the guard house. On their way they encountered one of the officers of the regiment walking with some ladies. The officer enquired what crime the prisoner had been guilty of. On hearing that he had left the ranks to chase a butterfly he thought he must be mad. One of the ladies, herself a naturalist, understood the case. At her request he was liberated.

At 20 years of age Thomas Edward left Aberdeen to work at his trade as a shoemaker at Banff. There he fell in love and married. This settled his roving propensities. His earnings were only 9s. 6d. per week, but through his wife's thrift and industry they managed to live respectably. Late in life, when Mr. Edward was speaking in public of his career, he declared that his wife was his real nugget, the only fortune he ever possessed.

Now that he was settled in a home of his own he began his work as a naturalist in earnest. He bought an old gun for 4s. 6d.—the barrel had to be tied to the stock with a piece of twine. His powder was carried in a horn, and the charges were measured out with the bowl of a tobacco pipe. Besides this he had a few bottles for insects, some boxes for moths and butterflies, and a book for putting his botancial specimens in. After his day's work was done, which was not until nine o'clock at night, he started out with his equipment, carrying his supper in his pocket. The nearest stream supplied him with water to drink with his frugal repast. He ignored all his neighbour's suggestions that "a wee drap o' whiskey would keep out the cold;" water was his only drink. As long as he could see he captured specimens, and studied the habits of the animals roaming about through the night. When it became too dark to pursue his investigations he lay down in a cave, or a fox's den, for an hour or two's sleep, returning to his work as soon as day dawned. At six o'clock he had to leave natural history to attend to his shoemaking. If the night was rainy it did not deter him. He would push himself feet foremost into some den or hole, leaving his head outside, and having his gun ready loaded to fire at any animal that came past. These midnight rambles gave him an excellent opportunity for seeing the animals moving about in their natural state. He soon learnt to distinguish their voices and signs. There was the *bark* of the roe-deer, the *bleak-bleak* of the hare, the *tap-tap* of the rabbit, the snarling *grunt* of the badger, the *squeak* of the otter, and the *blowing* or *hissing* sound made by the polecat, stoat, and weasel, when suddenly surprised. He was thoroughly at home among the animals. In the summer evenings he lay out in the open air with rats and mice running over him, and the larger animals sniffing about, especially if he had shot any birds and had them in his pockets.

His adventures were innumerable. Sometimes he had a fight with a weasel, or an encounter with a polecat. With the latter animal he had, on one occasion, a two hours' struggle. He was resting in a vault belonging to the ruined castle of the Boyne, when he heard a pit-pat near him. Presently the animal walked over him and began smelling. Edward caught hold of him and thrust him away. By his shriek he knew it was a polecat. He had in his breast pocket a water-hen which he had shot. This was what the polecat wanted. Edward lay still, being in readiness to secure him if he returned. Continuing the narrative, Mr. Edward writes: " I lay as still as death ; but, being forced to breathe, the movement of my chest made the brute raise his head, and at that moment I gript him by the throat! I sprang instantly to my feet, and held on. I actually thought that he would have torn my hands to pieces with his claws. I endeavoured to get him turned round, so as to get my hand to the back of his neck. Even then I had enough to do to hold him fast. How he screamed and yelled! What an unearthly noise in the dead of the night! The vault rang with his howlings! And then what an awful stench he emitted during his struggles! The very jackdaws in the upper stories of the castle began to caw! Still I kept my hold. But I could not prevent his yelling at the top of his voice. Although I gripped and squeezed with all my might and main, I could not choke him.

"Then I bethought me of another way of dealing with the brute. I had in my pocket about an ounce of chloroform, which I used for capturing insects. I took the bottle out, undid the cork, and thrust the ounce of chloroform down the truant's throat. It acted as a sleeping draught. He gradually lessened his struggles. Then I laid him down upon a stone, and pressing the iron heel of my boot upon his neck, dislocated his spine, and he struggled no more. I was quite exhausted when the struggle was over. The fight must have lasted nearly two hours." Mr. Edward was rewarded for this struggle by the beautiful specimen of the male polecat which he secured, and that without injury to its skin.

Mr. Edward had three different circuits for his natural history excursions. Two along the shores of the Moray

Firth, extending six or seven miles in each direction, and one inland to the distance of five or six miles. He usually contrived to visit each district twice a week, and his traps placed for catching beetles, grubs, and insects, he inspected at intervals. During five months of the year he slept out almost every night, except Saturday and Sunday. The winter nights he spent in preserving and arranging his specimens, working by the fire-light, as he could not afford a lamp. He made boxes for his specimens, glazing and polishing them himself. His only tools were his shoemaker's knife, a saw, and a hammer. He also stuffed his birds, and sometimes earned a trifle by stuffing some for other people.

After eight years of constant labour Thomas Edward had preserved nearly 2,000 specimens of living creatures found about Banff. Half of them consisted of quadrupeds, birds, reptiles, fishes, crustacea, starfish, zoophytes, corals, and sponges. He had, too, a large collection of plants, and insects filling twenty boxes and numbering 916. These were carefully fixed in their places and numbered, but a sad disaster befell them. Edward had put them in a garret to be, as he thought, in a safe place. What was his horror when one day on going to look at them he found the cases empty. There was nothing left but the pins which had fastened the insects and a stray wing or leg. This mischief was probably done by rats or mice. When his wife saw the empty cases she asked him what he would do next. "Weel," said he, "it is an awfu' disappointment, but I think the best thing will be to set to work and fill them up again." In four years he had nearly replaced the lost collection.

The idea occurred to him that he might make some money by exhibiting, as his house was pretty well filled with stuffed birds, quadrupeds, &c. So he began to prepare, cleaning his cases and brushing up his specimens. But he had another loss. He had put away 2,000 different kinds of dried plants in a box. The cats got at them, and the entire collection was spoilt.

He hired the Trades' Hall for his exhibition at the time of the Banff fair, May, 1845. It was a great success. The following year he exhibited again, and received still greater remuneration. This induced him to take his exhibition to Aberdeen. On the 31st of July, 1846, he had everything ready for the start. Six carriers' carts, the largest that could be found, were hired to convey the collection to Aberdeen; for there was no railroad. Edward, his wife, and five children accompanied the collection. They arrived safely in Aberdeen after a two days' journey. A shop, No. 132, in Union Street, was taken by Edward to hold his exhibition in. Bills and placards were posted about, and advertisements put in the local papers, but to no purpose. A very small number of visitors came. Edward had counted on a great success, but there was nothing but miserable failure. The Aberdeen people did not care for stuffed birds, &c. What was worst of all, many even questioned Edward's honesty. They said it was impossible for such a collection to have been made by a working man with a family to support, and that he was palming off a lie upon the public. His expenses were heavy, and how to pay all debts and get back to Banff he did not know. He started out one day to the sea-shore determined to end his life. He had thrown off part of his clothing, when a low shrill whistle arrested his attention. It was a sanderling. Away he went in chase of the bird, and forgot to commit suicide. His favourite study saved him. As things did not brighten by the middle of the sixth week he sold his entire collection for £20 10s., and paid off his debts.

He returned to his old home at Banff, and resumed his former habits. An amusing story is told of one of his adventures about this time. He was caught one night in a terrific thunderstorm. Wet to the skin he ran to the nearest cottage for shelter. He found two little girls inside, who told him that their mother was from home, but would return shortly. Meantime he went forward to the peat fire to dry his clothes. He examined his hat, which was two-storied. The upper part was separated from his head by a thin piece of board. In this he put his mosses, birds' eggs, butterflies, insects, and such like. He found them all right, and was congratulating himself on the fact when he noticed the children laughing. They ran out of the house to fetch their mother. Presently Edward saw her figure filling the doorway. She was a formidable virago, with red hair, bare legs, short petticoats, and had a pair of man's boots on. In her hand she held a hatchet with which she had been chopping wood. She stood for some minutes regarding Edward with clenched teeth. Then she yelled out, "Man, fat the sorra brocht ye in here, an' you in siccan a mess. Gang oot o' my hoose, I tell ye, this verra minit! Gang oot!" Edward apologised, and begged that she would allow him to remain until the rain ceased. "Not a minit," she shrieked, "ye'll pit my hoose afloat. Ye're a' vermin, and ye'll pit's in a hobble if ye dinna gang oot!" Edward said he had nothing to do with vermin; but at this crisis he put his hand to his cheek and found something crawling. He looked at his clothes—they, too, were covered with creeping things. He found on searching his pockets that his insect boxes had been soaked through by the rain, and all the creatures had escaped and were swarming about him. He fled from the house, glad to escape from its enraged occupant.

Edward's fame as a naturalist spread after he had exhibited. Before that time his neighbours looked upon him as rather a questionable character. His midnight rambles exposed him to a suspicion of poaching; but when the people saw his collection they understood him better. In order to extend his investigations farther into Aberdeenshire and Banffshire he obtained a licence from the authorities. The certificate ran as follows:—"These are to certify that the bearer, Thos. Edward, shoemaker, who is in height about 5 ft. 6 inches, has dark eyes and hair, much pock-pitted, round-shouldered, and about 35 years of age—is, in addition to his other calling, engaged in collecting and preserving various objects of natural history, particularly those objects which relate to ornithology (birds), oology (eggs), entomology (insects), helminthology (worms, &c.), conchology (shells); that for the purpose of procuring ornithological specimens, he is under the necessity of using a gun, but in doing so, we, the undersigned, have never heard of a single case of poaching being brought against him, and, as far as we know, he is not in the habit of killing game of any sort, nor of destroying property of any description, which, were he in the practice of so doing, being so frequently out with his gun, he could not, we think, have escaped public notice so long, having resided in this town for a period of 11 years, during which time he has borne an unimpeachable character.

"Banff, March, 1850.

"JAMES DUFF, J.P., &c., &c.'

About this time Edward met with a very serious accident. During one of his excursions he fell down a precipice, and was found by some working men wedged between two rocks. Fortunately his limbs were not broken; but he was too ill to work for a month afterwards. To meet the expenses of his illness and maintain his family, he was obliged to sell 100 cases out of his second collection. This was a severe blow to him.

Edward was obliged to rely on his friends for naming and classifying his specimens, as he could not afford to buy books on natural science. The Rev. James Smith, of the Manse of Monquhitter, about 10 miles from Banff, was his principal helper in this respect. It was he who first induced him to make notes of his observations. These were published from time to time in the *Banffshire Journal*. He also contributed papers to the *Naturalist*, the *Zoologist*, the *Ibis*, and the *Linnæan Journal*. They were most interesting and instructive. The great interest he felt in his subject enabled him to write graphically, although he knew little of grammar. All his knowledge was gained from personal observation. He studied the animals in their natural habitats, and was able to give to the public the most interesting details. Many a touching story did he tell of the devotion of animals to their young, and of their sympathy with each other in distress. On one occasion he shot at and wounded a tern which was busy fishing for food. Edward saw the bird fall into the water with its wing broken, and hastened to secure it; but some other terns came to the rescue. Two of them lifted him up out of the water and bore him away far out to sea. Concluding the narrative, Mr. Edward says:—"I was indeed rejoiced at the disappointment which they had occasioned, for they had thereby rendered me the witness of a scene which I could scarcely have believed, and which no length of time will efface from my recollection."

Edward had completed a third and most beautiful collection by the year 1858. The birds were arranged in their natural positions; pecking, feeding, fluttering, or flying, and sometimes with their nests and the young in them. His health, however, gave way from the excessive exposure to which he subjected himself; he became prostrate with rheumatic fever. To meet the extra expenses of his illness he had again to sell part of his collection. Nearly 40 cases of birds were sold, besides other things. On his recovery his doctor prohibited him from continuing his night wanderings. Therefore, he devoted his time to studying the natural history of the sea-shore. He corresponded with Mr. Macdonald, of Elgin, as to zoophytes; with Mr. Blackwood, of Aberdeen, as to algæ; and with Mr. Charles Bate, of Plymouth, as to crustacea. He laboured for many years in gathering marine objects from the Moray Firth, sending them to noted scientists to be named and classified. He could not afford a dredge, but used to lower buckets, pots, pans, anything he could get for the purpose, into the Moray Firth from some projecting rock. These were attached to ropes, and at intervals he drew them to land and took out any marine object that might have crept in. In this way he discovered many new specimens. His daughter, Maggie, went regularly to the fishing village to get the fish stomachs for her father. These he examined, and often found many valuable specimens in an undigested state. He also hunted amongst the refuse caught on the fishermen's lines. In short, he employed every means in his power to further science, and succeeded in discovering 26 new species among the crustacea in the Moray Firth; also a new midge, which was named by his friend, Mr. Couch, the "Edward's Midge," or the *Conchia Edwardii*.

In April, 1866, he was unanimously elected an Associate of the Linnean Society. Shortly after he was admitted a member of the Aberdeen Natural History Society, and in March, 1867, of the Glasgow Society. But as yet his scientific knowledge had not brought pecuniary benefit. His friends tried to get him a post as custodian of a museum, or as a coastguardsman, but without success. His health was much impaired, and he had a wife and eleven children to keep on scanty earnings. There was, however, no alternative but to continue at his trade as a shoemaker.

After the publication of Mr. Samuel Smiles' most charming biography, public attention was drawn to the poor Naturalist. The Queen was so touched by his story that she conferred upon him a pension of £50. A subscription was got up for him in Aberdeen, which was presented to him at a public meeting in his honour. He returned his thanks in a speech in broad Aberdeenshire Scotch, in which he alluded to the valuable help afforded him by his wife. She had sympathized with him in his pursuits, and given whatever aid was in her power. She was once asked what she thought of his night wanderings and queer ways· She replied, "Weel, he took such an interest in beasts that I didna' compleen. Shoemakers were then a very drucken set, but his beasts keepit him frae them. My man's been a sober man all his life; and he never neglected his wark. Sae I let him be."

Through the kindness of his friends, Thomas Edward lives peacefully and comfortably in his old age, pursuing in a quiet way his favourite studies. In addressing the boys at Yarlet School, near Liverpool, he thus summed up his life's history:—"In searching for living things my desire was not to destroy for destruction's sake, but simply that I might learn all I could concerning the beautiful and wonderful works of God. This was hard, though pleasant work; and remember, as I have told you before, I was uneducated, which you are not, or if you are, it must be your own fault. I was worse off, too, in another respect, if worse can be. I was very poor, very poor indeed. Neither had I any books, nor wherewithal to get books. I had no one to teach me, nor to advise me, nor to tell me a word of what I longed to know; I was like a ship set adrift on the ocean without a rudder, in fact, without a crew; but I still panted for knowledge. Yet, from the day when I got that terrible sore back from my last day-school teacher, I had nothing but to teach myself, or go untaught.

"But some of you may say, 'How did you do it?' Well, I had the will and I did it; and I suppose it was just by being, as I have told you, *never idle*. I was never at peace or rest unless I was at work, except sometimes when I was overpowered with sleep; and, take my word for it, that sleep vexed me most bitterly. I saw no good or use in it— though now I know better. I didn't want it, and I hated a sluggard. Sleep to me was only a waste and loss of time; but I had to succumb sometimes, though an hour or an hour and a half at most sufficed. I was up and at it again after that, either inside of the house or out. . . . With all this trouble and sacrifice, I must confess to you that I have lived a very happy life."

THOMAS CARLYLE.

THOMAS CARLYLE was born on the 4th of December, 1795, at Ecclefechan, a small market town in the south of Scotland, situated about 16 miles from Carlisle. His father was an honest, sober, God-fearing man, but with the sterner traits of Scotch character fully developed. He was a man to be feared rather than loved. The softer element, which was wanting in his father, Carlyle found in his mother. For her he had an unbounded affection. "If I had all the mothers I ever saw to choose from I would have chosen my own," he said, on one occasion. Later in life in writing to her, he breaks out into sudden rhapsody :—" Who is the one that never shrunk from me in my desolation, that never tired of my despondencies, or shut up, by a look or tone of impatience, the expression of my real or imaginary griefs? Who is it that loves me, and will love me for ever with an affection which no chance, no misery, no crime of mine can do away? It is you, my mother."

Although at the time of Thomas Carlyle's birth his parents were scarcely above the peasantry—his father being a mason by trade—the family of Carlyle was not without its noble ancestry. A few miles from Dumfries now stands the ruins of the ancient castle of Torthorwald, which the first Lord Carlyle received as a reward for a beating he gave the English during one of those frays, which, generations ago, devastated the "Fair Borderland." The Carlyles were originally English, their name being taken from Carlisle town. They first settled in Annandale in the reign of David II., when they were among the adherents of the Bruces. As time went by their lands were lost in lawsuits, their title lapsed, their descendants became simple yeomen, and Thomas

Carlyle, eventually to be the most illustrious of his line, ran barefoot in the streets of Ecclefechan.

He received his first instruction from his mother, who taught him to read. From his father he learnt arithmetic, and at five years old was sent to the village school. He soon displayed sufficient ability to make his parents feel that he might be made into a scholar. If there is one thing that delights the Scottish peasant above all others, it is to have a son who can push his way through the University. No self-denial, no amount of hard work will these education-loving people spare to advance a boy who shows promise of being a scholar. "I do not grudge thee thy schooling, Tom," said the elder Carlyle to his son one day, "now that thy uncle Frank owns thee a better arithmetician than himself." The boy of promise was accordingly transferred to the Annan Grammar School; a preparatory step before entering the Edinburgh University to train for a minister of the Scottish Kirk.

"Old Adam Hope," the master under whom Carlyle was now placed, was quite a notable in Annan. Among other things he had written a small *English* Grammar, which placed him high in the estimation of parents and scholars as a man of learning. Carlyle describes him as "A strong-built, bony, but rather lean kind of man, of brown complexion, and a pair of the sharpest, not the sweetest, black eyes. Walked in a lounging, stooping figure; in the street broad-brimmed and in clean frugal rustic clothes; in his school-room bareheaded, hands usually crossed over back, and with his effective leather strap hanging ready over his thumb if requisite anywhere. In my time he had a couple of his front teeth quite black, which was very visible, as his mouth usually wore a settled humanly contemptuous grin. 'Nothing good to be expected from you or from those you came of, ye little whelps; but we must get from you the best you have, and not complain of anything.' This was what the grin seemed to say; but the black teeth *(jet black*, for he chewed tobacco also to a slight extent, never spitting) were always mysterious to me, till at length I found they were of cork, the product of Adam's frugal penknife, and could be removed at pleasure. He was a man humanly contemptuous of the world, and valued 'suffrages' at a most low figure in comparison. I should judge an extremely proud man; for the rest an inexorable logician, a Calvinist at all points, and a Burgher Scotch Seceder to the backbone."

Carlyle entered Annan School on the 26th May, 1805. He was a shy, thoughtful boy, shrinking generally from rough companions, but possessing the hot temper of his race. His mother made him promise before he parted from her that he would never return a blow. It was only on an occasion of great provocation that he broke his word.

On Sundays he attended the Ecclefechan Meeting House with his parents. Mr. Johnston, a worthy man and a Seceder, was the minister. The Old Meeting House was attended by all the people round the country side who were dissatisfied with the Established Kirk. A grave and solemn assemblage it was ; many of the worshippers walked all the way from Carlisle, and others from Annan, there being no Secession Churches in those places. There was a stern, unyielding spirit in the old Seceders. A good story is told of one of them, David Hope, a relative of the schoolmaster, Adam. He had a little farm on the Solway shore. There had been a trying season for the harvest. David's "stuff" was standing out dry and ready to be carried in. He had just finished his frugal porridge breakfast and was about to "take the book," or conduct family worship, when a neighbour rushed in saying, "Such a raging wind risen as will drive the stooks [shocks] into the sea if let alone." "Wind !" answered David, slowly adjusting his spectacles; "Wind canna get ae straw that has been appointed mine. Sit down and let us worship God."

At the age of fourteen, in Nov., 1809, Thomas Carlyle, accompanied by an elder boy, called Tom Smail, who had already been at College, set out for the Edinburgh University. The Scotch students rarely indulged in riding in those days, but trudged along the road at the rate of 20 or 30 miles a day, relying on getting shelter for the night in the homes of the farmers or peasantry, whose doors were ever open to the poor scholar. In this way the poor Ecclefechan lad, yet to be the greatest thinker of his age, entered "Edinbugh Toon," after a journey of one hundred miles. He and his friend took a lodging in Simon Square, and after having a meal set out to see the wonderful city. After looking at the Cathedral of St. Giles and Parliament Square, the boys entered the law courts and saw the judges and the black gown advocates. All this made a profound impression on the mind of young Carlyle.

He was now to begin his University career. Five months out of the year were spent in attending the classes; the rest of the time was passed by the students in their country homes; or more generally in teaching, in order to earn money to meet their expenses. Their simple wants were supplied from the homestead. Relays of oatmeal, butter, eggs, &c., were duly forwarded to them by the country carrier, who took back, in return, their linen to be washed and mended by their mothers. It was only by such methods as these that poor men's sons could get an University education. Habits of thrift enabled them to subsist on the smallest means, and their poverty kept them from the temptations of the city. They got very little individual attention from the professors. The classes were too large to admit of the boys being readily distinguished one from the other. For the most part it rested entirely with themselves as to whether they became scholars or not.

Carlyle does not appear to have particularly distinguished himself. In mathematics he made good progress. Professor Leslie noticing his talents tried to advance him, but he could only do his best work when alone. The bustle of the class-room upset him. He rarely succeeded in carrying off prizes at the examinations.

His fellow-students held him in great esteem. Among the little clique who were his special friends he was called by such epithets as "Doctor," "Dean," or "Jonathan," as though they anticipated that he would develop into a second Dean Swift. He was the sober one among them, and always appealed to if money matters went wrong. All of them recognised him as above the common, and prophesied a brilliant future for him.

Carlyle finished his college course in 1814, and became Mathematical Tutor at Annan School. He carried on his studies in the intervals of teaching, presenting himself yearly at the University to read a discourse in the Divinity Hall. He was what was termed a rural divinity student. His first sermon was from the text, "Before I was afflicted

I went astray," &c. The professors complimented him upon it, but he felt very dissatisfied himself. His next attempt was a discourse in Latin on "Natural Religion;" whether there was or was not such a thing. It was while in Edinburgh delivering this discourse that he first made the acquaintance of Edward Irving, who had a'ready begun to show those marvellous powers of oratory which took London by storm.

Irving was at this time schoolmaster at Kirkcaldy, but some of the school patrons threw him over and started a rival school. Carlyle was invited to become its master. It was an awkward position, but he accepted it. Instead of meeting with coldness or resentment from Irving, he received from him the most cordial reception, and found in him his truest and best friend.

Carlyle began his life at Kirkcaldy in 1816. But he thoroughly disliked teaching, and the thought of entering the ministry was distasteful too. He entered little into society, but lived a solitary life, engrossed in his books. The outlook for the future was very dismal. Writing to a friend at this time he said, "Oh Tom, what a foolish flattering creature thou art! to talk of future eminence in connection with the literary history of the nineteenth century to such an one as me! Alas! my good lad, when I and all my fancies and reveries and speculations shall have been swept over with the besom of oblivion, the literary history of no century will feel itself the worse. Yet think not, because I talk thus, I am careless of literary fame. No; heaven knows, that ever since I have been able to form a wish, the wish of being known has been foremost."

The first romance of his life was at Kirkcaldy. He contracted a friendship with a beautiful Miss Gordon, which speedily ripened into an attachment. The lady's friends would not receive Carlyle as a suitor, and he was forced to relinquish her. A letter from Miss Gordon to her rejected lover gives a good idea of the impression which he left on the minds of others. "Cultivate the milder dispositions of the heart," wrote the lady; "subdue the more extravagant visions of the brain. In time your abilities must be known. Among your acquaintance they are already beheld with wonder and delight. By those whose opinion will be valuable, they hereafter will be appreciated. Genius will render you great. May virtue render you beloved. Remove the awful distance between you and ordinary men by kind and gentle manners. Deal gently with their inferiority, and be convinced they will respect you as much and like you more. Why conceal the real goodness that flows in your heart?"

In 1818 Carlyle finally determined to relinquish all thought of the ministry. He was not prepared to bind himself to the formulas of the Scottish Kirk. Teaching was also distasteful, and he purposed to study for the bar. By strict economy he had saved £90. With this he started once more for the Edinburgh University to begin his law studies. To support himself he taught pupils, and earned a little by writing for Dr. (afterwards Sir David) Brewster's "Encyclopædia."

His melancholy deepened, however, and the dyspepsia which tormented him throughout his life began its "gnawing pains" at his stomach. This, added to the uncertainties of his career, rendered him very morose. "He was gey [very] ill to live wi'" said his mother. His friend Edward Irving, tried to encourage him, and urged him to give "tongue" to his thoughts. Carlyle had accumulated a vast store of knowledge by his assiduous reading, but did not seem to know what to do with it. Irving wrote to him: "Known you must be before you can be employed. Known you will not be for a winning, attaching, accommodating man, but for an original, commanding, and rather self-willed man. Now, establish this last character, and you take a far higher grade than any other." Irving was the one friend to whom Carlyle in his gloom and despondency could unburden himself. The law had lost its charm for him, and everything seemed uncertain. It was at this time that he was introduced to Miss Welsh, the daughter of the chief medical man in Haddington. She was bent on literary pursuits, and Irving, who had been her tutor, recommended his friend Carlyle as one likely to help her in her studies. The friendship thus begun deepened until Miss Welsh became Mrs Carlyle.

Throwing aside all thought of any other profession, Carlyle now devoted himself to literature. He continued his articles to the "Encyclopædia," wrote on German literature, and translated "Legendre's Geometry." But, mainly through Irving's instrumentality, an unexpected good fortune befell him. He was offered a tutorship at £200 a year. It was by a Mr. Buller, who engaged him to superintend the studies of his sons while they were in Edinburgh. His relationship with the Bullers was a most cordial one. When they removed from Edinburgh to Kinnaird House, near Dunkeld, he accompanied them. But he had not yet found his true sphere. Before long he threw up the Buller tutorship, and started on a roving expedition. He visited London, Birmingham, Stratford-on-Avon, Dover, Paris, and finally returned again to London, and passed some time there.

Meanwhile he had written a "Life of Schiller," which came out in the *London Magazine* in 1823. He had also translated "Wilheim Meister," for which he received good pay, and from its author, the poet Goethe, a most flattering letter; so that Carlyle's hopes began to brighten; he felt that at last he was being recognised.

He now longed for a home of his own, where he could pursue his studies without interruption. An arrangement was made with his brother Alic for taking the farm of Hoddam Hill, in Annandale. There Carlyle lived for a short time, having his mother and sisters for housekeepers. But this was abandoned on account of his approaching marriage with Miss Welsh of Haddington.

She was a beautiful and accomplished lady, reared in a sphere very different to Carlyle. But she discerned in him a man of true genius, and was content to share his chequered career. Her father had been a doctor of some repute in Haddington, but died in the prime of manhood, leaving his wife, and only child. Miss Welsh could boast of descent from John Knox and the brave patriot Wallace. A story is told of one of her ancestors which shows the spirit of bravery which distinguished them. The lady was the daughter of John Knox and the wife of John Welsh. Her husband was banished by King James, but permission having been granted for his return on condition that he would acknowledge the authority of the bishops, she presented herself at Court, and on the terms being made known to her, with scornful gesture raised her apron, saying, "Please your Majesty, I'd rather kep his head here." The King, astounded, asked who she was. When told that she was a daughter of Knox, he exclaimed "Knox and Welsh! the devil never made such a match as that!" "It's right like, Sir," replied she, "for we never speered [asked] his advice."

Thomas Carlyle and the "Flower of Haddington," as Miss Welsh was called, were married in the year 1826. For two years they resided at No. 21, Comely Bank, Edinburgh. There they gathered round them a select company of friends. Lord Jeffrey, Dr. Brewster, and De Quincey were among their most frequent visitors. All were charmed by Mrs. Carlyle's exquisite grace of manner, and her husband's wonderful conversational powers, "unequalled," says Mr. Froude, "as far as my experience goes, by any other man."

During this period spent in Edinburgh he contributed papers to the *Edinburgh Review*. They were afterwards collected and published as the "Miscellanies." The first of the series was "Jean Paul." "German Literature" followed next, and created quite a sensation. Still Carlyle felt that his income was a very precarious one, and was anxious to secure some permanent appointment. He offered himself as a professor for the London University, but without success. A similar disappointment awaited him when he was induced by his friends to apply for the Professorship of Moral Philosophy in the University of St. Andrews, made vacant by the removal of Dr. Chalmers to London. Disappointed on all sides, and finding his means very straightened, Carlyle determined to leave Edinburgh.

Mrs. Carlyle had inherited the small estate of Craigenputtock. It was her father's birth-place, and had been the residence of her family for many generations. The manor house, a plain, quaint building, was situated on the moors, far away from civilized life. Dumfries, the nearest town, was sixteen miles distant. A drearier, sterner, and more desolate spot can hardly be imagined than was this melancholy Craigenputtock. But to this moorland farm Carlyle determined to go for the sake of economy, and to get quiet.

In May, 1828, he and his wife removed from Edinburgh and settled at this moorland house which was for seven years to be their home, and where, in the midst of that awful stillness, which Mrs. Carlyle says enabled her to hear the sheep nibbling the grass a quarter of a mile distant, the prophet was to think out his message to the world. To Mrs. Carlyle the change was great, and to Carlyle himself it does not appear to have been altogether pleasant. He noted in his diary of this time, " Finished a paper on Burns, September 16th, 1828, at this *Devil's Den*, Craigenputtock.

During the first part of their residence there, Carlyle's brother, Alic, lived in a cottage near, and managed the farm. Scotsbrig, where his parents lived, was only a few miles distant, and Templand, the home of Mrs. Carlyle's mother and uncles, was within easy access. The tedium of Craigenputtock was relieved by visits to one or other of these places. The journeys were usually made when Carlyle had completed some literary effort. He then gave himself a holiday. The horse and gig were made ready—special care being taken that the pipe and tobacco were conveniently placed underneath the splashboard to be dry and ready for use— and off he and Mrs. Carlyle rode to Scotsbrig or Templand. Lord Jeffrey occasionally paid them a visit and, on one memorable occasion, Emerson, the great American author, penetrated into their seclusion to enjoy a chat with the man whose writings he so admired. He thus describes Carlyle in his solitude:—" I found the house amid desolate heathery hills, where the lonely scholar nourished his mighty heart. Carlyle was a man from his youth, an author who did not need to hide from his readers, and as absolute a man of the world, unknown and exiled on that hill farm, as if holding on his own terms what is best in London. He was tall and gaunt, with a cliff-like brow, and holding his extraordinary powers of conversation in easy command ; clinging to his northern accent with evidentrelish ; full of lively anecdote, and with a streaming humour which floated everything he looked upon. His talk, playfully exalting the most familiar objects, put the companion at once into an acquaintance with his Lars and Lemurs, and it was very pleasant to learn what was destined to be a pretty mythology. Few were the objects and lonely the man, ' not a person to speak to within 16 miles except the minister of Dunscore ;' so that books inevitably made his topics."

In this solitude Carlyle wrote busily for the *Edinburgh Review*, *Fraser's Magazine*, and the *Foreign Review*.

But as his opinions grew more pronounced editors grew shy of him. "He had," as Mr. Froude says, "to form the taste by which he could be appreciated." "Hang them! hang them!" said he, as one disappointment followed another. "I have a book in me that will cause ears to tingle, and one day out it must and will issue. In this valley of the shadow of magazine editors we shall not always linger. Courage! not hope—for she was always a liar—but courage! courage!" Writing to his brother Robert, he said:—"I will not leave literature; neither should you leave it. Nay, had I but two potatoes in the world, and one true idea, I should hold it my duty to part with one potato for paper and ink, and live upon the other till I got it written." A man with so high an ideal was not likely to be crushed down, or made to toady to popular opinion. He would write what he held to be truth or not at all. "Knowing how you abhor all affectation," had been said to him when a mere boy. The feeling grew upon him until it seemed that his whole energy was directed against "shams." He had to bear the consequences of his honesty and originality. "Sartor Resartus" was written, and with the manuscript in his pocket he set out from Glencaple Quay on the Solway to sail to London. But not a publisher would look at it. "It is a work of genius, dear," said his noble wife, as she finished reading the last page. The genius, however, was too original to be appreciated.

Mrs. Carlyle joined him in London, and remained for the winter. During that time he found a publisher for his "History of German Literature," but "Sartor" was condemned. One publisher had agreed to bring it out, but got scared when the first sheet was printed, and gave up the enterprise. Thoroughly disheartened, they returned to their moorland home to hide their poverty. Lord Jeffrey offered money, and Carlyle was at length forced to accept from him a loan of £50.

The winter of 1833 he spent in Edinburgh for the purpose of reading in the Advocates' Library, preparatory to writing the "French Revolution." During his stay he arranged for the publication of "Sartor Resartus" in *Fraser's Magazine.* No sooner did it appear than the unfortunate editor felt the impending ruin of his magazine.

The public could not understand so novel a kind of writing. One gentleman wrote that if that kind of stuff continued to appear he would not take in *Fraser*. But across the Atlantic was one who could appreciate. Ralph Waldo Emerson wrote requesting that the magazine should be sent him as long as anything of Carlyle's appeared in it.

"Sartor Resartus" ("The Tailor Done Over," the name of an old Scotch ballad) was composed by Carlyle at Craigenputtock. He spent intervals of five years upon it. The hero, Professor Tenfelsdroeckh ("Devil's Dirt") seems in part to be a portrait of human nature, but a great deal of Carlyle's own life and experiences are set forth in the history of Tenfelsdroeckh. All that had been seething in his mind, from his very boyhood, came out in this book. He worked out his theory of "the clothes philosophy," and showed how poor a mask were mere clothes. The ermine of the king did not make him a nobler man than those around him. True nobility lay in man's inner self, not in the outward guise. It was one tremendous protest against shams, and a passionate call to the world to flee from falsehood to truth.

In 1834 Carlyle, finding himself possessed of about £200, determined to try his fortune in London. He set out to find a house, leaving Mrs. Carlyle to pack up and follow. They settled in an old-fashioned house, built in the reign of Queen Anne, situated in a quiet street of Chelsea called Cheyne Row. This continued to be Carlyle's home until the day of his death. He had for near neighbours Maclise, the artist, and Leigh Hunt. Besides these friends, others soon came. Among them John Stuart Mill, Charles Buller— Carlyle's old pupil and now a brilliant parliamentary man— the Marquis of Lansdowne, Lord Ashburton, Mrs. Austin, Erasmus Darwin, Miss Martineau, Allan Cunningham, and John Sterling. Carlyle's marvellous conversational powers acted as a charm on all who came under its influence. It was almost an impossibility for others to talk when he once started on a subject. He bore every one else down by the mighty torrent of his eloquence. At times he would be in a grimly humorous mood, telling his stories in a strong Scotch dialect, and with a quiet enjoyment. Or his ire would be roused by some act of toadyism, and the unfortunate offender would feel the wordy torrent of his wrath. His high philosophy sometimes formed the subject of his harangues. Then his long full sentences flowed out, lit up by strange imagery and poetic fancy, until it seemed as though some ancient seer was pouring forth his impassioned utterances. He had a peculiar, sharp, short way of putting the extinguisher upon any person who spoke in what he thought a foolish manner. On one occasion he was at a dinner party in Berlin, when some of the guests—mistaken pietists—were expressing their regret that so godlike a genius as Emerson had not devoted himself more to Christianity. Carlyle sat grim, eyeing the speakers, twisting his dinner napkin, and ominously silent. At last he broke out in a slow emphatic manner, "Meine Herren, did you never hear the story of that man who vilified the sun because it would not light his cigar?" This put a most complete stop to the discussion.

Sharp, cutting sarcasm he certainly had, and would at times indulge in it past all endurance. Yet withal there was in him a deep compassion—a humanness of feeling that illuminated his otherwise stern character. Leigh Hunt, who had ample opportunity for judging his peculiarities of temperament, says :—"I believe that what Mr. Carlyle loves better than his fault-finding, with all its eloquence, is the face of any human creature that looks suffering, and loving, and sincere; and I believe further, that if the fellow-creature were suffering only, and neither loving nor sincere, but had come to a pass of agony in this life which put him at the mercies of some good man for some last help and consolation towards his grave, even at the risk of loss to repute, and a sure amount of pain and vexation, that man, if the groan reached him in its forlornness, would be Thomas Carlyle." To his own kindred he was particularly generous, helping them with money when it meant deprivation to himself. His brother Robert was educated as a doctor almost entirely at his expense. To his aged parents he was ever kind and thoughtful. No honest man in distress ever sought his help in vain.

After settling in London the "French Revolution" was his first literary effort. If that failed, he meant to bury himself in the Far West. John Mill took deep interest in the book, and supplied Carlyle with materials for it. But a sad misfortune befell the first volume. Mr. Mill had it at his house for perusal. It was left carelessly lying about, and a servant lit the fire with it. This catastrophe almost broke Carlyle's heart. His little store of money was melting away, and he was relying on this book to bring in more. All his time and trouble had gone for naught. It was weeks before he could re-commence the task. Mr. Mill generously sent him £200, but he would only accept £100, which was the sum taken to keep his house while the volume was being written. In the spring of 1837 the completed work was published. "The last paragraph," says Carlyle, "I well remember writing upstairs in the drawing-room that now is, which was then my writing-room; beside her there, and in a grey evening, soon after tea, whereupon, with her dear blessing on me, going out to walk. I had said before going out, 'What will they do with this book? none knows, my Jeannie, lass; but they have not had, for 200 years, any book that came more truly from a man's very heart, and so let them trample it under foot and hoof as they see best." But they did not trample it under feet. The public were taken by storm with this marvellous history of the French Revolution, which had the fascination of some thrilling romance, and the music of some grand epic poem.

For the next three or four years Carlyle gave annual courses of lectures in Willis's Rooms. All the *élite* of London society flocked to hear this Annandale peasant. They were fascinated by the man's earnestness. He had not, like his friend Irving—whose star had set—the gift of oratory, but held them spell bound by the intensity of his nature. "You can almost fancy," said one of his listeners, "in some of his most enthusiastic and energetic moments, that you see his inmost soul in his face." His movements were very ungraceful, and he spoke in his harsh Scotch accent. The lectures on "Heroes and Hero Worship" created the greatest sensation.

In 1845 "The Life and Letters of Oliver Cromwell" appeared. If there had been any doubt about Carlyle's genius as a writer this book dispelled it. His fame was made. Years of unceasing toil he had given in gathering together these letters and speeches of Cromwell. He succeeded in throwing an altogether different light upon the motives and actions of the hitherto much maligned Protector.

Twenty years later his great work of "Frederick the Great" was published. For thirteen years he had laboured at it, taking trips to Germany to glean information. During this period he became quite a recluse. He had his study at the top of the house, and there he sat day after day "silent and aloft," writing his "Frederick." Riding was his only diversion. His wife saw little of him except for half-an-hour in the evening, when he took his pipe beside her and talked of his book. Always his book—his mind could dwell on nothing else. Wife, friends, everything was forgotten in this one absorbing idea.

In the same year as the publication of "The Life of Frederick the Great" took place, Carlyle was appointed Lord Rector of the University of Edinburgh, as successor to Mr. Gladstone. He had emerged from his long spell of work in a shattered state of health, and had grown more and more averse to public appearances. But this was an honour that even he was not altogether prepared to refuse. Great was the enthusiasm in Edinburgh when it was known that he had accepted the office, and would deliver the Rectorial address. Mrs. Carlyle was too ill to accompany him. For many years her health had been giving way, and she was quite unfit for so exciting a scene. Professor Tyndall took her place, and escorted the "Prophet" to his native land, promising to keep her informed by telegram as to how he passed through the ordeal.

The largest public room in the city was taken for the occasion. Tickets were sold for every available space. The Scotch ministers flocked in from their country manses and mingled with the London clergy in the general rush to see and hear. It was a moment never to be forgotten by those who were present when Carlyle, in his Rectorial robes, accompanied by the Principal of the University, the Members of the Senate, the Lord Provost, and a file of notables, advanced towards the platform. His face still wore the country bronze which had marked it fifty-six years before, when a nameless Annandale lad he came to the "grey city" to study for the Kirk. The Kirk had lost a true and honest man, but the world had gained a seer.

Before the address the degree of LL.D. was conferred upon Mr. Erskine of Linlathen, Carlyle's old friend ; on Professors Huxley, Tyndall, and Ramsay, and on Mr. Rae, the Arctic explorer. It had also been offered to Carlyle, but refused it, laughingly saying that it might cause confusion in Paradise if there were to be two Dr. Carlyles. His brother had entered the medical profession. This ceremony over, he arose amid waving of hats and a tempest of cheering to address the students, first throwing off the robe of office which the writer of the "Clothes Philosophy" could ill endure.

The address was given without any notes, and came from his lips easily and fluently. It was characterized by simplicity and a desire to implant in the minds of the students practical lessons to guide them in their studies, and above all, in their choice of books.

Hardly had this brilliant ceremony ended than the principal figure in it was overtaken with a sorrow that blighted the remainder of his career. Carlyle had travelled to Dumfries from Edinburgh, and there the melancholy news reached him that his wife was dead. Her death had occurred suddenly, while taking her drive in Hyde Park. Sad and sorrowful he returned to London in order to accompany her remains to Haddington, where, according to Scottish custom, they were *silently* laid in the choir of the old cathedral. On her tombstone her many virtues were set forth by her husband, "In her bright existence," he wrote. "she had more sorrows than are common, but also a soft invincibility, a capacity of discernment, and a noble loyalty of heart which are rare. For 40 years she was the true and loving helpmate of her husband, and by act and word unweariedly forwarded him as none else could in all of worthy that he did or attempted."

The light of his life had gone out. Desolate, forlorn, he returned to the old house at Chelsea, there to live out the remainder of his days in one long wail of melancholy. Already a man well advanced in years, and somewhat worn by the intense life he had lived, this great blow fell upon him with unusual severity. The cry of remorse and sorrow which tinges every page of his "Reminiscences," shows only too sadly how desolate his life had become. Scholars and men of mark still found their way to Chelsea, and strove to dissipate his gloom, but it deepened as the years went by. He varied the monotony of his life by occasional trips abroad, or in visiting his sister, Mrs. Aitken, at Dumfries. Riding along the beautiful Dumfries lanes, his gaunt figure and sorrow-worn face were often seen. He looked like a man with his heart buried in the past. As he strolled from his house at Chelsea along the river side the children came fearlessly about him, and many a story is told of the aged philosopher visiting the confectioner's shop at the corner of the street where he lived to buy sweetmeats for them.

On the 5th of February, 1881, he passed away in his 86th year. Dean Stanley immediately suggested Westminster Abbey as a fitting burial place, but Carlyle's wish had been to lie with his forefathers. In accordance with it he was buried in the quiet little churchyard of Ecclefechan, by the side of his parents, and with only a simple stone to mark his resting place.

HENRY SCOTT RIDDELL.

THE career of Henry Scott Riddell, who has been aptly termed the "Last Border Minstrel," although not terminating in any very marked distinction, is full of interest. His life is another tribute to man's power of overcoming adverse circumstances by moulding them to himself instead of being moulded by them.

He was the son of a simple shepherd, and was born on the 23rd of September, 1798, at Sorbie, near Langholm, in Selkirkshire. His parents left Sorbie when he was quite young and settled at Langshawburn. While there he received lessons, in the winter months, from a young man who was employed by several shepherds to instruct their families. He went round them in turn, boarding at their houses as payment for his services. In summer time lessons were laid aside and young Riddell roamed the hills and dales learning to tend sheep. He made very little progress in his studies, loving foot-ball better than the spelling-book. He was boarded, for short periods, at the schools of Davington, Roberton, and Newmill, but with very poor results,

His education as a poet began during those early years. James Hogg, the Ettrick Shepherd, was a frequent visitor at his father's house; he would listen to his talk in wrapt delight. He could repeat a great part of the "Shepherd's" poems from hearing them read; he was himself unable to read. His mind was well stored with the tales and ballads of the Border, which he heard from his father's friends as they chatted round the ingle.

At an early age he took a situation as shepherd in the neighbourhood of Deloraine, and was proud of his employment. With all the poet's rapture he enjoyed the beauties of hill and dale, mountain and stream, as he tended his herd. He had begun to make verses, and in summer days sat on the hill-side writing them using his knees for a desk. There was nothing to disturb the calm serenity of the place save the caresses of his faithful dog or the stir of the sheep grazing in the vale below. He had his regular halting places, which were well known to his dog, who had also his chosen place of repose close to his master's seat. Trotting in advance of the shepherd, the faithful creature would stop when he reached an accustomed resting place, and if his master walked past it would, by dumb show, express his surprise.

Some of young Riddell's poetry took the form of satire, which was directed against any person round the countryside who had been guilty of mean or cruel actions. He usually carried a number of these squibs in the crown of his hat for his *private* perusal, but fate ordered it otherwise. One day a rude gust of wind swept his hat from his head, and away went the papers over hill and dale. Some he rescued, but others were picked up by the very persons against whom they were directed. One man, finding his actions set forth in verse, complained to his neighbours, who in turn stated like grievances. The affair spread until it reached the ears of the poet's father, who rated him soundly upon his imprudent conduct. Not knowing what reparation to make he ended the episode by making a satire upon himself.

Leaving Deloraine at the end of two years he became shepherd to Mr. Knox, of Todrigg. Life now began to have more interest for him. He met with a warm friend and admirer in his master's son, who praised his verses and prophesied that he would one day become a noted poet.

Through the kindness of this friend he was able to extend his reading, which had hitherto been very limited. While at his former situation he had borrowed the "Pilgrim's Progress," "The Holy War," and a romance entitled, "Prissimus, the Renowned King of Bohemia," from a shepherd's wife. He had profited greatly by this old woman's conversation; she was singularly intelligent and a devout Christian. The more he read, the greater became his longing for knowledge. He determined to get further education. He had saved a little money, and to this was added a small sum left him by his father, whose death occurred at this time. Gathering his small stores together, he bade farewell to the crook and plaid, and set himself to study.

He now entered the parish school of Biggar, in Clydesdale, where he met with a true friend in his teacher, Mr. Scott. He soon became known in the district as a bard from the mountains. His song of "The Crook and Plaid," written at this time, obtained a widespread popularity, associated as it was with his shepherd's life. In addition to his poetry, he wrote "A Border Romance," and contributed some papers to the *Clydesdale Magazine*. His studies progressed favourably, and he gained many friends of literary and cultivated tastes.

He determined, after leaving Biggar, to pursue his studies at the Edinburgh University. His entrance there was a turning-point in his career. Under the tuition he obtained his powers were enlarged, and he threw off the rustic manners and expressions which had marked his early youth. In his autobiography he gratefully refers to his tutors, especially Professor Wilson, and the Greek professor, Mr. Dunbar. On one occasion he placed on the table of Mr. Dunbar a translation of one of the odes of Anacreon. An enquiry was made for the author, but Riddell remained silent, until, upon repeated questioning, he was obliged to admit that it was his. Its excellence was greatly commented upon. In Professor Wilson he found a kind friend. He would not receive any fees for his classes, and invited him to his house, introduced him to his friends, and furthered his advancement in every possible way.

The warm-heartedness and amiability of Riddell's character made him a favourite in whatever society he entered. After he had been a short time in Edinburgh, he had gathered round him a number of congenial friends, many of them members of a literary club, which he joined. He always tried to cultivate both sides of his being, the head and *the heart*. In this Professor Wilson encouraged him; he was one of the few friends who sympathized with Riddell's poetic sentiments and love of nature. Speaking of the poet's education, the Professor often remarked that "He would not have given the education which Riddell had received afar in the green bosom of mountain solitude, and among the haunts and homes of the shepherd, for all that he had received at colleges."

For a time Mr. Riddell pursued his studies at St. Andrew's University, where he studied moral philosophy in the class of Dr. Chalmers. Returning to Edinburgh, he completed his University career, and resolved to enter the ministry.

Meantime he had been engaged by Mr. R. A. Smith, the musical composer, and the friend of Tannahill the poet, to write some songs for the *Select Melodies* and for *The Irish Minstrel*. Mr. McLeod also asked him to contribute some songs to a work on which he was engaged. He sent, amongst others, "Oh, why left I my Hame," and "Scotland Yet." The latter became very popular; it was full of national enthusiasm :—

> "The thistle wags upon the fields,
>   Where Wallace bore his blade;
> That gave her foeman's dearest bluid
>   To dye her auld grey plaid;
> And looking to the left, my lads,
>   He sang this doughty glee:
> 'Auld Scotland's right, and Scotland's might,
>   And Scotland's hills for me;
> We'll drink a cup for Scotland yet
>   Wi' a' the honours three.'
>
> "They tell o' lands wi' brighter skies,
>   Where freedom's voice ne'er rang;
> Gie me the hills where Ossian lies
>   And Coila's minstrel sang;
> For I've nae skill o' lands, my lads,
>   That kenna to be free;
> 'Then Scotland's right, and Scotland's might,
>   And Scotland's hills for me;
> We'll drink a cup for Scotland yet
>   Wi' a' the honours three.'"

Edinburgh, with its historical associations, its palaces and towers, and its crowded streets, had been to young Riddell a city of wonder. Fresh from his native vales and hills, the sight of the city slums, teeming with miserable and degraded men and women, made him melancholy. Writing of it he says : "I had seen nothing of the sort, nor yet even so much as a semblance of it, and therefore I had no idea that there existed such a miserable shred of degradation, for example, as a cinder woman—desolate and dirty as her employment—busily prone, beneath the sheely night sky, to find out and fasten upon the crumb, whose pilgrimage certainly had not improved it since falling from the rich man's table.

Compassion, though not naturally so, becomes painful when entertained towards those whom we believe labouring under suffering which we fain would, but cannot alleviate." He delighted to explore places of historic interest in company with some of his friends. On one occasion he, with his friend Mr. Harrower, and two English gentlemen, went to inspect the battle-field of Pinkie. The Englishmen bantered the Scotch friends at the chastisement Scotland received at that memorable battle. Riddell remembered the advice an old Scotchman gave to his son, who was about to leave his native land for England—" dinna forget to avenge the battle o' Pinkie on them"—and composed the song, "Ours is the land of gallant hearts," by way of taking *his* revenge :—

> "Ours is the land of gallant hearts,
>   The land of lovely forms;
> The island of the mountain harp,
>   The torrents and the storms ;
> The land that bears the freeman's tread,
>   And never bore the slave's ;
> Where far and deep the greenwoods spread,
>   And wild the thistle waves.
>   *   *   *   *
> What need we say how Wallace fought,
>   Or how his foemen fell?
> Or how on glorious Bannockburn
>   The freeborn bore them well?
> Ours is the land of gallant hearts,
>   The land of honoured graves,
> Whose wreath of fame shall ne'er depart
>   While yet the thistle waves."

At the end of his college course Mr. Riddell prepared a volume of his verses which were published, in 1831, by Mr. Blackwood, under the title of " Songs of the Ark." Previous to that he had published a long poem on Lord Byron, soon after hearing of that poet's death. One stanza will show the sympathy he felt for his unhappy life :—

> " His life was separation, and his death
> Hath been of the same fortune ;—he was torn
> From all congenial, as, with his last breath,
> Hath been his heart from its own bosom ;* worn
> With many sorrows from the living scorn
> Of those whose love forbade him to despise.
> And he hath trod a pilgrimage forlorn,
> Though known to thousands ;—all life's dearer ties
> Were seared or severed, till were none to sympathize."

---

* When Byron died, the newspapers said that his heart was taken out to be preserved.

Mr. Riddell was in the habit of spending his vacations with his brother at Brookside, and on that relative's removal to Teviothead, accompanied him. He now became a probationer for the ministry of the Established Church of Scotland. On the death of the minister at Teviothead, the congregation of that place invited Mr. Riddell to fill the vacancy. For a time he devoted himself entirely to his incumbent duties, which were very arduous. There was no manse provided for him, and no available house within nine miles of the church. This distance he was compelled to walk each Sunday, often arriving at the church drenched with rain. The wet poured from his sleeves on to the Bible before him, and oozed out of his shoes if he stirred his feet on the pulpit floor. After a time the Duke of Buccleuch built him a manse.

Now that he was comfortably settled at Teviothead, Mr. Riddell married the lady to whom he had been engaged for fourteen long years, during which time her love had never faltered, although her hand had been sought by wealthier suitors. She was the daughter of Mr. Clark, of Biggar, and the "Eliza" of the poet's songs. In lines "To Eliza" he thus expresses himself:—

> "But years of silent time have now
>   With joys and sorrows passed away,
> Since love and love's most tender vow
>   Bore o'er our hearts a mutual sway.
> And should this form be wan and cold,
>   Couched in the chamber of the tomb,
> Before that time by hope foretold,
>   To realize our bliss shall come.
>
> "Still say not thou, as some have said,
>   That love and friendship are a lie ;
> Or that their power can never fade
>   Unless the human mind can die.
> My love for thee is centred there,
>   And whether fettered here or free,
> His soul can never wander where
>   It may not long, as now, for thee."

In 1841 Mr. Riddell became seriously ill through an idle report very damaging to his character. It preyed upon his mind until he became insane, and was removed to the Crichton Asylum, Dumfries. He was under the care of Dr. Crichton Brown, who, to divert the minds of his patients started a paper to be contributed to by the inmates of the asylum. Mr. Riddell wrote largely for it, and this occupation was some little solace to his perturbed mind.

After a period of skilful treatment he was quite restored to health, and returned to his much-loved wife. He did not resume his ministerial duties, but lived a retired life, devoting himself to literature. Through the kindness of the Duke of Buccleuch he continued to live in the house which had been built for him when he became minister of Teviothead.

He took great delight in farming his little piece of land, composing his verses as he handled the hoe and spade. The people round the district loved and honoured him as their Border poet. Occasionally he appeared on the platform of one of the neighbouring towns as a lecturer, but he loved best to live in the quiet retirement of his home writing his poetry, or affording hospitality to his friends.

In 1847 he contributed a sketch of James Hogg, the Ettrick Shepherd, to "Hogg's Instructor." In 1855 he translated the Gospel of St. Matthew, and in 1857 the Psalms, into Lowland Scotch for Prince Lucien Bonaparte. He wrote a number of tales, chiefly on Border subjects, as they were to him the most interesting.

He never lost his interest in sheep. In 1848 he published a series of papers on "Store-farming in the South of Scotland," and about the same time sent an "Essay on Foot-rot in Sheep" to the Highland and Agricultural Society, for which he was awarded £10.

He was an enthusiastic antiquary, and by his excavations brought to light many valuable remains of the early inhabitants of his district.

In 1866 Mr. Riddell was elected an honorary member of the Border Counties Association. It was a pleasing sight to see the old poet listening, in the meetings of his fellow-borderers, to the applause which the singing of his own songs elicited. The last local meeting of the Association took place at Hawick, 28th of July, 1870. Mr. Riddell was expected to act as chairman, but a sudden attack of illness prevented him, and a few days afterwards he died.

His funeral was attended by a large concourse of friends and admirers, chiefly from his own district. His life had been so retired that he was little known outside the Borderland. Many people expressed surprise when told of the recent death of the author of "Scotland Yet," thinking that it had taken place years before.

Mr. Riddell's general appearance was one of great muscular strength. There was an expression about his irregular features—hard to define—which rivetted a stranger's attention, and made him feel that he was gazing on no ordinary man. A few years before his death he visited the widow of Robert Burns, who, on taking leave of him, gazed intently upon him as she held his hand and said, that "She had never seen anyone who reminded her so much of her husband."

In "Geordie Tait's Courtship" and in "The Wee Auld Man" Mr. Riddell displays a fine power of humour. He wrote many religious poems, but the greater part were devoted to love and to the praises of his native land. A quotation from his poem on "Scotland" will form a fit ending to the story of the life of one who did not desire any greater distinction than to be known as a humble bard of fair Scotia.

"For thou, my native land, though lone and grey,

* * * * * *

Hold'st fast thy meed what many lands have lost,
And own'st the virtues they could never boast.
For thee the generous, loving life obtains
That best can tell where sacred freedom reigns;
Nor fail thy works of Nature and of Art
To lure the eye and fascinate the heart:
Thy rivers bold, and hills and forests deep,
Enhance the valley and adorn the steep;
Fair smiles the home with banks and bowers between,
The stone-built city and the woodland scene:
And if by cliff and cairn, on moor and dale,
The high hill breezes speak with proud avail,
The voice awakens o'er the warrior's grave,
That stood and fell thy native rights to save.
So, too, though solitude her throne may raise
Lonely and far amid the moorland's maze,
Still are thy homes, by mountain and by glen,
The homes of freeborn and unconquered men;
No task o'er toils, no tyranny o'er runs,
Thy lovely daughters and thy doughty sons:
Fair as the light, when darker days depart,
Thy queen herself, 'mid love from every heart,
Delights upon thy mountains wild to stand
And see the sceptre borne on Freedom's land."

WILLIAM LEIGHTON LEITCH.

WILLIAM LEIGHTON LEITCH was one of our greatest painters in water-colours. He had scarcely any advantages in early life, but attained to the highest position in his art by his own industry and perseverance. It was his aim to make his last drawing his best. Ever striving to attain greater excellence in his art, he worked on until within a few weeks of his death. "Work, work, work," was ever his advice to the aspiring artist.

He was born on the 2nd of November, 1804, at Glasgow. His parents were in humble circumstances, but greatly respected by their neighbours for their upright conduct and plodding industry. They possessed some of the finest traits of Scottish character; frugality united to hardihood and independence. His father was a soldier, but at the conclusion of the war, by the battle of Waterloo, 1815, settled in Glasgow with his wife and family.

Young Leitch received a plain, but sound education. His taste for drawing was early shown by his attempts to copy the pictures on his grandmother's china tea cups, and the fascination which a Bible containing a print of Jacob's ladder had for him. He was always doing something with pen or pencil. On one occasion he made copies of the portraits of the Emperor Alexander of Russia, and of the King of Prussia, from some prints he had seen in the window of a shop in the Trongate. These he took with him when he was taken on a visit to the "skipper's leddy," a well-to-do relative, by "Aunty Bell," a good-natured old maid, who was very kind to young Leitch in his early years. His drawings were greatly admired by both ladies, who prophesied that his father would not be able to make a writer or a spinner of him. His talent for penmanship brought him a small commission from a Mrs. Gray, who kept a little shop at the head of the close where he lived, to print a bill for her shop window in large Roman letters, PENS, INK, AND PAPER SOLD HERE. The little woman was delighted with it, when young Leitch showed it to her, and gave him twopence for his trouble, remarking to his mother that " he was not like the rest of the deevil's buckies o' laddies that ran mad about the plainstanes and causeway."

Mr. Leitch's mother was a very sweet singer of the old Scotch songs; one of her favourites was "Wandering Willie." In the evenings he delighted to sit by her side, and listen to her. The impression of the admiration he then felt remained with him in after years, even when mingling with the highest in the land, and established as instructor to the Queen herself. Young Leitch appears to have inherited some of his mother's musical ability. When a boy he took lessons on the violin from an eccentric character named Jack Shaw, and made considerable progress; but his greater gift for painting absorbed all his time in after years, and he gave up the study of music.

Heraldry was one of his favourite studies as a boy. As the carriages passed him in the streets he would gaze eagerly at the coats of arms. On one occasion seeing a carriage waiting at the entrance to the Infirmary, which was opposite his home, he ran across the street with his paper and pencil and rapidly drew a copy of the armorial bearings on the panels of the carriage. The lady who was sitting inside asked to see what he had drawn. She was much pleased with it, and detained the young artist until the gentleman for whom she was waiting joined her. He also expressed his approval, and gave young Leitch sixpence. This, with the exception of the twopence he received from Mrs. Gray, was the first money he had of his own.

One of the favourite sports of young Leitch and his companions was climbing the monuments surrounding the Cathedral. On one occasion he had a great fright; part of an old monument which he was climbing gave way. Aunty Bell heard of this exploit, and for fear of something worse happening, persuaded him to employ himself in making a sketch of the Cathedral. Gladly did he begin this congenial task ; but, alas! unforeseen difficulties arose. He had no idea of perspective, and soon found that his paper was covered before half the Cathedral was depicted. Hastening down from the monument, where he had perched himself with his paper and pencil, he carried his miserable failure to Aunty Bell. The good woman could not understand where the difficulty lay. She showed him a picture of the sacred edifice printed on a much smaller piece of paper than the one he had used, and on which he had not been able to get in the top nor the bottom, the east nor the west, but only the central part of the building. Discouraged by this failure he did not again attempt to draw from objects out of doors.

After leaving school he was sent to a lawyer's office ; it was his father's intention for him to follow the law. In six weeks he left, as it was very distasteful to him. His parents next sent him to learn the art of weaving; but this he disliked more than the law, and having had the misfortune to drop a lighted candle on the web as he sat at work it brought matters to a crisis; his master thrashed him for his carelessness, and so ended his engagement with the weaver. Being now left to follow his own bent he chose the trade of a house painter, and was accordingly apprenticed to a Mr. Harbut, who had his shop in Broad Close, in the High Street.

The love of art was growing fast upon young Leitch at this time, but unfortunately he had to blunder his way without any guidance. One of his companions at this time was Daniel Macnee, afterwards Sir Daniel Macnee, and President of the Royal Scottish Academy. The two boys, both such passionate students of art, spent their evenings together practising drawing. An amusing story is told regarding the fate of one of young Leitch's early paintings. He had made an elaborate copy in water-colours of a coloured engraving, and after carefully trimming the edges, presented it unmounted to a young girl of his acquaintance. She received it very graciously, but, to the young artist's unspeakable horror, folded and re-folded it, drawing her nail along the folded edge each time until she had made it a convenient size for putting into her pocket. Leitch looked on silently, but with what feelings can be readily imagined.

He was very fond of reading, and such books as "Hudibras," "Don Quixote," "Gil Blas," the poems of Goldsmith, Campbell, Thompson, Beattie, and Walter Scott were great favourites. He and a companion made, between them, a copy of "The Lady of the Lake."

During the first year of his apprenticeship, he visited a circus, and was so attracted by the scenery, that he determined to become a scene painter.

In 1824, when only 20 years of age, Mr. Leitch married Miss Susannah Smellie, a young lady whom he had fallen in love with while attending a choral class. The marriage proved a most happy one ; Mrs. Leitch was a real help and adviser to her husband throughout his chequered career. They had only 15s. a week to live on when they started life together, but through the help, encouragement, and forethought of his young wife, Mr. Leitch was able to struggle on until his long-worked for success came. It was their rule never to get into debt, nor to eat a meal until they had earned it.

Shortly after his marriage, when his engagement with Mr. Harbut ended, he applied for the place of scene-painter at the Theatre Royal, Queen Street, Glasgow. Mr. Byrne, the manager, after seeing a specimen of his work, engaged him with the offer of £1 a week for the first six months, and 25s. afterwards.

He now made rapid improvement in his art ; the continual practice, and the opportunity he had for studying the paintings of Patrick Nasmyth and of David Roberts, greatly benefitted him. During this engagement he had, occasionally, to take minor parts in the plays, and to help in the choruses. This was very distasteful to him ; he never appeared upon the stage willingly.

The Theatre Royal was not in a flourishing condition financially, consequently the employés had to wait a long time for their hard-earned wages. Mr. Leitch and his young wife were often in great need through these delays. One Saturday morning the wages were many weeks in arrears, and the men were getting angry and dissatisfied as they waited for the manager. Mr. Byrne came in upon them, and, without offering them any money, ordered the machinist, Macklin, and Mr. Leitch, to start by the three o'clock coach for Ayr, where they were to prepare the theatre for the performance of "Blue Beard." They asked for their wages "Have'nt I told you," replied the manager, "that all your expenses are paid for? be off with you at once. I'll be down at the coach office directly." There was no alternative; they were obliged to set out without a farthing in their pockets.

They reached Ayr at nine o'clock at night, cold and faint with the journey. After getting shelter for the night at the house of a friend, who gave them a simple Scotch supper, they began their work at the theatre at six o'clock the following morning. It was Sunday, and they were obliged to start out early in order to reach the theatre without observation, or they would probably have been punished for desecrating the Lord's Day.

Their task was not a pleasant one. The theatre was cold and damp, besides being miserably dirty. Mr. Leitch set himself to re-touch the scenery, which was in a most dilapidated condition. He worked until he became so faint from hunger that he had not power to do any more; his companion was even worse. A tapping at the stage door aroused them from their misery. "That must be Jim," said old Macklin, opening the door; and there sure enough was Jim, a poor half-witted fellow, who had come to seek them out. Finding some empty beer bottles amongst the rubbish under the stage, which, from their greasy condition, had evidently been used for candlesticks, they sent him to sell them, and buy food with the money they brought. In a short time he returned with a few potatoes and three small salted herrings, which he had bought with the $3\frac{1}{2}$d. he received for the bottles. The next difficulty was to cook them. Mr. Leitch discovered an old helmet, which was fortunately water-tight; in this he cooked the potatoes and herrings over a fire he had kindled in the green-room. Poor old Macklin could hardly believe that at last there was something to eat; many times he thanked God over that simple repast.

Shortly after this Mr. Leitch was thrown out of employment through Mr. Byrne running away from the theatre, and leaving his company in the lurch. He now managed to earn a little by portrait painting; but, having heard that Macnee and several of his companions were employed in snuff-box painting, he went to Cumnock, where that branch of the trade was largely carried on. He started alone, but was soon joined by Mrs. Leitch and their infant daughter. He worked for several dealers during the twelve months he passed in Cumnock. At the end of that time a Mr. Smith, the head of a large establishment in Mauchline, was so struck with his painting, that he engaged him to superintend the painting department in his establishment. While there Mr. Leitch executed some beautiful work in box painting. It is interesting to know that among his friends in Mauchline were Robert Armour, the brother of Robert Burns' "Jean," and Willie Fisher, son of Burns' "Holy Willie."

At this time he attracted the notice of the Marquis of Hastings, and of Dr. Young of Irvine. They strongly advised him to go to London; this he determined to do. Leaving his wife with her friends, he set out for the Metropolis, and, through the influence of David Roberts, obtained an engagement as scene-painter at the Prince of Wales' Theatre, Tottenham Court Road. At that time it was called the Queen's. The work was hard and the pay poor. After toiling from 15 to 17 hours per day, he had to live on less than half that number of shillings per week, and support a wife and three children. Writing of this time Mr. Leitch says:—"We got up the pretty story of 'Cherry and Fair Star,' and this, I think, was the only piece at this theatre the scenery of which I painted entirely myself. I begged the manager to let me have a chance of doing justice to my intentions, as I thought I could produce something better than the ordinary work in this part of the city. I was allowed to do it, and it was successful. All the papers spoke well of it, and some of them in very flattering terms. About a week after the first performance, Mr. Forrester ('Alfred Crowquill') came to me and told me that a number of the *cognoscenti*, including, he said, my countryman, Bill Gordon, had been in the pit, and were admiring the scenery, when Gordon exclaimed, 'Hang it if I like Leitch's work; all his scenes are so confoundedly like pictures!' Forrester said, gravely, 'Well, Gordon, you are quite right. Leitch has certainly a trick of getting a good deal of the picturesque into his scenes; but, take comfort, my good friend, for we all know there is not one in the profession so guiltless of that quality as yourself.'"

Although Mr. Leitch's friends praised his work, *he* was not satisfied, but felt that he needed further instruction. It was about this time that he first saw some of Stanfield's paintings at Drury Lane. They were a revelation to him; long and earnestly he studied them, and having obtained permission to repaint a scene for a piece then in preparation, painted it after Stanfield's methods. It was a great success, everyone was praising it. One night the manager, Mr. Macfarren, told him that a gentleman wished to speak to him. On going into the box lobby he was met by a tall, thin gentleman, to whom the manager said, "Mr. Stanfield, this is the young man who painted the scene you have admired so much." "He shook me kindly by the hand," writes Mr. Leitch, "and told me how much he had been pleased with my scene. He had seen it himself, he said, three times, and he had now brought his wife and children to see it it also." Mr. Leitch told Mr. Stanfield of the help he had received through studying his paintings at Drury Lane. Mr. Stanfield gave him great praise for his work, and some valuable hints for the pursuance of his art.

In 1832 he was obliged to leave the Queen's Theatre, the funds were so low. He then entered upon an engagement at the Pavilion Theatre, where he obtained good and regular pay.

At this time he was noticed by Mr. Anderden, a London stockbroker, who gave him several commissions for drawings, and advised him to get some lessons from Copley Fielding, which he did. On one occasion that eminent painter gave him a very simple looking picture to copy. When Mr. Leitch began to work at it, he found it more difficult than he imagined. Showing his copy to Mr. Fielding, he told him of the difficulty he had had, saying, "I went over that sky six times." "Ah, there it is," said Fielding; "you think it looks very simple because it does not show any labour. You say you went over the sky six times. I believe I am within the mark when I say that I went over mine 60 times."

In 1832 Mr. Leitch's pictures obtained admission into the Royal Academy, and in the Suffolk Street Gallery. The following year he set out for Italy.

His friend Mr. Anderden provided him with money to

start. He was away for four years travelling through Holland, Italy, and Switzerland, visiting the art galleries, and studying the paintings of the great masters. At first he was sorely pressed for money; he could not obtain employment, and some part of the time had to live on 2s. 6d. per week.

Through the kindness of the British Consul he obtained introductions to several families, who employed him to teach. From that time he prospered, and was able to pursue his studies in comfort. At Rome he became acquainted with several noted artists, including Gibson, Thorwaldsen, the Baron Carmucini, and Horace Vernet; he also made some valuable friendships among the English nobility who were visiting the Continent.

In 1837 Mr. Leitch rejoined his wife and family in London. His reputation as a rising artist had reached there through the reports of his pupils abroad, so that on his return he found plenty of employment as a teacher. His first pupil in London was the Honourable Edward Bouverie, who introduced him to other families of distinction.

The Duchess of Sutherland having seen a portfolio of Mr. Leitch's drawings was so struck with their beauty that she took them to the Palace to show them to Her Majesty and the Prince Consort. They admired them very much, especially two studies, of which Her Majesty commanded Mr. Leitch to make her copies.

Shortly after this he received a note from Lady Canning, one of his pupils, telling him that the Queen wished him to go to Windsor to give her lessons in water-colours. Her Majesty had been so delighted with some paintings done by Lady Canning that she desired to know who her instructor was, and when she was told it was Mr. Leitch, wished that he should give her lessons also. Mr. Leitch felt some trepidation at the thought of instructing Royalty, but the pleasant manner of the Queen set him at ease. Upon his introduction to her presence she said, "Mr. Leitch, there are a good many of your pupils here who are my friends, among them Lady Canning, and I admire their talent for water-colour painting. I have therefore sent for you, and hope I may have the benefit of your lessons." Mr. Leitch replied suitably to these kind words, and after having adjusted the table, with the help of Her Majesty and Lady Canning, so as to get the proper light, he proceeded to give the lesson. He was afraid of wearying Her Majesty with the introductory remarks, but she put him at ease by saying, "You will tell me what to do just as you told Lady Canning, and I will do it. I am very conscientious in my work."

The Queen made very great progress under Mr. Leitch's instruction. He had taken a sketch of hers to his studio to be mounted. His friend Stanfield noticed it, and asked by whom it was painted. "By a pupil of mine" said Mr. Leitch. "Oh nonsense," replied Stanfield. "Yes," said Mr. Leitch, "and it is by a lady." Stanfield examined it more closely and said, "Well, she paints too well for an amateur. She will be soon entering the ranks as a professional artist."

For 22 years Mr. Leitch attended at the palace. He gave lessons to all the Queen's children, who attained great proficiency in drawing and painting under his tuition. The Princess Alice was his most gifted pupil.

During his latter years he was obliged to discontinue teaching, so many demands were made upon him in connection with the higher practice of his art. He made an exception in the case of the Princess of Wales, to whom he gave lessons long after he had retired from teaching. She was very kind to him, and showed her regard for his memory by sending a wreath of white flowers to be placed upon his coffin.

With his brother artists he was always on good terms, and ever ready to encourage young beginners. He gives an amusing account of his first encounter with Turner, the landscape painter. It was shortly after his return from Italy, when he went to dine with Mr. Pickersgill, in Soho Square. "Mr. Pickersgill, when he invited me," writes Mr. Leitch, "said he should like me to bring a folio of the studies I had done in Italy, as he thought his friends would be pleased to see them, and especially Chantry and Turner. I accordingly took with me some drawings, and when we came up to the drawing-room they were produced. I was seated between Turner and Sir Martin Shee. Jones and Mr. Hilton were opposite, and as they had the folio they handed out the drawings separately to pass round the table. I don't recollect anything particular being said of the first 10 or 12 subjects. Sir Martin Shee always said something

R

polite and pleasant, but Turner, when I put the drawings into his hand, gave only a hasty glance at them and a subdued grunt, and passed them to Mr. Pickersgill without any remark. I think it was about the middle of my folio that I observed Mr. Hilton and Mr. Jones whispering together, and looking with more than ordinary attention at one of the drawings, and when Sir Martin put it into my hands he gave me a pleasant smile. I passed it to Turner, who held it for some time, regarding it attentively with knitted brows. Then turning to me he said in a brusque manner, 'Where did you get that?' I was taken a little aback at the rough manner of the question and did not immediately answer, and he said again, ' Where did you get that?' All were now silent and listening. I answered, 'To tell the truth, Mr. Turner, that drawing was done from memory. It is an impression of a subject and effect which I saw in the Abruzzi mountains, near the town of Salmona, in the middle of the Apennines.' He looked at me for a moment with a very unsatisfactory expression, and said, ' I don't believe a word of it.' Nothing more was said. Significant looks were exchanged amongst the company, and the rest of the drawings were passed over without much remark. After Turner left, Sir Martin Shee said to me, 'You have given us a great pleasure in showing us these interesting studies, but I need not say anything in commendation of them after the compliment that has just been paid you.' I replied that if Sir Martin alluded to what Mr. Turner had said, it was surely an extraordinary way of paying a compliment, and that I could not imagine what he meant. Sir Martin replied, ' Mr. Turner is an extraordinary man, and I cannot tell you what he meant, but this I am sure of, that had he not thought your drawing more than ordinarily good, and true, and beautiful, he would not have said a word about it.'"

Mr. Leitch became a Member of the Institute of Watercolour Painters in 1845, and was afterwards made Vice-President. His pictures were frequently exhibited in the galleries, but many of his finest ones were bought direct from his studio, without public exhibition.

He passed away on the 25th of April, 1883, at his residence in Alexandra Road, St. John's Wood, in his 79th year. A large number of friends, from among the most cultured in the land, mourned his loss. He was a general favourite in society from his kindly disposition and well-cultivated mind. He had, too, a great fund of drollery, and used to entertain his friends by imitating quaint Scottish characters. To his piety the late Princess Alice has borne testimony; in one of her letters she refers to Mr. Leitch as being the one who first led her to think seriously on religion.

He worked to the last at his beloved art, leaving many beautiful pictures in his studio. His aim in his painting was to make it a true representation of nature. The advice which he gave to a pupil will best illustrate his manner of work:—"Avoid bad works as you would fly from evil. Come back again to nature, again and again, and you will have the greatest comfort. Work, work, work, is the word, both with head and hand. We cannot get anything good or true and beautiful without going through suffering for it; and work is the price we must pay for all enjoyment we may have from the divine art of painting."

HENRY M. STANLEY.

IT has often been stated that Henry Stanley, the discoverer of Livingstone, and the fearless explorer of Africa, was an American by birth. America was, however, only the country of his adoption. His birthplace was the thriving town of Denbigh, North Wales. He was born there in 1843, and was christened John Rowlands after his father. "Stanley" was adopted by him as a name after he settled in America.

As a child John Rowlands displayed great ability, and was distinguished among his fellows as a bright, quick boy, fond of adventure, and full of daring. He attended the public school of St. Asaph, and made such rapid progress that he was employed by the master to assist in keeping accounts. The Bishop, who was in the habit of visiting the school, noticed him, and suggested to the master the advisability of putting him to some trade. Turning and patting John on the head, he said, "Well, my lad, what trade would you like to be apprenticed to?" "To that of a Bishop," was the prompt reply.

On the 13th of May, 1856, he left the school of St. Asaph, and became a pupil teacher in the National School of Brynford. His cousin was the head master. He afterwards removed with his cousin to the National School at Mold. A gentleman of Llandudno, who knew him well at this period, speaks of him as possessed of "an indomitable will," that really knew no impediment to its purpose. "I knew," he says, "every ingredient in his nature. I thought, and used to sum him up as a full-faced, stubborn, self-willed, round-headed, uncompromising, deep fellow. In conversation with you his black eyes would roll away from you as if he was really in deep meditation about half-a-dozen things

besides the subject of conversation. He was particularly strong in trunk, but not very smart or elegant about the legs, which were slightly disproportionately short. His temperament was unusually sensitive; he could stand no chaff, nor the least bit of humour."

When nearly sixteen years of age he left his cousin, owing to a dispute between them. He had been put to do some menial tasks; this was very galling to his high spirit. Without telling anyone of his intention, he started for Liverpool, determined to sail for America. He was penniless and friendless, but his resolution was made, and he tramped steadily on, mile after mile of unknown country, until Liverpool was reached. He had only a few pence, and could not afford to pay for a night's lodging. Wonderingly he gazed at the crowds as they hurried past him in the thoroughfares of the city. At the docks he eagerly watched the sailors, and the crowds of emigrants getting ready to sail. Wearied with the journey he was glad to coil himself up on the step of a sheltered door, where he slept soundly until the morning.

It was impossible for him to get to the New World in his penniless state unless he worked his way across. This he determined to do. After trying one ship and then another, he succeeded in obtaining employment as a cabin-boy with the captain of a New Orleans trader. His experiences during the voyage were very rough, but he did not mind. He was filled with hope. As, in calm weather, he listened to the sailors' tales of far off lands, and of the mighty Mississippi, and the wonders of the West, he longed to rove amidst their grandeur, and the trials of the voyage were forgotten as he thought of the future.

After nearly two months at sea he landed at New Orleans, free to seek his fortune.

He soon secured an appointment in the office of a merchant named *Stanley*. His ability, and the story of his friendless condition, touched the feelings of his employer, and having no children of his own he, in course of time, adopted John Rowlands as his son and heir. From that time John Rowlands became known as Henry Stanley. He changed his own name for that of his benefactor.

All seemed smooth before him, but it was not to last. The death of his kind friend, before he had executed his will, threw Stanley upon his own resources. The relatives of the deceased gentleman did not look with kindness upon a young man who had so nearly deprived them of their possessions, so he was forced to leave the office of his late master, and try his fortunes elsewhere. The name he had adopted he cherished too fondly ever to give it up. It was his wish to be known only as Henry Stanley.

His friends and relatives at Denbigh were not particularly surprised to hear that he had changed his name, as it is a very common thing in Wales for a man to adopt a new name.

When the American Civil War broke out Henry Stanley joined the Confederate Army. He fought in all the engagements up to the battle of Pittsburgh, April, 1862, when, with a number of others, he was taken prisoner. While being conveyed to the prison he made his escape by a daring manœuvre. Watching a favourable opportunity he burst through the armed escort, plunged into the river, and swam safely across. Shots were fired after him, but he escaped without a scratch.

After this adventure he returned home to visit his friends. His reception in Wales not being very encouraging, he set out again for America. He was at this time in nearly as poor a condition as when he tramped his way to Liverpool bent on seeking the Far West.

He landed in New York. It was a Federal State, and there he was liable to arrest as a Confederate prisoner. His ready mind quickly furnished him with a plan. He enlisted in the Federal Navy as a common seaman, thus securing safety. This was in 1863. From that time he obtained rapid promotion in the Navy. He was made clerk to the ship, and four months afterwards secretary to the Admiral. His next promotion was a reward for his bravery. During the heat of an action he swam 500 yards under the fire from the fort, and succeeded in attaching a rope to a Confederate steamer which his ship (the *Ticonderoga*) was enabled to secure as a prize. For this he was made an ensign with a salary of £350 per annum.

He concluded his career as a naval officer by taking part in the second attack on Fort Fisher, 1865. After this he obtained leave of absence and visited his mother at Bodelwyddan. His old friends received him more graciously than they had done during his former visit. He visited the school of St. Asaph; entertained the boys with sweetmeats and buns, and addressed some words of advice to them. The sight of this handsome young man in his naval uniform made a great impression on the boys, who remembered that a few years before he had been like one of them. He was looked on as quite a hero during this visit, and a great future was prophesied for him by his friends. The old applewoman, whose stall he frequented in his school days, wisely remarked:—" Did I not tell you he would come to something? I knew he would." During this visit he assumed his old name of John Rowlands, but on his return to America discarded it again for Henry Stanley, which name he has ever since adhered to.

On his return to New York he resigned his commission, as the civil war was at an end. It was about this time that, in company with Mr. Noe and Mr. Cook, he made an excursion across Asia. It was a daring expedition. They started from Smyrna, and, without knowing anything of the country, hired horses and rode into the interior. After a skirmish with a gang of brigands, they galloped off to the mountains, and following an unknown route rode straight into the robbers' head-quarters. They were at once seized and stripped of all their possessions. The robbers detained them for several days hoping to get more money from them. They imagined that they might have hidden some of their valuables before they were captured. To find out this they subjected them to a variety of tortures, and sharpened their tulwars in their presence, and threatened to cut their throats if they did not confess. After coming to the conclusion that they had got all, the robbers took their prisoners before the Cadi, and accused them of attempted murder and robbery. They thought that this course of action would prevent any suspicion from being attached to themselves.

Mr. Stanley addressed the Cadi, and told him of the treatment to which they had been subjected by their accusers, and, pointing to one of the robbers, said, that evidence of the truth of his statement would be found by searching the man. Search was made, and the property of the travellers was found as Mr. Stanley had said. The Turks were then placed under arrest, and Mr. Stanley and his friends pursued their journey. They were in a sorry plight, having no money and very little clothing. By the help of a gentleman in connection with the Ottoman Bank, who lent them money and clothes, they reached Constantinople. Mr. Stanley quickly laid his grievances before the American Consul, who advanced £150 without any security, so moved was he by the forlorn appearance of the three youths. The robbers were tried and sentenced to punishment, and the Turkish Government paid over to Mr. Stanley and his two friends a sum of money to compensate for their losses.

In 1867 Mr. Stanley returned to the United States and was, for some time, correspondent of the *Missouri Democrat* and of the *New York Tribune*, during General Hancock's expedition against the Kwioa and Cheyenne Indians. He had many adventures while travelling with this expedition, and his letters were full of the horrible cruelty experienced by the white men from the Indians.

On his return from this expedition, he built a raft and, in company with a friend, floated down the river Platte for a distance of 700 miles.

He obtained, on his return to New York, the appointment of travelling correspondent to the *New York Herald*, at a salary of £600 per year. In this capacity he accompanied the forces under Sir Charles Napier, who were going to the relief of the English captives detained at Magdala by King Theodore. The "Yankee," as the officers called Stanley, won universal praise during this Abyssinian expedition for his skill in travelling. He was an adept at managing his tent and baggage.

After a visit to London and Denbigh, he was despatched, by the proprietors of the *New York Herald*, to Madrid, to report on the Spanish Revolution. On the 16th of October, 1869, he received a telegram from Mr. James Gordon Bennett, jun., the manager of the *New York Herald*, summoning him to Paris. In a few hours he was on his way and reached Paris the following night. With his usual promptitude he hastened to the Grand Hotel, and knocked at the door of Mr. Bennett's room. He thus describes what took place:

"Come in," I heard a voice say.
Entering, I found Mr. Bennett in bed.
"Who are you?" he asked.
"My name is Stanley," I answered.

"Ah yes, sit down ; I have important business on hand for you."

After throwing over his shoulders his robe-de-chambre, Mr. Bennett asked :

"Where do you think Livingstone is ? "

" I really do not know, sir."

" Do you think he is alive ?"

" He may be and he may not be," I answered.

"Well, I think he is alive, and that he can be found, and I am going to send you to find him."

"What," said I, "do you really think I can find Doctor Livingstone ? Do you mean me to go to Central Africa ?"

" Yes ; I mean that you shall go and find him wherever you may hear that he is, and to get what news you can of him, and perhaps "—delivering himself thoughtfully and deliberately—" the old man may be in want : take enough with you to help him, should he require it. Of course you will act according to your own plans, and do what you think best—BUT FIND LIVINGSTONE ! "

I wondered at the cool order of sending one to Central Africa to search for a man whom I, in common with almost all other men, believed to be dead :

" Have you considered seriously the great expense you are likely to incur on account of this little journey ? "

" What will it cost ? " he asked abruptly.

" Burton and Speke's journey to Central Africa cost between £3,000 and £5,000, and I fear it cannot be done under £2,500."

" Well, I tell you what you will do. Draw £1,000 now ; and, when you have gone through that, draw another £1,000, and when you have finished that, draw another £1,000, and so on ; but, FIND LIVINGSTONE ! "

After receiving instructions to go to the inauguration of the Suez Canal, and to visit Jerusalem and Constantinople, and finally to push his way through Persia to India, and thence to Zanzibar to start for Africa, Mr. Stanley parted with his chief, saying :—" Good-night, sir ; what it is in the power of human nature to do I will do ; and on such an errand as I go upon, God will be with me."

Mr. Stanley arrived in India in the month of August, 1870, and on the 12th of October sailed in the barque *Polly* from Bombay for the Mauritius. He was full of the great enterprise which he had before him. The first mate on the vessel, William Lawrence Farquhar, from Leith, Scotland, was an excellent navigator. Mr. Stanley secured his services for his expedition to Africa, and also those of Selim, a Christian Arab boy, to act as interpreter.

They reached Zanzibar on the 6th of January, 1871. There Mr. Stanley proceeded to organize his expedition.

Zanzibar is the capital of the island of that name, and situated 25 miles from the continent of Africa. It is the centre of the ivory trade. The Arab traders carry to its markets their stores of ivory, gum opal, hides, timber, and slaves obtained from Africa.

Seeking out the American Consul, Dr. Kirk, Stanley made enquiries about Dr. Livingstone, but could get little information. Many of the Zanzibar people felt confident that Livingstone was dead. Mr. Stanley kept his own counsel, telling no one of his object in penetrating the Dark Continent. It was generally supposed that he was going merely for a survey of the country.

After 28 days of anxious labour he had everything ready for the start. His purchases amounted to six tons of luggage. As he looked upon these, "piled up, tier after tier, row upon row, here a mass of cooking utensils, there bundles of rope, tents, saddles, a pile of portmanteaus and boxes, containing every imaginable thing," he adds, "I confess I was rather abashed at my own temerity. Here were at least six tons of material! How will it ever be possible, thought I, to move this inert mass across the wilderness stretching between the sea and the great lakes of Africa? Bah! cast all doubts away, man, and have at them! 'Sufficient for the day is the evil thereof,' without borrowing from the morrow."

It was necessary to start fully equipped for such a hazardous journey. Once fairly started on his journey into the interior, all hope of supplying his needs was at an end. He required to take with him just what a ship bound for a long voyage must have. To convey this large amount of luggage 160 men were required.

On the 4th of February, 1870, "The New York Herald Expedition" sailed from Zanzibar. The American flag waved from the mast. The consul, his lady, and their two children bade them adieu, with many prayers for their safety; and the native population grouped around to see the last of the white man and his wonderful cargo.

In a short time the African continent rose to view, and in 10 hours they dropped anchor on the top of the coral reef, within a few yards of the beach of Bagamoyo.

Mr. Stanley selected a house, and proceeded to get ready his caravans to start for the interior. After a great deal of trouble with the lying, cheating Arabs, he secured a sufficient number of pagazis (carriers) to accompany him. He had in all five caravans, comprising 192 souls, 10 donkeys, 17 asses, 2 horses, and a dog. The pagazis were loaded with the bales of cloth and beads which it was necessary to take in place of money to trade with the natives in the villages on their route, and also for paying "honga," or tribute to the chiefs.

Mr. Stanley started four caravans, and then followed with the fifth. He chose a route hitherto unknown to travellers. From the news he had gathered at Zanzibar, it seemed probable that Dr. Livingstone was to be found in the neighbourhood of Ujiji. To that place he resolved to march regardless of all difficulties.

His patience was greatly tried by the laziness of his men. He could only get them forward at the rate of four miles per day. Sickness attacked some of them, obliging the fourth caravan to remain behind for some days. When the difficulties of the way showed themselves, some of the natives deserted. It required the greatest tact and skill on the part of Mr. Stanley to keep his company together. His two horses died at an early stage of the journey. Again and again he was prostrated by fever, but struggled on, ever keeping a brave heart. Streams and swamps had to be crossed, no easy matter with so large a quantity of baggage and sick men to care for.

At length they reached the Mikata river, which was swollen with the rains, as it was the rainy or Masika season. It took five hours to cross over the unsteady bridge, half buried in the water. After a brief rest they proceeded across the Mikata plain, which was one great swamp after the heavy rains. For two days they trudged through this frightful region, in some places plunging into holes four and five feet deep. At the end of that time they reached the Rudewa river. Crossing a branch of that river they came upon a reedy marsh, and for three hours had to splash through four feet of water before reaching dry ground. So ended the crossing of the swamp of Makata; but the effects soon showed themselves. The animals died, until only five remained of the 30 which set out from Bagamoyo. The soldiers and pagazis sickened of innumerable diseases, and Mr. Stanley himself was brought to death's door by an acute attack of dysentery.

After a few days rest they proceeded to the hill country and on to Ugogo. The breezes from the mountains somewhat refreshed the jaded travellers after the horrors of the Makata swamp. But difficulties of another kind beset them. The jungles were thick with the thorn bushes, which tore their clothes from their limbs as they passed through them. Their stores of provisions were nearly exhausted. For 57 days their food was Matama porridge and tough goat. Reaching the country of Ugogo they obtained supplies of good food.

They had now a dangerous country before them. It was peopled by fierce Africans ready to attack them as they passed through their villages, and demanding heavy tribute.

The flies, ants, and ear-wigs were a source of constant annoyance. There were long, weary marches, without the possibility of getting water. But at last Unyanyembe was reached, and with banners flying and trumpets sounding the caravan entered the Arab town of Kwikuru. Mr. Stanley received quite an ovation as he walked beside the governor to his tembe, or residence.

During his stay Mr. Stanley was laid prostrate with fever and was faithfully attended by the Arab boy, Selim, until his recovery. Selim was then laid low by the same disease.

By the morning of the 29th of July, Mr. Stanley and his company were ready to march to Ujiji. The country through which they passed was in terror about Mirambo, a mighty chief, who was making war upon the people. Stanley's men were so terrified lest they should meet the dread Mirambo, that it was with difficulty he urged them forward.

It was during this journey that he received as a present, from an Arab, the boy Kalulu, who became Mr. Stanley's faithful attendant.

On the 3rd of November, they were told by some travellers from Ujiji that a white man had just arrived there.

Eagerly did Mr. Stanley enquire his age and appearance. From the answers given he felt certain that the white man was Dr. Livingstone. Assembling his men together he, for the first time, told them the real motive for his journey into Africa, and asked them if they were willing to march to Ujiji without a halt. All answered in the affirmative, and with a bounding heart the intrepid traveller set out.

His supply of cloth and beads was nearly gone. He had scarcely enough to satisfy the exorbitant demands of the chiefs through whose country he passed. It seemed at one time that he would be unable to proceed, having nothing with which to pay tribute. But by bribing a native to guide them through a jungle, they escaped without further trouble.

On the 10th of November, Mr. Stanley sighted the waters of the Tanganika, and pressed on to Ujiji. "At this grand moment," writes Mr. Stanley, "we do not think of the hundreds of miles we have marched, of the hundreds of hills that we have ascended and descended, of the many forests we have traversed, of the jungles and thickets that annoyed us, of the fervid salt plains that blistered our feet, of the hot suns that scorched us, nor the dangers and difficulties, now happily surmounted. At last the sublime hour has arrived! —our dreams, our hopes and anticipations are about to be realized! Our hearts and our feelings are with our eyes, as we peer into the palms and try to make out in which hut or house lives the white man with the grey beard we heard about on the Malagarazi."

The flags were unfurled, and a volley from nearly 50 guns, fired as a salute, roused the people of Ujiji. They flocked out to meet the caravan, as it marched into the village with the "Stars and Stripes" waving above them.

Mr. Stanley was speedily accosted by Susi, the trusty servant of Dr. Livingstone. All doubts were now at an end, the Dr. was alive and at Ujiji. "What would I have given," writes Mr. Stanley, "for a bit of friendly wilderness, where, unseen, I might vent my joy in some mad freak, such as idiotically biting my hand, turning a somersault, or slashing at trees, in order to allay those exciting feelings that were well nigh uncontrollable. My heart beats fast, but I must not let my face betray my emotions, lest it shall detract from the dignity of a white man appearing under such extraordinary circumstances."

"So I did that which I thought most dignified. I pushed back the crowds, and passing from the rear, walked down a living avenue of people, until I came in front of the semicircle of Arabs, in the front of which stood the white man with the grey beard. As I advanced slowly towards him I noticed he was pale, looked wearied, had a grey beard, wore a bluish cap with a faded gold band round it, had on a red-sleeved waistcoat, and a pair of grey tweed trousers. I would have run to him, only I was a coward in the presence of such a mob—would have embraced him, only, he being an Englishman, I did not know how he would receive me; so I did what cowardice and false pride suggested was the best thing—walked deliberately to him, took off my hat, and said:

"Dr. Livingstone I presume?"

"Yes," said he, with a kind smile, lifting his cap slightly.

I replace my hat on my head, and he puts on his cap, and we both grasp hands, and I then say aloud:—

"Thank God, Doctor, I have been permitted to see you."

He answered, "I feel thankful that I am here to welcome you."

Mr. Stanley had now accomplished his task. He spent several months with Dr. Livingstone, and explored, with him, the northern head of Lake Tanganika, and then started for home. His march from Bagamoyo had taken 236 days.

Dr. Livingstone accompanied him on his homeward journey as far as Unyanyembe. There the friends parted, Livingstone to continue his explorations, and Stanley to convey the joyful tidings of his successful expedition.

The Royal Geographical Society of England rewarded Mr. Stanley, for his gallant relief of Livingstone, with a medal and their warmest thanks. Her Majesty forwarded her expression of satisfaction and regard through the following letter from Earl Granville.

"Foreign Office, August 27.

"SIR,—I have great satisfaction in conveying to you, by command of the Queen, Her Majesty's high appreciation of the prudence and zeal which you have displayed in opening a communication with Dr. Livingstone, and relieving Her Majesty from the anxiety which, in common with her subjects, she had felt in regard to the fate of that distinguished traveller.

"The Queen desires me to express her thanks for the service you have thus rendered, together with Her Majesty's congratulations on your having so successfully carried on the mission which you fearlessly undertook. Her Majesty also desires me to request your acceptance of the memorial which accompanies this letter.
"I am Sir,
"Your obedient servant,
"GRANVILLE."

The letter was accompanied by a beautiful gold snuff-box set with brilliants, as a memorial from Her Majesty to Mr. Stanley.

During the Ashantee War, Mr. Stanley accompanied the forces under Sir Garnet Wolseley, as special correspondent for the *New York Herald.* On his return to England from that expedition, April, 1874, the news reached him of the death of his friend, Dr. Livingstone. He had died on the shores of Lake Bemba, just on the verge of the region he was intending to explore. At the burial of the great traveller in Westminster Abbey, Mr. Stanley was one of the pall-bearers. It was with a sorrowful heart that he turned from the grave of the noble man whom he had learnt to reverence and love in those days they spent together at Ujiji. He felt, too, that the work Livingstone had begun in exploring the Dark Continent was stopped at its very commencement. It was his determination to take it up. Night and day he laboured at his book, "Coomassie and Magdala," and when that literary work was completed, began a study of Africa. One day, when passing an old book shop, he noticed a volume entitled, "How to Observe." He purchased it, found it full of useful hints, and it led him to buy quite a library of books on Africa. They amounted to 130 in number, and these he studied assiduously. He became acquainted with all that had been written on the geography, geology, botany, and ethnology of the Dark Continent. Full of the subject, he entered the office of the *Daily Telegraph*, and was discussing with one of the staff when the editor entered. Mr. Stanley was talking of Livingstone's uncompleted work.

"Could you, and would you, complete the work?" asked the editor. "And what is there to do?"

Mr. Stanley answered:—

"The outlet of Lake Tanganika is undiscovered. We know nothing scarcely—except what Speke has sketched out—of Lake Victoria; we do not even know whether it consists of one or many lakes, and therefore the sources of the Nile are still unknown. Moreover, the western half of the African continent is still a white blank."

"Do you think you can settle all this, if we commission you?"

"While I live there will be something done. If I survive the time required to perform all the work, all shall be done."

"The matter was for the moment suspended, because Mr. James Gordon Bennett, of the *New York Herald*, had prior claims on my services," writes Mr. Stanley. Continuing the narrative, he says:—"A telegram was despatched to New York to him. 'Would he join the *Daily Telegraph* in sending Stanley out to Africa, to complete the discoveries of Speke, Burton, and Livingstone?' and, within 24 hours, my 'new mission' to Africa was determined on as a joint expedition, by the laconic answer which the cable flashed under the Atlantic—'Yes; Bennett.'"

Two weeks were allowed Mr. Stanley for making his purchases for the expedition. He had a beautiful barge built, which could be divided into five sections to admit of easy carriage over land. It was named the *Lady Alice*. In this he hoped to navigate the African lakes and rivers. He secured the services of three young English boatmen, Francis John Pocock, Edward Pocock, and Richard Barker, to accompany the expedition. They set out on the 15th of August, 1874, and reached the Island of Zanzibar—25 miles distant from the African coast—on September 21st, 1874.

At Zanzibar Mr. Stanley had to lay in stores of cloth, beads, wire, medicine and miscellaneous articles, until his total weight of goods amounted to over 18,000 lbs., requiring the carrying capacity of 300 men. On the 12th of November all was ready to sail for the African port, Bagamoyo. After five days there, the expedition was ready to set out on its march across the "Dark Continent."

"Accordingly, at 9 a.m. of the 17th," writes Mr. Stanley, "five days after leaving Zanzibar we filed out from the town, receiving some complimentary and not a few uncomplimentary parting words from the inhabitants, male and female,

who are out in strong force to view the procession as follows:
—Four chiefs, a few hundred yards in front; next the twelve
guides, clad in red robes of Joho, bearing the wire coils; then
a long file, 270 strong, bearing cloth, wire, beads, and sections
of the *Lady Alice*; after them thirty-six women and ten boys,
children of some of the chiefs and boat-bearers, following their
mothers and assisting them with trifling loads of utensils,
followed by the riding-asses, Europeans, and gun-bearers;
the long line closed by sixteen chiefs, who acted as rear-guard,
and whose duties are to pick up stragglers, and to act as
supernumeraries until other men can be procured; in all, 356
souls connected with the Anglo-American Expedition."

Mr. Stanley intended to lead the expedition, in the first
place, to Lake Victoria Nyanza, where he proposed to begin his
explorations. But he had much to contend with before he
reached his destination. As soon as the perils of the way
showed themselves the natives began to desert, and those
who remained were full of complainings. It required all
Mr. Stanley's tact to keep the expedition in marching
order. On one occasion, while hunting, he was confronted
by lions. He and his attendants lay down in the long grass,
and waited the approach of the foremost. Mr. Stanley fired
—it fell, and the others disappeared with a rush. They had
much to endure from the rainy season, and at one time the
provisions were so low that starvation seemed inevitable.
Mr. Stanley searched for game, but there was none to be
found. The men looked about for edible roots and berries,
and at last, in desperation, gorged themselves on the carcase
of a putrid elephant, sickness following as a consequence.
At last, to Mr. Stanley's great joy, he discovered that he had
sufficient oatmeal "to give every soul two cupfuls of thin
gruel." A "Torquay dress-trunk" of sheet iron was filled
with 25 gallons of water, into which the oatmeal was put.
The people heaped fuel under it, anxious to hasten its boiling,
and then gathered round for their share, clamouring eagerly
as only half-starved people could. During this terrible
march Edward Pocock, one of the English boatmen, died
of typhus fever. Thirty of the men were at one time on
the sick list from various causes. At last, all difficulties
surmounted, they sighted the silvery lake, Victoria Nyanza,
and the natives struck up a song of triumph, which Mr.
Stanley has translated:—

"Sing, O Sing, friends; the journey is ended;
Sing aloud, O friends; sing to the great Nyanza;
Sing all, sing loud, O friends; sing to the great sea;
Give your last look to the lands behind, and then turn to the sea.
Long time ago you left your lands,
Your wives and children, your brothers and your friends;
Tell me, have you seen a sea like this
Since you left the great salt sea?
This sea is fresh, is good, and sweet;
Your sea is salt and bad, unfit to drink;
This sea is like wine to drink for thirsty men;
The salt sea—bah! it makes me sick.
Lift up your heads, O men, and gaze around;
Try if you can see its end.
See, it stretches moons away,
This great, sweet, fresh-water sea.
Kaduma's land is just below;
He is rich in cattle, sheep, and goats.
The Msunga [Stanley] is rich in cloth and beads;
His hand is open, and his heart is free.
To-morrow the Msunga must make us strong
With meat and beer, wine and grain;
We shall dance and play the live-long day,
And eat, and drink, and sing, and play.

The expedition now halted at Kagehyi, on the edge of the lake, after a journey of 720 miles. The time occupied being from November 17th, 1874, to February 27th, 1875.

After a period of rest Mr. Stanley started, with a portion of his men, on the 8th of March, 1875, to circumnavigate the lake in the *Lady Alice*. He penetrated every bay, inlet, and creek, and became acquainted with the wild tribes which lived on the shores: five times he and his crew suffered terribly at the hands of these savages. In the following account he gives a description of one, among the many, of his hair-breadth escapes:—He had encountered a hostile tribe on the island of Bumbireh. The king and chief men of the tribe were holding a consultation as to the action they should take against the crew of the *Lady Alice*, "when," writes Mr. Stanley, " An audacious party came round the stern of the boat, and with superlatively hideous jestures affronted me; one of them even gave a tug at my hair, thinking it was a wig. I revenged myself by seizing his hand, and suddenly bending it back almost dislocated it, causing him to howl with pain. His comrades swayed their lances, but I smilingly looked at them, for all idea of self-preservation had now almost fled."

"The issue had surely arrived. There had been just one brief moment of agony when I reflected how unlovely death appears in such guise as that in which it threatened me. What would my people think as they anxiously waited for the never returning master? What would Pocock and Barker say when they heard of the tragedy of Bumbireh? And my friends in America and Europe? 'Tut, it is only a brief moment of pain, and then what can the ferocious dogs do more?' It is a consolation that, if anything, it will be short, sharp, sudden—a gasp, and then a silence—for ever and ever!" And after that I was ready for the fight, and for death. At this crisis the native chiefs beckoned Safeni, Mr. Stanley's coxswain, as though they wished to discuss terms with him. Shortly he returned with the intelligence that they were to be detained on the island until the morrow. Mr. Stanley felt the awfulness of the situation, and seeing evident signs for the beginning of hostilities, he conceived a daring plan for launching his boat and escaping. "Here, Safeni," he said, "take these two fine red cloths in your hand; walk slowly up after them [the chiefs] a little way, and the minute you hear my voice run back; and you, my boys, this is for life and death mind; range yourselves on each side of the boat, lay your hands ou each side of it carelessly, but with a firm grip, and when I give the word, push it with the force of a hundred men down the hill into the water. Are you all ready, and do you think you can do it? Otherwise we might as well begin fighting where we are."

"Yes, Inshallah, master," they cried with one voice.

"Go, Safeni!"

I waited until he had walked 50 yards away, and saw that he acted precisely as I had instructed him.

"Push, my boys; push for your lives!"

"The crew bent their heads and strained their arms; the boat began to move, and there was a hissing, grinding noise below me. I seized my double-barrelled elephant rifle and shouted "Safeni! Safeni! return."

The natives were quick-eyed. They saw the boat moving, and with one accord they swept down the hill, uttering the most fearful cries.

"My boat was at the water's edge. 'Shoot her into the lake, my men; never mind the water;' and clear of all obstructions she darted out upon the lake.

"Safeni stood for an instant on the water's edge, with the cloths in his hand. The foremost of a crowd of natives was about 20 yards from him. He raised his spear and balanced himself.

"Spring into the water, man, head first," I cried.

"The balanced spear was about to fly, and another man was preparing his weapon for a deadly cast, when I raised my gun, and the bullet ploughed through him, and through the second. The bowmen halted and drew their bows. I sent two charges of buck-shot into their midst with terrible effect. The natives retreated from the beach on which the boat had lately lain."

Mr. Stanley succeeded in launching his boat, but the natives determined not to let him escape. They rushed round to a creek to intercept him. Meantime Mr. Stanley and his men had to fight two hippopotami, which they saw advancing open-mouthed. Having shot these animals, they had to give battle to the savages, who had manned their canoes and were pursuing them. After a severe conflict the *Lady Alice* was free and sailing peacefully, once more, upon the bosom of the lake.

While at Uganda, Mr. Stanley had met Colonel Linant de Bellefonds, one of Colonel Gordon's party. He was staying with Mtesa, the Emperor of Uganda, who most hospitably entertained Mr. Stanley. Mtesa was a very fine specimen of a heathen monarch, and subsequently, through Mr. Stanley's efforts, was converted to Christianity. He had also promised to furnish Mr. Stanley with an escort to pursue his explorations, after his return from the circumnavigation of the lake Nyanza.

Fifty-seven days from the time Mr. Stanley set out from Kagehyi for his voyage, he returned to that place, where the larger portion of his company were awaiting him, having thoroughly explored the Victoria Nyanza.

After an interval the expedition set out for Uganda to solicit help from Mtesa. That monarch was engaged in a war, and Mr. Stanley was obliged to wait until it was over. It was during this stay that Mtesa embraced Christianity. Mr. Stanley made him a copy of portions of the Bible in his native language, and was the means of persuading him to govern his subjects more justly and humanely.

The war over, Mr. Stanley set out for the exploration

of the country between Muta Nzigé and Lake Victoria, accompanied by a party of men under the command of Sambuzi, one of Mtesa's chiefs, who was to guide the way. All went well for a time, when the escort became unmanageable, and Mr. Stanley was obliged to send them back to the emperor, and, in consequence, was unable to pursue his discoveries in that region. Reluctantly he resumed his journey in a southerly direction, and, bidding adieu to the lands which supply the Nile, proceeded to Lake Tanganika April 7th, 1876.

Mr. Stanley started for his cruise on Lake Tanganika on the 11th of June, 1876, and returned to Ujiji, after an absence of 51 days, on July 31st, having sailed a distance of 810 miles without illness or disaster. He found the entire coast line of the Tanganika to be about 930 miles, its breadth from 10 to 45 miles, averaging 28 miles, and its superficial area covering a space of 9,240 square miles.

On the morning of the 25th of August, after repairing the canoes and getting the boat ready, the expedition set out again; this time to cross the Tanganika, and to commence the stupendous task of exploring the mighty River Congo, or Livingstone, to its union with the Atlantic Ocean. Before many days had elapsed Mr. Stanley was deserted by 41 of his men, among them Kalulu, who had been his attendant from a child. They were pursued, and Kalulu, with six others, were recovered. Dangers innumerable had now to be faced. The shores of the mighty river were invested by cannibals, with whom the expedition had again and again most terrible encounters. Mr. Stanley believes himself to have been saved from death many times through his colour. The cannibals were awestruck at the sight of a white man, and sometimes with "their fingers pressing the triggers of their deadly muskets," aimed full at Mr. Stanley, they forgot to fire, becoming absorbed in contemplating the "white man." As they pursued the course of the river, they found that it abounded in cataracts, rapids, and deceptive whirlpools. Some were quite impassable, and the men had to drag the boat and the canoes through the tangled masses of vegetation along the shores until a place could be found where it was safe to again embark. Often they found themselves placed between two dangers—the fearful cataract roaring in the distance, to enter which was certain death; and the cannibals lining the banks of the river and thirsting for their blood. They were often obliged to fight their way through the savages; there was no alternative. Before entering the first cataract of the Livingstone Falls, they came to a large expanse of water, embracing about 30 square miles, which Pocock suggested should be called "Stanley Pool," and the white cliffs which rose up above it were named the "Dover Cliffs." After battling with the Livingstone Falls, they entered upon a series of cataracts in the "Stanley Falls." Many brave men fell victims to the treacherous whirlpools; among them Kalulu, and the English boatswain, Pocock. Mr. Stanley saw his ranks getting thinner and thinner from disease, hardships, and accidents; but at last they reached a district where the people told them that the "great salt sea" was only a few miles distant. Mr. Stanley writes:—"The freshness and ardour of feeling with which I had set out from the Indian Ocean had by this time been quite worn away. Fevers had sapped the frame, overmuch trouble had strained the spirit, hunger had debilitated the body, anxiety preyed upon the mind. My people were groaning aloud; their sunken eyes and unfleshed bodies were a living reproach to me; their vigour was now gone, though their fidelity was unquestionable; their knees were bent with weakness, and their backs were no longer rigid with the vigour of youth, and life, and strength, and fire of devotion. Hollow-eyed, sallow, and gaunt, unspeakably miserable in aspect, we yielded at length to imperious nature, and had but one thought only—to trudge on for one look more at the blue ocean." Hearing that there were four more rapids before the river reached the Atlantic, Mr. Stanley determined to complete the remainder of the journey overland. The *Lady Alice*, after a journey of 7,000 miles up and down Africa, "was consigned to a resting-place above the Isangila cataract, to bleach and rot to dust," 31st of July, 1877. The emaciated expedition, after being revived by food sent them by the Europeans at Embomma, set out on foot for the Atlantic coast. After a short stay at Kabinda, where the Europeans showed them the utmost kindness, the expedition sailed for the Cape of Good Hope, and from thence to Zanzibar, where Mr. Stanley had the painful task of taking leave of his brave followers, whom the perils and privations of the way had strangely endeared to him. The chiefs had served him in his first expedition when he found Livingstone, and the poor fellows were sad at the parting. "And for years and years to come," writes Mr. Stanley, "in many homes in Zanzibar there will be told the great story of our journey, and the actors in it will be heroes among their kith and kin. For me, too, they are heroes,—these poor ignorant children of Africa, for, from the first deadly struggle with the savage I turn to the last staggering rush into Embomma, they had rallied to my voice like veterans, and in the hour of need had never failed me. And thus, aided by their willing hands and by their loyal hearts, the expedition had been successful, and the three great problems of the Dark Continent's geography had been fairly solved."

On his return to England Mr. Stanley was becomingly honoured by Royalty, and by the Geographical Society of London, which gave him a public reception. The various Geographical Societies of the Continent bestowed their honours upon him, and the Government of the United States passed a unanimous vote of thanks for his services.

At the request of the International Association, formed by Leopold, King of the Belgians, Mr. Stanley started again for Africa, to explore the Congo, and to open up the "Dark Continent" for European commerce. Through his efforts the region of the Congo is becoming the home of civilization. Missionaries have their settlements on its banks, and are fast Christianizing the savage tribes.

Mr. Stanley came home for a short time in 1882; he has since returned, and is now (1884) continuing his exploration of the River Congo. His head-quarters are at Leopoldville, a flourishing town at Stanley Pool, named after the Belgian king, who has recently provided Mr. Stanley with a steam-boat, to be called *Le Stanley*, to facilitate the navigation of the river.

EDWARD IRVING.

FEW men have risen to fame so quickly as Edward Irving. But it was a popularity which died away almost as suddenly as it came to life, leaving its victim a melancholy picture of an honest, fervent enthusiast, forsaken, down-trodden, and crushed by those who had been his closest friends.

Edward Irving was born of respectable Scotch parentage. His father, Gavin Irving, was a tanner, in the quiet, sober-looking old town of Annan. Mary Lowther, his mother, was a handsome, sprightly woman, who ruled her house and family of eight children with great shrewdness. She was the daughter of a small landed proprietor. Most of her kinsfolk held similar positions in life, for the Lowthers were a family of some importance, ranking rather above the Irvings.

Young Edward's home was in the beautiful and fruitful Annandale, which has sent forth so many of its stalwart sons to make their mark in the world's history. He was born in a little house close by the old town cross of Annan, on the 4th of August, 1792. In his rude wooden cradle he lay and basked in the sunshine which entered his mother's bedchamber. But unfortunately the pleasant sunshine glared too full upon the one eye of baby Edward—the other was shaded by the side of the cradle—causing a squint, the only defect in those dark, handsome features inherited from his mother.

He received his first instruction at a dame school kept by "Peggy Paine," who had some notoriety in the place from being a relative of Tom Paine, of French Revolution fame. Irving's characteristic good nature exhibited itself among his school-fellows. A little Hannah could not learn her letters.

He sat by her day after day and helped her through the difficulty. In after years the same Hannah became a domestic servant in London. Her school-fellow had risen to be the renowned preacher, but he disdained not to grasp her warmly by the hand when he passed her one day at her work. The girl's master and mistress sought for the honour of entertaining the famous Mr. Irving. Hannah interceded, and, to please his old school-fellow, the great orator graced the table of her employers.

Another story is told of Irving's boyish generosity. His mother was a guest at one of the little tea parties which the Annan folk delighted in, when she was summoned from her friends by the importunities of little Edward, who pleaded at the street door to be allowed to speak to his mother. She went to him, expecting to hear of some domestic accident. But no, his anxiety was to gain her permission to take some of his linen to a sick lad! Having secured it, he ran off with a bounding heart on his errand of mercy.

So his early years passed in the old-fashioned market town, almost out of reach of the busy world. He played with his companions at the Waterfoot, the little port where the river Annan enters the Solway, and had, at least, one narrow escape from a watery grave. There was nothing much to distinguish him from the other lads of the place. Like them he roved about the country, swam, rowed, and delighted in all kinds of outdoor sports. There was one exception. On the Sunday he left his young companions to join a band of devotees who walked from Annan to Ecclefechan to attend the ministry of the Rev. Mr. Johnstone, a Secession minister. Possibly the little Edward had a special friend among these devout pilgrims, who, true to their convictions, tramped their six miles rather than attend the Annan church, where the minister was regarded as a loose character. Or he might have been drawn to join the band in order to listen to the stirring tales of Covenanting times, which not unfrequently formed the topic of conversation among these reverent worshippers.

In the meeting-house of Ecclefechan sat another small boy destined to attain world-wide fame. Thomas Carlyle recalls the time when he watched this little band of pilgrims from Annan, with their eager boy-companion, file into the meeting-house, and saw, in stormy weather, their "streaming plaids" hung up to dry during service.

Irving's parents designed him for the ministry. Accordingly, after some preparatory training at the Annan Grammar School, under the worthy domine, Adam Hope, he was sent to the Edinburgh University. He was 13 years old when he began his studies in the old grey city. His brother, John, destined for the medical profession, accompanied him. As was usual with Scotch students, they tramped their way from Annan to Edinburgh, getting a night's rest and refreshment at the houses as they passed. Their supplies of oatmeal, eggs, butter, and general home produce were forwarded by the carrier's cart, by which also their linen was taken home to be washed and mended. They had no personal expenses beyond the few shillings paid for a room. This was situated in a lofty flat in the old town, near the college.

The Scotch University "Session" lasted from November to May. The remainder of the year was spent by the students in their country homes, or in teaching. A divinity student had to study, for four years, the branches of classical and philosophical education. He then began the study of theology, which consumed four years more. At the age of 21 he went through his "trials" before the Presbytery, and was licensed to preach. This was the course of study now entered upon by Edward Irving.

In April, 1809, when 17 years of age, he took his degree of M.A. There is no record that he was a particularly diligent student. He, however, passed creditably through the University, and attracted the notice of Professor Christison, and of the mathematical professor, Sir John Leslie. Among the students he was liked as a generous, warm-hearted fellow. It was his habit to carry in his pocket a miniature copy of "Ossian," from which, in his country rambles, he would read or recite extracts to his companions with all the vehement and grandiloquent style at his command; thus indicating something of the oratorical powers which were destined to arouse the London world of fashion.

In the spring of 1810, Irving became teacher of a school at Haddington. He had still to pursue his divinity studies, going up to the University each year to preach a sermon before the professors in the Divinity Hall. About this time fresh from college, with prizes and honours, he paid a visit to the Annan Grammar School. His old master, Adam Hope, received him with much show of attention. The scholars eyed him admiringly. Among the small boys who gazed upon him and envied him his glory was young Thomas Carlyle. He thus describes Irving's appearance at that time:—"He was scrupulously dressed; black coat, tight pantaloons, in the fashion of the day, and looked very neat, self-possessed, and amiable; a flourishing strip of a youth, with coal-black hair, swarthy, clear complexion, very straight on his feet, and, except for the glaring squint, decidedly handsome." He entered upon his duties at Haddington school with every advantage. Sir John Leslie had recommended him as a distinguished student. His great affability gained him many friends. Among them was Doctor Welsh, the principal medical man of the place.

The Doctor's only daughter, Jane, afterwards Mrs. Thomas Carlyle, had shown an aptitude for Latin. It was her ambition to be educated like a boy. Latin she imagined to be the first step in that direction. Accordingly, having found an old copy of the *rudiments* in a lumber room, she engaged the services of some humble student and secretly began her study of the language. Having mastered a little, she chose a fitting opportunity for displaying her newly acquired learning. The Doctor and his wife sat enjoying a cosy after-dinner hour around the fire. The little Jane cunningly concealed herself under the table, behind the crimson folds of the cover. Presently her childish voice gave forth, "*penna, pennæ, pennam.*" The good doctor caught her in his arms, smothered her with kisses, and decided then and there that the Latin studies should be continued, and a fitting tutor sought. The choice fell upon Irving. Henceforward the young master of Haddington school attended each morning and evening at Doctor Welsh's house to instruct his little daughter. A warm attachment sprang up between master and pupil which seemed, at one time, likely to end in marriage. But circumstances intervened, and Miss Welsh eventually became the wife of Irving's friend, Thomas Carlyle.

As a teacher, Irving had the character of being very severe. Perhaps his giant-like appearance tended to invest him with the character of an unmerciful pedagogue. A story is told of the fright one girl received who had occasion to return to the school-room during recess. Irving was there alone, and was practising his oratorical powers by reciting one of Satan's speeches out of "Paradise Lost." The effect was so real that the girl, coming suddenly upon him, fled back to her companions affrighted, as though she had seen Satan himself.

It was while at Haddington that he first heard the celebrated Dr. Chalmers, whose assistant he afterwards became. Chalmers was announced to preach at St. George's, Edinburgh. It was on a week night evening, and Irving, with a band of his pupils, set out to hear the great preacher, walking the distance of 35 miles without any rest, except what was obtained during the service. On arriving at the church they found it already well filled. Spying a vacant pew in the gallery, Irving strode forward to secure it. The pew opener drew his arm across the pew, saying it was engaged. But Irving insisted that at such a time all seats must be open to the public. As the man still objected, he lost all patience, and exclaimed, with all the grandiloquent style and gesture at his command, "Remove your arm, or I will shatter it to pieces." The pew opener beat a speedy retreat before the infuriated young giant, and Irving and his party took possession of the pew.

In 1812 he removed from Haddington to Kirkcaldy, to become master of the academy there. In time some of his patrons got dissatisfied, and started a rival school. Of this school Thomas Carlyle was appointed master. It is greatly to Irving's credit that he showed no resentment at this appointment. Carlyle, referring to his friendship with Irving, says: "Irving was for years my senior, the *facile princeps* for success and reputation among the Edinburgh students, famed mathematician, famed teacher, first at Haddington, then here [Kirkcaldy], a flourishing man whom cross fortune was beginning to nibble at. He received me with open arms, and was a brother to me, and a friend there and elsewhere afterwards—such friend as I never had again or before in this world, at heart constant till he died."

Irving passed successfully through his "trials" before the Kirkcaldy Presbytery, and, in 1815, was fully licensed to preach. His first sermon was preached in his native town of Annan, and caused great commotion. All the town turned out to hear him When part way through his discourse, by an incautious movement, he tilted the Bible, and away went his sermon, fluttering down on to the precentor's desk. All wondered what the young licentiate would do. Stooping his long figure over the pulpit he calmly picked up the manuscript from where it lay; crushed it up in his great hands, thrust it in his pocket, and went on more fluently than before. A young man who could show himself so independent of the magic "paper" was a marvel to the Annan folk. Irving's name was made in his native town from that day.

At Kirkcaldy the good people thought he had "over muckle granner." A baker of the place kicked open his pew door and went in anger from the church whenever the young preacher with "too much grandeur" made his appearance in the pulpit. Irving's fervid eloquence was a mystery to his sedate countrymen. His impassioned utterances, striking figure—he was over six feet high, handsome and showy in appearance—deep ringing voice, and awful earnestness, were novel, and, to them, unministerial. So time passed by, and he received no "call."

Wearied of waiting, and tired of teaching, he left Kirkcaldy for Edinburgh. Thoroughly disheartened at remaining so long unsought, 'he was beginning to contemplate entering the mission field, when he received a summons from Dr. Andrew Thomson to preach in his pulpit at St. George's. The letter further intimated that Dr. Chalmers, who was in want of an assistant minister, would be present. With a beating heart Irving obeyed the summons. But the days passed by, and he heard nothing further from Dr. Chalmers. In despair he sailed for Ireland, seeking to drown his disappointment in adventure. A great crime had been recently committed in Ireland. The police were on the alert, watching all strangers who came into port at Belfast. When Irving landed his striking appearance, which partook somewhat of the desperado, drew their attention, and he was arrested. The Rev. Mr. Hanna—father of Dr. Hanna—Presbyterian minister of the place, procured his liberation, and took him as a guest to his house.

In Ireland he roamed about among the peasantry, sharing

their potatoes, and charming them with his free-heartedness. On his return to Coleraine, *en route* for Scotland, he found a letter awaiting him which caused his gloom to disappear, and the future to grow bright and promising. It was a letter from Dr. Chalmers, inviting him to become his assistant minister. In that capacity Irving settled in Glasgow, 1819.

His appearance created some little stir among Dr. Chalmers' congregation. A lady tells how, on one occasion, being particularly engaged in some domestic duty, she gave orders to her servants not to admit visitors. Her occupation was suddenly interrupted by one of her maids coming in, in a great state of excitement, saying :" Mem! there's a wonderful gentleman called. I couldna say you were engaged to *him*. I think he maun be a highland chief!" The visitor was Edward Irving. A gentleman said to Dr. Chalmers, "Do you know, Doctor, what people are saying about your new assistant? They say he's like a brigand chief."

There was small chance for Irving to draw much attention in the pulpit, occupying as he did the difficult post of assistant to so popular a preacher as Dr. Chalmers. He was a young nobody, whose presence people endured in the pulpit as a necessity. Nevertheless he made warm friends everywhere. Especially was he a welcome guest in the homes of the Glasgow poor.

The care of the poor was made a special study by Dr. Chalmers in the working of his parish. The majority of his parishioners were weavers, labourers, and factory-workers, and to the amelioration of their condition he devoted himself. The weekly offerings of his church were spent in the erection of schools and other charitable schemes. In this noble work he met with a most efficient helper in his new assistant. In and out of the homes of the labouring poor Irving went, gaining their love and confidence. He disdained not to share their simple meals, and was ready at all times and seasons to answer the call of sickness or distress.

His manner of visitation was marked by many peculiarities. "Peace be to this house" was his invariable greeting as he entered. On the heads of the children he laid his hands, repeating the priestly benediction, "The Lord bless thee and keep thee." All this took wonderfully with the Glasgow people. They looked forward to seeing his giant form entering their houses, and blessing them as he did so. It was little money he had to give, but he always brought a warm heart and ready sympathy. When an unexpected legacy came to him, which tradition makes somewhere between £30 and £100, he changed it into the £1 notes of Scotland, and each day as he started on his visits put one into his pocket to be distributed among the needy. So he continued day after day, until the legacy was all gone.

A good story is told of the way in which he won over an infidel shoemaker. The man's wife was a church member, and received Irving's visits graciously, but he always sat sullen and moody at his work. Irving, bent on drawing him into conversation, picked up a piece of patent leather, then a new invention, and began talking about it. "What do ye ken about leather?" asked the man, with great contempt, and without raising his eyes. Irving being a tanner's son, was able to enter upon the subject intelligently, and interested the shoemaker in an account of a process for making shoes by machinery. He had studied it up for the purpose. As the conversation proceeded the man suspended his work, and, raising his eyes to the great figure bent over him, said, "Od' you're a decent kind o' fellow!—do you preach?" The next Sunday he and his family were at church, and from that time he became quite a changed character. His usual remark about Irving was, "He's a sensible man, yon; he kens about leather."

Much beloved as Irving was in the homes of the poor, in the pulpit he had still to feel himself in the shade. People would turn from the church door when they knew that he was to preach and not Dr. Chalmers. This was hard to bear, but he struggled on, hoping that some other sphere would open out to him. He was on the eve of accepting an invitation to go to Kingston in Jamaica, as pastor of a Presbyterian church, when the unlooked for "call" came from the Caledonian Church, Hatton Garden, henceforward to be the scene of his marvellous success.

The Caledonian Church was not of any importance at that time beyond the fact that it was attached to a large charitable institution, the Caledonian Asylum, intended for the orphan children of soldiers and sailors. The flock was small and insignificant. It was scarcely able to offer a fixed stipend to the minister whom they had invited. Still Irving was eager for a field of labour where he could be free to act on his own lines. After an affectionate farewell to Dr. Chalmers' congregation, the young probationer went through the final "trials" before the Presbytery of Annan, and was ordained a minister of the Scottish Kirk.

He began his ministry at the little Caledonian Chapel, Hatton Garden, on the 2nd Sunday of July, 1822. His congregation consisted of the 50 members of the church, together with a small sprinkling of strangers. He preached from the text, "Therefore came I unto you without gainsaying, as soon as I was sent for. I ask you therefore for what intent you have sent for me?" It was an impressive discourse. In a mysterious manner his fame spread; the people were taken by storm; each Sunday the crowd of hearers increased until the hitherto unknown chapel was crowded from end to end, and hundreds went away unable to gain admission. The great of the land were amongst the crowd. Scholars, statesmen, and noble lords flocked around the young preacher. High-born ladies were content to sit upon his pulpit steps that they might catch his burning, earnest words of eloquence. It was not some short and flowery discourse that they came to listen to, but for three hours Irving prayed, preached, and exhorted in the measured, stately language of the bye-gone ages. A success so instantaneous, startling, and brilliant has rarely been recorded.

The immediate cause of the flow of rank and fashion to Hatton Garden Chapel was a speech of Canning's in the House of Commons. He was taken to hear Irving by his friend Sir James Mackintosh, who had been struck by the preacher's reference in his prayer to a family of orphans, as being now "thrown upon the Fatherhood of God." Canning was delighted, and shortly afterwards told the House of Commons that the most eloquent sermon he ever heard was preached by the minister of one of the poorest churches in Christendom. This aroused "society," who flocked immediately to hear the wonderful orator. Thus the despised "assistant" of St. John's, Glasgow, found himself the most popular London preacher.

In 1823 he published his first book, "The Orations and an Argument for Judgment to come." In the September of the same year he married Miss Isabella Martin, the daughter of the minister at Kirkcaldy. They settled in an unpretentious house in Middleton Terrace, Pentonville. There, on the 22nd of July, 1824, was born their first child, little Edward, the child of hope and promise to be so soon torn from its sorrowing parents' side.

Irving's popularity did not spoil him. He was ever humble and conscientious in his work. His house was thrown open to all comers. Not only did his congregation visit him, but his home was the general asylum for all struggling Scotchmen who came to London to seek their fortunes. Countless stories might be told of his generosity to the poor, the outcast, the sinning, and the needy, who sought his hospitable roof. On one occasion two Greek youths were entrusted to his care. "Joseph Wolff, my much-esteemed friend," he writes, "and Lady George Wolff, also my much-esteemed friend, have given me another proof of their esteem by sending me two Greeks. . . . . These two Greeks has Joseph Wolff sent—wholly entrusted to me—so that I am to them as father and guardian, and provider and everything, which also I am right happy to be. . . . . By the blessing of God, poor though I am, yet rich in faith, by His grace I will take upon myself the responsibility of their charges until they return to their native Cyprus again." It is hardly probable that Irving was allowed to bear all their expenses, at the same time his generous soul would not have flinched from it.

His labours were of a most exhaustive kind. His dining room was crowded before breakfast by devout ladies, elders of his church, struggling young Scotchmen, and the waifs and strays he had picked up. He talked with them, had family worship, and for all who cared to remain breakfast was provided. After these early visitors had left, he spent the morning in his study. His early frugal dinner over, he began his round of visitations. In the evening there were meetings to attend, and more visitations. It was generally midnight before he reached home. The strain on Sundays was tremendous. His services lasted for three hours and a-half in the morning, and two and a-half in the evening. The interval between was filled up with visitations, or some other kind of work. His only relaxation seems to have been carrying the baby Edward, hoisted in his great arms, along the Pentonville lanes. He was

T

passionately attached to his child. Its death, which occurred in 1825, was a severe blow to him.

It took place at the manse at Kirkcaldy, Mrs. Irving's paternal home, whether she had taken him for change. Irving's grief was overpowering. Although a numerous family was given him, many of whom he followed to the grave, the memory of baby Edward remained green as ever.

Mrs. Irving stayed for some time in her father's house after this sad event. Her husband was in London at his regular duties. But he wrote her an epistle each day, which took the form of a diary. This journal gives a graphic account of how each hour of his days was spent. It teems with holy thought and feeling. None could read it without being impressed by the intense earnestness of Irving's life, and by his noble self-sacrificing spirit.

The little church in Hatton Garden soon became too small to hold his congregation. In 1827 a new one was opened in Regent Square. One thousand sittings were taken at once. The orator's popularity continued, although the stream of fashionable life began to flow in other directions. Forsaken by the noble lords and coronetted ladies he still was a power in the vast Metropolis, and pursued his way with humility and single-mindedness.

His fame had travelled to Scotland, and when, in 1828, he made an apostolic journey through his native land the excitement was intense. At Annan he addressed the farmers and traders in their weekly market, and went in and out of the homes of the peasantry proclaiming his message of love and mercy. On the Sunday he preached from the " tent," a movable wooden pulpit used in Scotland on great ecclesiastical occasions. The neighbouring ministers closed their churches and joined in the crowd which flocked to listen to that voice which had no equal in Annandale. Proceeding to Edinburgh, he began his twelve lectures on the Apocalypse in St. Andrew's Church. But it proved too small to accommodate the eager crowds, and a change to the West Church was necessitated. The General Assembly was then sitting in Edinburgh, and the old grey city was full of Presbyterian divines. To meet their convenience Irving's services were held at six o'clock in the morning. Long before that hour, when the rising sun was flooding the beautiful city with rosy light, the crowd of sober Scotch divines, the *élite* of Edinburgh society, and people from all ranks streamed along the road to the West Church. Some, more enthusiastic than the rest, bore their little ones along, thinking to impress upon their young minds the wonderful eloquence which they may never hear excelled.

From Edinburgh Irving continued his journey through Glasgow and the neighbouring towns to Kirkcaldy, where his wife was staying. He was announced to preach on the Sacramental Fast-day. The church was crowded with expectant listeners. As he walked along in the calm of the lovely evening to the church he was startled by the news that the galleries, over-crowded with people, had given way. There was a fearful panic, the dead and the dying being borne out into the adjacent churchyard. Amid this awful scene some excited individual taunted Irving with being the cause of the disaster. This was a bitter sting to his sensitive heart. He is said to have withdrawn to his chamber in tears and humiliation, exclaiming, "God hath put me to shame this day before all the people." So ended, in disaster and confusion, this otherwise brilliant apostolic journey. After ministering to the sufferers, he returned to his regular labours in London.

Great as was the fame of the preacher, it did not protect him from harsh criticism. Already there was a whisper of heresy against him. This soon grew into an open attack. Irving, in his published works and in his sermons, taught that Christ took upon him our sinful nature when he came to earth as the Redeemer. Ill-natured people twisted this into meaning that Christ was sinful. Nothing could be further from Irving's mind than that. While believing that it was essential for the Redeemer to assume our present nature, with all its evil propensities, he, at the same time, maintained that the Son of God was pure and sinless through the Holy Spirit which dwelt in him. A mean fellow named Cole, who was always ready for mischief-making, called upon Irving, and remonstrated with him on teaching this monstrous doctrine of "the sinfulness of Christ." Patiently and lovingly Irving explained his views, but his treacherous questioner was not convinced, and, in a short time, wrote against him a grave charge of heresy. Others who had felt suspicious joined. Before long the cloud, at first no bigger than a man's hand, burst in all its fury upon Edward Irving. Secure in the approval of his own conscience, he beheld it in amazement. The London Presbytery censured him, but Regent Square Church held to their pastor and separated themselves from it. The case was brought before the General Assembly of the Church of Scotland. While that august gathering of learned divines held their sittings in Edinburgh, Irving and his followers were holding early morning prayer-meetings to ask that God's blessing might rest upon it and guide it in its deliberations.

It was an Assembly to be remembered in the history of Presbyterianism. Four cases of heresy were dealt with by it. Alexander Scott, a young probationer, was forbidden to preach; Mr. Maclean was reprimanded, and sent back to be dealt with by his Presbytery; John Macleod Campbell, minister of Row, was expelled, because he preached that Christ died for all men, in opposition to the Calvanistic creed; lastly, Edward Irving was censured on account of his published writings, which were deemed heretical.

This was unspeakably bitter; he felt the humiliation keenly. Few men had tried more earnestly than he to fulfil the duties of a Christian minister. His whole life had been consecrated to his high calling. Turning sorrowfully away from all this ecclesiastical bigotry he met daily with his flock to pray for the outpouring of the Holy Spirit. For many years the study of prophecy had had a special interest for him. At the house of his friend, Henry Drummond, yearly meetings had been held for the special study of the ancient prophecies. These were known as the "Albury Conferences." Irving was the leading spirit in them. His studies led him to expect the coming of Christ at an early period. Many things transpired to strengthen his belief. News was coming from Scotland of marvellous manifestations of miraculous power by devout persons. One, Mary Campbell, was raised from her bed of sickness at the command of an earnest Christian, and other cures, equally extraordinary, were taking place. Surely, thought Irving, the day of the Lord is at hand, and God is enduing His saints with miraculous powers. So in faith he and his church prayed that the Lord would bestow upon them His gracious spirit, as He had done in the days of old upon the apostles. The answer to their prayers seemed to be fulfilled; many professed to have received the gift of prophesying, and began to speak with "tongues."

The scenes in Regent Square Church became indescribable. Hysteric females were rushing from the church, during service time, to burst forth in the vestry into incoherent ravings in the "unknown tongue," which they declared themselves unable to restrain. The excitement increased. One after another, both male and female, were seized with this spirit of prophesying. The crowds of London flocked to see the new phenomena. The press took it up, jeered and ridiculed, and accused Irving of having resorted to this exhibition as a mere trick to draw out the people. Meantime, he looked on and wondered. Had not the saints been praying for an outpouring of the Holy Spirit? This must be an answer to their prayers; it was the voice of God. So he reasoned, and feeling this, he could do none other than listen to it. The speakers with "tongues" no longer sought the seclusion of the vestry for their outbreaks, but spake out openly in the middle of the public services, Irving pausing in his sermon or prayer to let them be heard; for was it not the voice of God? So he firmly believed, for the characters of these people professing to have miraculous powers were unimpeachable.

At length the trustees of Regent Square Church deposed Irving for having broken the provisions of the trust deed by allowing these disorderly proceedings to take place. The greater part of his congregation went out with him, and formed themselves into the body since known as "The Catholic Apostolic Church."

The bitterest day of all to Irving was that on which he was formally expelled from the Scottish Church. In the little church of Annan, where he had been baptized, where he had taken his ordination vows, he was declared by the Presbytery unfit to be a minister. Friends and relatives forsook him, and even the speakers with "tongues," who had brought about the scandal, heaped indignities upon him. Humbly he bore it, believing with honest child-like spirit that God was ordering all.

The newly-formed 'Apostolic Church" erected a chapel in Newman Street. Irving conducted the services according to the new regulations; but his ways were too lofty and pure for the fanatics who gathered around him. He laboured on, often preaching seven times a week, besides numerous other engagements. The strain was too great even for his strong frame. His health gave way, and, during a visit he paid to Glasgow to establish a church, broke down completely. Many a pitying, sorrowing glance followed him as he crawled along the Glasgow streets. "That is the great Mr. Irving," said the people, with bated breath, as they saw his emaciated form pass by.

On a gloomy December Sunday the end came. He passed peacefully away, saying with his last breath, "If I die, I die unto the Lord. Amen." He was buried in the silent crypt of Glasgow Cathedral. The clergy and the leading people of the city attended his funeral. The peculiarities of his creed were forgotten in the love which a life so pure, unselfish and sincere drew from all ranks. "Scarce any man who knew him," writes Mrs. Oliphant, "can yet name, without a softened voice and dimmed eye, the name of Edward Irving—true friend and tender heart, martyr and saint."

BIBLIOLIFE

Old Books Deserve a New Life
www.bibliolife.com

Did you know that you can get most of our titles in our trademark **EasyScript**[TM] print format? **EasyScript**[TM] provides readers with a larger than average typeface, for a reading experience that's easier on the eyes.

Did you know that we have an ever-growing collection of books in many languages?

Order online:
www.bibliolife.com/store

Or to exclusively browse our **EasyScript**[TM] collection:
www.bibliogrande.com

At BiblioLife, we aim to make knowledge more accessible by making thousands of titles available to you – quickly and affordably.

Contact us:
BiblioLife
PO Box 21206
Charleston, SC 29413

LaVergne, TN USA
20 December 2009

167654LV00006BA/48/A